Property

JESSE HAMM
18932 Benedict Dr.
Woodbridge, CA 95258
(209) 368-5936

SHAM PEARLS FOR REAL SWINE

SHAM PEARLS FOR REAL SWINE

FRANKY·SCHAEFFER

Wolgemuth & Hyatt, Publishers, Inc.
Brentwood, Tennessee

Unless otherwise noted, all scripture quotations are from the New King James Version
of the Bible, © 1979, 1980, 1982, 1984 by Thomas Nelson, Inc., Nashville, Tennessee
and are used by permission.

Appendix A is taken from *The War Against the Intellect* by Peter Shaw.
Copyright © 1989 by Peter Shaw and used by permission of the University of Iowa
Press.

Appendix B is taken from *Amusing Ourselves to Death* by Neil Postman.
Copyright © 1985 by Neil Postman and used by permission of Viking Penguin, a division of Penguin Books, USA, Inc.

Wolgemuth & Hyatt, Publishers, Inc.
1749 Mallory Lane, Suite 110, Brentwood, Tennessee 37027.

Library of Congress Cataloging-in-Publication Data

Schaeffer, Franky.
    Sham pearls for real swine / Franky Schaeffer. — 1st ed.
        p. cm.
    ISBN 0-943497-89-2
    1. Christianity and the arts. I. Title.
    BR115.A8S32 1990
    261.5'7 — dc20
                                                        90-31541
                                                          CIP

For my patient daughter Jessica

CONTENTS

ACKNOWLEDGMENTS

First, I would like to thank a number of people who specifically encouraged me to write this book: John Cox, John Whitehead, Thom Howard, Steven Hawley, Paul and Kristina McGuire, my wife, Genie Schaeffer, and my mother, Edith Schaeffer.

Second, I would like to thank Michael Hyatt for his wonderful encouragement throughout this project. His support has been unusual in its kindness and understanding. I would also like to acknowledge the friendship and support of Robert Wolgemuth as he stood behind me in the writing of this book. Russ Sorensen, my editor, and Susan Kirby, who copyedited my book, were both tremendously helpful and pleasant to work with. Thank you!

A "thank you" is also in order to my children, Jessica, Francis, and John (and, again, to my wife Genie), for all the love, patience, and affection with which I am undeservedly surrounded.

Thank you, Paul and Kristina McGuire for providing a home away from home for me in Hollywood. And thank you to Jim and Judy Buchfuehfer for your long, loyal friendship. Thank you, Lori Ambacher and Genie Schaeffer for typing my many handwritten drafts (more than a dozen) of this book when I needed them done rather than when it was convenient to you both. I also wish to express my gratitude to Peter Shaw and Neil Postman for allowing me to use their material in the appendices. I would also like to thank Norman Podhoretz, editor of *Commentary* magazine, for so generously allowing me to quote at length from several articles published in *Commentary* (published monthly by the American Jewish Committee, 165 East 56th St., New York, NY 10022), as well as to the other publishers and authors quoted in this book. Last but not least, I would like to thank my minister Tom Oats, the rector of Christ Church Episcopal, Hamilton, Massachusetts, for his teaching and friendship.

Franky Schaeffer
February 1990

FOREWORD

I was surprised, a bit overwhelmed, and honored, when my son asked me to write a foreword for this book. The request plunged me into a thorough reading of his manuscript. I carried it with me into the isolation of a plane trip and into other hours protected from interruption. It is a book that is impossible to put down — a book that needs the kind of concentration required when looking at familiar objects through a microscope. The microscope brings forth breathtaking detail that one has never considered before because the detail had been lost in the blur of familiarity. Ideas, like cells, need to be examined so thoroughly as to startle the mind with seeing something from a new perspective, and that is exactly what this book does.

When my late husband, Francis Schaeffer, began to express his ideas, which were developed through discussions with people who came to him from various disciplines, what he was saying did not meet with approval on the part of many of his theological colleagues. From 1948 on, one of the frequent participants in these discussions was Professor Hans Rookmaaker, head of the Department of Art History in the Free University of Amsterdam. Professor Rookmaaker was an expert in the history of jazz and was often asked to write the notes on jazz record jackets as well as articles for newspapers on both art and jazz. As a young man Franky was a close friend of Dr. Rookmaaker, and I well remember the many long hours that Fran and my son and the professor spent discussing art.

Franky's ideas, like his father's before him, may also draw some criticism. However, the arguments in the book extend and build upon the work of Francis Schaeffer in a helpful way and hopefully will stimulate and set in motion a discussion about the arts and media with a depth of understanding which is long overdue.

A microscopic view can be startling. The probing of false ideas, as well as unchangeable truth, needs an approach of drastic honesty. I wish I had been exposed to this thought-provoking and scrutinizing process at a very early period in my own life, when I was full of questions as to what really was basic and what had been added as man-made regulations to the teaching of Christianity regarding the arts and humanities.

As I read this book, I was stunned by Franky's brutal honesty and scrupulousness in giving a history of his own life, ambitions, and determination for increasing integrity in his own movie directing and screenwriting. I had always known of his striking quality of perseverance, but this honesty struck me forcibly. He writes from the experiences of disappointment, frustration, and successes known by every creative person who has struggled to be heard or seen in some area. He unveils his own film experiences from the reality of the blood, sweat, and tears involved in slogging work—not from the fantasy of a romantic but from the context of real-life struggles. For me, as a writer, Franky's book brings a recognition of a truthful portrayal of reality.

Sham Pearls For Real Swine is not something to read for mere entertainment but a book to reread, each time shifting the lens of the microscope a bit to examine one's own understanding—separating it from the comfortable rut of cliché.

Thank you, Franky.

Edith Schaeffer
February 1990

All you have to do is write one true sentence.

Ernest Hemingway

PROLOGUE

S ir Winston Churchill coined the phrase "sham pearls for real swine" in reference to the British public school (private prep school to Americans) he attended. He said of the teaching there that it was a place "where sham pearls were fed to real swine." Unfortunately, the same can be said of a great deal of teaching in the Christian church concerning the arts, media, and our culture in general.

Perhaps I have, by using this title, handed my critics, "the carping censures of the world" (Shakespeare, *Richard III*), an easy turn of phrase with which to dismiss the book on the basis of the title being an apt description of my book's contents! If so, well and good. I aim to please and what better way to do this than to hand one's head to a critic on a platter with, as Bertie Wooster would say, "watercress all 'round it!"

Since writing my first book, *Addicted to Mediocrity*, in 1980, I have been on some strange adventures. For one thing, I have changed careers from that of a documentary filmmaker to that of a feature film director and screenwriter.

The movie industry is a tough, strange, and often lonely business. As a Christian working in the arts, I have naturally looked to the church for encouragement, yet there are problems within Christendom concerning its understanding of the arts. Middle America and its religious expression, evangelical fundamentalist or Roman Catholic Christianity, is often unsympathetic to the arts and to cultural endeavor. Where, then, is the Christian pursuing a career in the arts to turn for inspiration, help, and advice?

As for the arts, what are they for? What do they "do"? Mainly, as far as many Christians are concerned, they scandalize, perplex, and anger. Strange priorities rule the sensibilities of some Christians. Four-letter words used in films outrage the brethren, yet routine lies in the church hardly cause comment. Nudity on the stage, screen, or canvas arouses fundamentalists to fury, yet a carnival atmosphere of debauched materialism reigns unchallenged in much of the church.

The values of middle America are replacing Biblical absolutes in the church. If it were thinkable, God would be blamed by some Christians for creating too much — too much lusty flesh, too many pretty women, too much natural diversity. If Shakespeare were understood today, his plays, the glorious pinnacle of Christian morality expressed through drama, would be banned as "unsuitable" by much of the modern fundamentalist church. If Leonardo da Vinci and Michelangelo were working as our contemporaries, they would face hostility from some quarters in the church. The Bible itself, if read as a book and not as a spiritual devotional mantra, would be rejected as a profane oddity, filled with sexual and violent images.

Some Christians have said that they want to "restore and reclaim America," to return to an earlier innocence, to "go back." But, we may ask, back to what? The 1950s? What other age beyond our own of anesthetized, plastic propriety could accommodate us? What past leaders would meet our standards of piety? Luther? We would find him vulgar. Shakespeare? Filthy. Bach? Secular. Verdi? Catholic. Joan of Arc? Insane. Winston Churchill? A drunken warmonger. George Washington? A reactionary chauvinist. Jesus of Nazareth? Rude, sexist, offensive, and inscrutable. All of these would be too complicated, too real, too human for the "nice," the timid, the shallow, the ignorant — the church.

The dedicated Christian pursuing a career in the arts or media is caught between a hammer and an anvil — the hammer of *closed-minded* secularism and the anvil of *closed-minded* fundamentalist Christianity. Please don't misunderstand me. I believe in the fundamentals of the Faith, and I do not have an axe to grind with evangelical fundamentalism or Roman Catholicism as such. I object only to the closed-mindedness and the anti-cultural baggage that today is often characteristic of both. The Christian in the arts has a narrow and precarious road to walk. I attempt to walk that road in my profession as a movie director and screenwriter; I proceed with many a stumble. I hope this book will perhaps serve others engaged in the arts, and other walks of life, who share that elusive path with me. This book necessarily draws lessons from my film-making experiences which I trust will be applicable to my readers in their own lives and work. I hope that others will find that events in my life will relate to their own and that my conclusions, drawn from experience, study, and long reflection, will help them.

My intention in writing this book is to help generate a robust discussion of the problems and ideas I set forth in this volume. My intention is *not* to set myself up as an "expert" of some sort or to present my book as the only opinion or the last word on the subject. My voice is only one among many.

As G. K. Chesterton remarked in the introduction to his book, *St. Thomas Aquinas,* "I can only express the hope, and indeed the confidence, that those that regard me as the heretic will hardly blame me for expressing my own conviction."

My angel — his name is Freedom.
Choose him to be your king;
He shall cut pathways east and west,
And fend you with his wing.

Emerson, *Boston Hymn*

1

FISH IN BOILING WATER

C. S. Lewis once said that he wrote the *Narnia* stories because they were the books he would have liked to have read as a child. I have written this book because it is the book that, during the first five years of turmoil as I jumped full-time into the movie business, I would have loved to have read.

A Voice From the Past

I am not the only believing Christian to have recently taken a hard, critical look at Christians' efforts in the arts and media. For instance, my late father (theologian Francis Schaeffer) had a great interest in the subject. While looking through some of his old correspondence recently, I found a letter dated August 19, 1982. Dad was writing to a Mr. French of Ann Arbor, Michigan, to advise him regarding a conflict with the elders of his church who were refusing to take a stand on sanctity-of-life issues. Yet, somewhat surprisingly, Dad's comments began by focusing on another issue: the arts. He wrote:

> What you are up against in your church there is all too tragically common in many of our Bible-believing churches. As you know, I speak of *the false view of pietism and spirituality.* . . . There is

no doubt in my mind that biblically it is just that—it is a false
view of spirituality. The price for this, as for all things less than
God calls us to, has been overwhelmingly costly, first in individual lives. We have had so many young people come here to
L'Abri [the religious study center my late father founded] who
become Christians and then [return to a] . . . church holding this
false view of spirituality . . . [that] told them that their art,
music, or poetry . . . is subspiritual. Through the years literally
hundreds of them have come here destroyed and wiped out.
Happily, for many of them we have seen them set free and they
are now creating again.

It is interesting to note that my father began a letter on why a
church and its elders would be silent on a major medical ethical
issue, abortion, by stating his views on the tragedy of the lack of
understanding of the arts by many Christians, and equating the
two problems.

My father always encouraged artists' aspirations. And my
mother saw to it that instead of pocket money, I had art supplies
and lessons when I was a child. This encouragement to create
continued over the years. I well remember my father, on a trip to
Florence, Italy, hiring a model, out of his meager funds, for me to
use as part of an experimental movie I was shooting as a fifteen-
year-old "director." I also remember him as someone who defended freedom of expression, including the artistic freedom necessary to experiment and make mistakes.

Yet as I have learned to my sorrow, people in the Christian
church, both evangelical fundamentalist and Roman Catholic, are
often far from sharing my father's enlightened appreciation of the
arts, let alone supporting those of us pursuing artistic careers.

Plastic Churches

Most contemporary American church buildings are symbolically
ugly, accurately reflecting the taste of pastor and people alike. In

Los Angeles, Atlanta, and Dallas, for example, one finds a number of so-called superchurches—churches with five thousand to ten thousand members. These churches house congregations with the money, power, and means to build contemporary Chartres cathedrals, if they had the vision. The profound ugliness of these churches is not the result of budget priorities. These buildings are expensive; studied ugliness does not come cheap. Many of these church buildings seem to express the same sense of aesthetics as that of the living-room/kitchen set from the old "Dick Van Dyke Show." They constitute an assault on the senses: a nightmare of red velvet and prefab ceiling "tile," StainWare carpet in pastel shades from hell and the Easter Bunny, a Mt. Everest of canned sweet corn and lime Jell-o.

Distorted echoes of a now-pacified Christianity ring out in an electronic clarion call to middle America. These churches are the elevator music of religion, the counseling rooms in which the latest psycho-babble is used to assuage the anxieties of the pre- and post-mid-life crises menopausal congregation. They provide child-care facilities to assist families in staying apart. In Christian bookstores, greeting cards and wall plaques decorated with pious sayings compete for space with the latest cassette tape wisdom of the local Protestant "pope" of the superchurch ministry outreach, worldwide international evangelism, counseling/suicide prevention hotline, daycare, elementary school, high school, senior citizen center, Bible school, fund raising, youth center, parking lot ghetto. If these churches were food, they would have a shelf life of one hundred years—all sugar and preservatives, the two basic evangelical fundamentalist intellectual food groups. They are giant cash registers in which sham pearls are fed to the enlightened who in turn excrete money to feed the machine. Here, the artist has as much chance of thriving as the plastic plants do in the artificial light of the "sanctuary."

Art

The arts ask hard questions. Art incinerates polyester/velvet dreams of inner healing and cheap grace. Art hurts, slaps, and defines. Art is interested in truth: in bad words spoken by bad people, in good words spoken by good people, in sin and goodness, in life, sex, birth, color, texture, death, love, hate, nature, man, religion, music, God, fire, water, and air. Art tears down, builds up, and redefines. Art is uncomfortable. Good art (which, among other things, means truth-telling art) is good in itself, *even when it is about bad things.*

Good art expresses an interest in everything. Art, like the Bible, is not defined by one period of history. Art explores immorality and immortality. There are no taboo subjects for good art, any more than there is taboo news for newspapers, because art is unafraid of the truth. Art, like Christ, comes to sinners in an imperfect world. People who imagine themselves to be perfect do not like art. The middle-class church, living in a cocoon of false expectations, resents people who wield sharp razor blades or worse, disturb their sleep. Art is fleshly yet eternal. Art is human. Art is a mirror to the world. Art is the bridge between flesh and soul. "Art is science in the flesh," as Jean Cocteau wrote in *Le Rappel a l'Ordre.*

Because art destroys a false sense of security, it is looked on with suspicion, even perceived as an enemy by the middle class and its spokespersons in the church, who, through ignorance, subdue artists and discourage talent. "Do not offend your brother" is a Bible verse often misused to intimidate the artist in the same way as "turn the other cheek" is sometimes taken out of Biblical context to justify "Christian" pacifism. There is a Bible verse handily available for every tyrannical cause, to be exploited by those who use the Bible as an ideological weapon.

Literature

The Bible

Only by giving the Bible a devotional spin when we read it, by taking isolated verses out of context and ignoring the raw whole, by filtering and interpreting, do we "civilize" it. Civilized, the Bible has become a devotional prop of middle-class values instead of being the rude challenge to false propriety it actually is. The Bible is a dangerous, uncivilized, abrasive, raw, complicated, aggressive, scandalous, and offensive book. The Bible is the literature of God, and literature, as every book burner knows, is dangerous. The Bible is the drama of God; it is God's *Hamlet, Canterbury Tales,* and *Wuthering Heights.* The Bible is, among other things, about God, men, women, sex, lies, truth, sin, goodness, fornication, adultery, murder, childbearing, virgins, whores, blasphemy, prayer, wine, food, history, nature, poetry, rape, love, salvation, damnation, temptation, and angels. Today the Bible is widely studied but rarely read. If the Bible were a film, it would be R-rated in some parts, X-rated in others. The Bible is not middle class. The Bible is not "nice." The Bible's tone is closer to that of the late Lenny Bruce than to that of the hushed piety of some ministers.

In some centuries, the church did not allow the common people to read the Bible. Now by spiritualizing it and taming it through devotional and theological interpretations, the church once again muzzles the book in a "damage control" exercise. We now study the Bible but through a filter of piety that castrates its virility.

When the unfiltered power of Biblical understanding has occasionally broken into the open, there have been cultural results. The powerful, Biblically based Dutch paintings of Rembrandt and Vermeer serve as examples with their reflections of raw, genuine life. For instance, there are the exquisite nude paintings of Rembrandt's wife. We see portraits of friends, simple scenes from everyday life, as in Vermeer's *Girl Interrupted at her Music,* in which common events of life are portrayed as luminous events. Odd, earthy moments are depicted as well; an old man and woman urinating by the roadside is captured in a Rembrandt etching. Life as a whole—the good, the bad, the indifferent, the odd, the funny—was painted by great artists who *were* believing Christians. These were artists who loved Jesus and looked to Him for salvation, who understood the cultural and artistic basis that Biblical belief gives to those in the arts.

Shakespeare

The painters, scholars, sculptors, and philosophers were not the only Christians and Jews who shaped our culture. Consider Shakespeare, the truth-seeker, the glory of the English-speaking peoples; Shakespeare, who created both that saint of chaste Christianity, Desdemona in *Othello,* and the ribald sexual humor and double meanings in *The Comedy of Errors;* Shakespeare, who gives us truth about life—life theatrically painted as lovingly, humorously, and truly as it ever will be. His was drama based on a sense of Jewish-Christian morality, drama that today the ignorant, *a-cultural* church would reject as *un-Christian* if it were reproduced in language we understood. *Un-Christian* because it does not reflect middle-class nicety and propriety. Yet in Shakespeare's life and writing, we see a testimony to the Christian faith and its cultural fruit. S. Schoenbaum, Franklyn Bliss Snyder Professor of English at Northwestern University and one of the most world-renowned Elizabethan scholars, writes of Shakespeare's Christian faith:

> Inculcated from the formative years of early childhood, the Bible and Book of Common Prayer . . . profoundly nourished Shakespeare's imagination. One learned Biblical scholar, ranging through all the works . . . has identified quotations from, or references to, forty-two books of the Bible—eighteen each from the Old and New Testaments, and six from the Apocrypha. Scarcely a phrase from the first three chapters of Genesis escapes allusion in the plays. Job and Ecclesiastes were favorite

books, but Cain left an especially powerful impression — Shakespeare refers to him at least twenty-five times. . . . Shakespeare's range of religious reference is not limited to the Bible. Sometimes he quotes Scripture by way of the Prayer Book, as when the Fifth Commandment becomes "Thou shalt do no murder," and the words of the Psalmist, "We bring our years to an end, as it were a tale that is told" ("We have spent our yeeres as a thought," in the Genevan Bible) metamorphose into the "tale told by an idiot." . . . Our most thorough student of the Homilies takes them to be "A New Shakespearean Source-Book," and concludes that the dramatist derived his ideas of the divine right of kings, the subject's duty to obey, and the mischief and wickedness of rebellion — ideas that so powerfully inform the English history plays — not from his narrative sources . . . but either directly or indirectly from the [Christian-Anglican] politico-religious creed set forth in the Homilies. The services at Holy Trinity, Morning Prayer and Evening Prayer, Baptism and Holy Communion — indeed all the occasions of worship — remained with Shakespeare, and echo through the plays. (From *William Shakespeare, A Documentary Life* [New York: Oxford University Press, 1975], 48-49)

The breast of the church once also nurtured the composers: Vivaldi, Mozart, Bach, Corelli, Albinoni, Handel, Verdi, to name just a few of hundreds. Many looked to the historic Jesus for their personal salvation; all worked in an atmosphere informed by Jewish-Christian sensibilities. The Bible, the truth, set many free to be the people they were created to be, to use the talents God gave them. The traditions of the church provided a moral framework which was the foundation of the great artistic achievements of Western culture.

History

Our own time of studied indifference and ignorance toward the arts and humanities by Christians is fortunately not typical of church history — Protestant, Roman Catholic, or Orthodox. In contrast to our own era, one thinks of the High Middle Ages or the Florentine Renaissance led by the Medici family, or the pious Marsilio Ficino and his Platonic Institute. Christian belief informed the quest for knowledge in what was then understood as an orderly created universe. Therefore, as Leonardo dissected cadavers and illustrated his anatomy drawings, he could assume he was involved in a valid quest for knowledge. The pious and sublime frescos of Fra Angelico and the power of myth renewed by Venus as she comes to us in her seashell, led to the shore of our desire by the hand of Botticelli, were all inspired by the light of a rational, Biblical understanding, even when the subject at hand was an interpretation of a classic Greek myth.

The Dilemma

Yet today it seems that truth expressed through the arts is at war with a false spirituality which pervades the church. The servants of hypocrisy, found in abundance in the bosom of Christianized middle America, are not the friends of the arts or Western culture.

Loneliness is a constant reality for Christians who seriously pursue an artistic career. We are caught on the horns of a miserable dilemma. On the one hand is the church; on the other is the larger world and its art community. The nonbelieving art community, be it in the field of painting, theater, writing, film, music, or dance, has little interest in those who would express orthodox Jewish-Christian themes through their personal lives or their artworks. Yet the church is no better; it has lost vital contact with art and culture and has even lost the cultural vocabulary to discuss art and the humanities, let alone encourage artists.

To better understand the dilemma faced by believing Christian and Jewish artists, let us look at an analogous example. There are some African languages in which the future tense does not exist.

(This linguistically reflects a theological belief in animistic fatalism.) Thus for some tribes there is no way to discuss the future as we would understand it; what the ancestors did of old will be done again tomorrow. An African health worker who is confronted by such linguistic barriers to progress and tries to explain some future project, for instance changing a tribal custom in a way that will be of benefit hygienically, has a nearly impossible task. The very words do not exist with which to describe a different future reality.

Many Christians in the arts face the same frustrating dilemma today. Because Christian contact with the arts has recently been so minimal and hostile, the artist cannot discuss his or her art with fellow believers in a way that will be understood. There is no common vocabulary.

The contemporary, middle-class church is living in a historical vacuum. The church, both Protestant and Catholic, is largely unaware of its own cultural past. With each successive split and realignment within Protestantism, the church has moved further away from its cultural inheritance. Within the Catholic community, liberal theology and leftist politics have served to undermine its traditional commitment to the arts as the church has focused on "political relevance" at the expense of spirituality and culture. Today, with only a few exceptions, the church and church-related educational institutions are not centers of interest in history of any kind, let alone the history of art and culture. Nor are church institutions mounting a coherent defense of Western culture against the anti-Western tide that is sweeping the intellectual world.

The Great Divorce

The church is now thoroughly divorced from its historic culture. While claiming to wish to "reach mankind," it often fails because our culture *cannot* be reached from outside by outsiders who do not even bother to learn the cultural language. Ironically, because the church does not understand or even care about its own cultural artistic history, it does not understand its own finest, nonreligious creation: Western culture. In this way, the church is like a bad parent who has abandoned its child. Robert Nisbet writes, "Western philosophy can be declared a series of footnotes on St. Augustine" (*History of the Idea of Progress* [New York: Basic Books, 1980], 71). Nisbet expresses a sentiment as a secular scholar that many Christians seem to have forgotten: Western art and culture *are* Jewish-Christian at their roots.

Believing Christians who work in the secular art community are not only misunderstood by the church, because of its ignorance about art, but worse, are often rejected as "unspiritual" for concentrating on a "worldly" pursuit instead of a "spiritual" or "humanitarian" one.

The modern church, when it sees a contemporary Christian's artwork, has little knowledge and negligible historical perspective with which to judge it. It simply passes judgments based on current middle-class ideas of what is "appropriate" or in "good taste" or what represents ideological "right thinking."

Since today's middle American ideas of virtue are not those that have historically inspired great art, there is a conflict between members of the middle-class church and those who would be serious artists. For instance, current middle American, post-Victorian ideas of propriety hold that all nudity in art is "bad." Yet an artist who does not draw the nude figure cannot learn the traditional, accumulated skills of thousands of years of figurative Western art history—much of it church-supported, Christian art history—and pays a severe artistic price for such willful ignorance.

However, there are much deeper problems preventing the church from having a positive cultural influence. The church, both "liberal" and "conservative," is now living in a historical vacuum; it wants instant results when it seeks to change culture. The idea of a historical unfolding such as the Renaissance, that took four hundred years to mature, is totally foreign to the modern church that measures everything in TV "sound bite" increments.

Hans Rookmaaker, the late Dutch evangelical Christian art historian and head of the art history department at the Free University of Amsterdam, has explained that any significant influence believing Christians in our time might have in the arts would take *generations.* This idea does not play well to a church that wants its problems solved in one weekend retreat, wants the world converted in one evangelistic rally, or sees its mission as encouraging the redistribution of wealth between people to achieve instant "justice."

Middle America, politically left and right, in cutting itself off from a historical understanding of Western culture, has become an aesthetic nightmare. Thus, even when it comes to personal taste, individuals in the church are rarely sympathetic to good art. Middle America knows what it likes, and it's awful!

In this tasteless world, the artist is condemned for being "secular" by the church and is ostracized by his or her nonbelieving contemporaries for being foolishly "religious." In the smooth world that is Christianity in America today, how many people can feel the poignancy of Emily Dickinson's immortal line, "I died for beauty" or the depth of the artistic struggle described by Graham Greene in what he called "the despair of never getting anything right"?

Visual, as well as literary, expression is foreign to most of today's church. This lack of understanding is exacerbated by the fact that few leaders in the church come from a background that would give them any particular knowledge of, or sympathy for, the visual arts. As a result, we have a legion of theologically trained but artistically boorish Christians who are the leaders of evangelical fundamentalist and Roman Catholic Christianity.

Some Christians have called for more involvement in the culture by the church. However, usually when Christian leaders have called for a Christian presence in the arts or media, what they have actually had in mind is the making of gospel propaganda or so-called family entertainment that embodies what they are pleased to call "traditional values." More often than not, what these offerings turn out to be is middle-class pablum that will offend no one, cause no one to think, mean nothing, and leave its audience as comfortable and mindless as before they were fleetingly entertained by it. In other words, the "traditional values" turn out to be the values of the 1950s middle America, not the far more robust traditions of Western culture. What most Christians seem to crave when they call for a Christian presence in the arts is a return to middle American sentimentality, the kind of sentimentality that confuses virtue with niceness. This is a long way from the expressionist realism we find in the Bible itself, a long way from a concept of truth that traditional Jesuit *and* Calvinist scholarship once would have defended as the basis for a self-confident Western civilization.

Overreaction to Secularization

Christians are threatened by the aggressive secularism of our time, often with good reason. Unfortunately, our reaction to disturbing trends of secularization has led to the creation of defensive Christian ghettos in education, the church, and the mind. Our own confused reactions in this respect are not much different than those of Christians in the fourteenth century, a similarly convulsed period of history, of which the late historian Barbara Tuchman wrote:

> Times of anxiety nourish belief in conspiracies of evil, which in the 14th century were seen as the work of persons or groups with access to diabolical aid. . . . The Church was on the defensive, torn apart by the schism, challenged in authority and doctrine by aggressive movements of dissent, beset by cries for reform. Like the ordinary man, it felt surrounded by malevolent forces. (*A Distant Mirror* [New York: Knopf, 1978], 514-515)

No better description could be written with reference to the attitudes of many Christians in our own day to the secularist onslaught. In the most unfortunate reaction possible, many Christians find false security through collective ignorance and deny rather than affirm, run rather than shape, endlessly say no rather than present good alternatives. The Christian who is serious about being an artist occupies, in this reactionary ghetto, a place as comfortable as that of a live fish placed in boiling water.

The church is ugly when it begins to defend itself rather than truth. This ugliness is not unique to our day. Looking back in history, it is easy to understand the distress Molière must have felt when some of his "brothers" in the church plotted to have him burnt for *blasphemy* because he wrote a play, *Le Tartuffe,* in which a character dressed as a priest was portrayed as devious and hypocritical. Ironically, the play itself was intended as a corrective satire to help reform the institution of the church. In another instance of religiosity perverting art, when Botticelli came under the spiritual influence of the fiery priest, Savonarola, he, at the fevered priest's bidding, burnt some of his earlier "nonreligious," "sinful" artwork! He then painted a gloomy series of second-rate religious paintings. Bad art but right-minded theology. Savonarola was gratified; the human race became a little poorer.

Yet, in spite of the tragic examples of intolerance of the arts by some Christians past and present, the glory of the historical church that *did* understand the arts stands in stark contrast to our own inward-looking time.

Woe to him that is alone when he falleth; for he hath not another to help him up.

Ecclesiastes 4:10 KJV

2

FLYING SOLO

Self-employment is full of fear and dread. For me, as a movie director, every project has a well-worn cycle, not too different, I imagine, than that faced by other people working in the arts: initial euphoria over an idea or opportunity; the first pain of inevitable compromise, caused by such things as the reality of limited budget and time constraints; then the actual work, which, for me, is divided into three parts: preproduction, the chaos of production (the shoot), and the relative calm after the storm, postproduction, in which one tries to repair the damage. The last desperate hope is that the movie's music score will fix what was unrepaired during the editing! Then comes the end of the production, the surprise of a good review or the sinking sense of the inevitable fates at work in a bad one, a rush of hype, self-selling, marketing, and then silence.

Alone again, with a never-ending internal conversation: Will I ever work again? If I do get the chance, will I be able to remember what I learned from the last production and make a better movie? Will the next project, Hydra-like, take on a life of its own and get away from me? Is there life after movies? How long will my dwindling funds hold out? Is my agent doing *anything*? Why doesn't he call? Am I well-connected enough? Am I any good at what I do at all? Why don't I know more "important" people who can help me get another directing job? Does God answer prayer? Then I preach a now-too-familiar sermon to myself. I recall that God has faithfully provided for my wife, our three children, and me for many years. I ask myself, how many years longer does God have to supply our needs and wants before I begin to trust Him?

Artists spend more time worrying about money than about art. At least I know I do. Money is *the* artistic problem — money to live on, money to buy artistic freedom, money to buy time to be creative. What have I learned about money and the arts? Pay cash! Avoid debt! *Never* count your chickens before they hatch. Live below your means. Never rely on anything until the money is in the bank. As a Christian, I know that I should believe that "The Lord is my shepherd," but in practice my attitude is more often like that of Palladas, who wrote, "The life of man is the plaything of fortune, a wretched life and a vagrant, tossed between riches and poverty" (*Greek Anthology,* Bk. X [Epigram], 80).

Most artistic work is of a plodding, practical nature — one foot in front of the other. The one constant of the life of the artist is anxiety — financial and artistic. This gloom of worry is punctured by occasional light, which leaves the dark even murkier when the light is gone. Living with the dread of not working again becomes the central work of faith in the creative life.

As my own best-laid plans have often lain in ruins about me, I have slowly learned to look for God's blessing, marking my life in places I was not concentrating on as much as I should have been.

"Fame and Fortune"

One of the first attempts I made to get into the feature film business seemed to be a sure route to success, a shortcut to fame and fortune. I had co-written a script that I believed was perfect for a one-man tour de force by some well-known actor *if* I could find one willing to work with an unknown director. The very first agent I contacted sent the script to his client, James Mason. Mason read it and loved it! God was in heaven smiling down upon me! *All was well in my soul*!

I worked on the script with James Mason at his home in Vevey, Switzerland. Like all the good old British actors, not to be confused with the young, TV-generated American brat-packers, he was gentle courtesy itself. He even offered to "read" for me, not that I asked him, but he offered nonetheless, as if I were some famous director considering various unknown actors for the part.

My producer and partner, Jim Buchfuehrer, and I raised the cash for this low-budget movie, signed a deal with Mason's agent, and prepared to win an Oscar for him!

Then he died! I was outraged. How could God "lead" me all this way, then capriciously take James Mason home to *his* reward *before* I had *used* him to get *mine*?

My project died with James Mason. It turned out other agents hated the script. I had stumbled onto the one *name* actor who liked it, and he had died.

I have a photograph of Mason in his garden, standing next to a favorite, retired, old Fiat next to which he had planted vines. The vine-covered car sat quietly rusting away as the tendrils of Virginia creeper climbed up its sides. The picture is my souvenir of lost hope.

I am learning that God does lead but does not necessarily share our immediate ambitions. Just because something we are doing appears to be working does not mean that we are being "led." Believing Christians, like everyone else, live in the real world, a world of disappointments and fear.

The constant dread of the artistic life remains with me even after many more years of experience. For me, as a Christian, the fear remains, but what is slowly changing is my ability to bring my fear to the feet of Jesus, rather than to delude myself into thinking that I can plan or pray my way to success.

Trusting God

The true rewards in life are not usually where we look for them. They are often in altogether less dramatic places than the winning of Oscars. Perhaps we become grateful to God for the fact that against all odds we have remained faithful to our spouses with His help. Or that we have, in spite of the temptation to become workaholics, been forced by events to put our children first and our careers second. In these fundamentally simple areas of life, we can see God's blessing, His grace, and His love for us. The work itself, most of the time, is just a job—a job whose success depends on the ever-shifting winds of fortune. Our spouses, our children, obeying Christ—these are an end in themselves. Our artistic careers will careen up and down, but loving children, the love of our spouse, a thankful heart—these can be enjoyed now and eternally.

Sexual fidelity, loyalty to our children, love of God, trusting God to provide money, or at least trying to trust—these are the hardest challenges of the artistic life for Christians. The rest is a question of talent and luck. Luck? But "surely God sees even every sparrow of the air." Yes, but perhaps we should avoid the temptation of dignifying our every whim and ambition with some fondly imagined heavenly plan, as if destiny stands or falls on the basis of our small, ego-driven creations. Hyper-Calvinists and pietists of all stripes may spin in their graves, but I do not believe that God necessarily cares about every trivial incident of our lives in the self-centered way we wish He would. It seems to me a mistake to view God as a predictable slot machine into which we put our prayers and from which we then extract what we want. In my own experience it has been too easy to dignify my selfish struggles and failings with the trappings of so-called spiritual warfare. I believe things usually happen for simple reasons, the natural results of a cause-and-effect universe. For instance, if I choose to pin all my career hopes on a frail, old actor, I am not being particularly bright. Old people die. If I fail at what I am doing, it may not be because I am being persecuted or because God is trying to teach me something. It is probably because I am not very good at what I do and am going about it in a stupid way.

I believe that the anxiety, the cycles of creative energy, and the slogging through everyday work, disappointments, and failures are universal characteristics in all artists' lives. The constant rekindling of enthusiasm for a new project, opportunity, movie, play, screenplay, painting, book, or piece of music, in spite of disappointments, is evidence of our being created in the image of the Creator. Artists *are* driven. Despite insurmountable odds, we continue to dream, plan, scheme, and move ahead. We even will wallow in the depths of failure, if need be, rather than abandon our art in favor of an easier life. A project on which we have labored for months, even years, may utterly come unstuck and collapse, leaving us with debt and embarrassment. We will mourn its passing for a time and then remarkably get up off the floor and start another project.

The artistic life is hard. It is fraught with artistic and financial setbacks, and each artist has his or her own horror stories. The now-defunct Empire Pictures owes me $8,000 that I will never see for months of hard work on a movie. As a result of the refusal of Empire to honor its contract, I was unable to make tuition payments for my children and had to borrow money. One of my friends, a painter, just sold a work he has slaved over for a year. The New York gallery that represents him takes a 50 percent cut of his earnings. The collector who bought the artwork is paying in two installments. My friend worries that the gallery will take its 50 percent commission by taking the whole of the first payment, rather than dividing it with him and then dividing the second installment. What will he live on in the meantime? How will he support his wife and children? Yet he, like thousands before him, will continue to paint regardless of the attendant financial vagaries and myriad disappointments.

In fact, he and I are some of the fortunate few who have worked at all. In the February 1990 issue of *Art in America* the conclusions of several studies on artists and their incomes were published. In these studies, 4,136 artists and writers were surveyed and asked over one hundred questions relative to their financial and professional status. Among the findings was the fact that 70 percent said they had to work at other jobs besides their art or writing to support themselves. Only 20 percent earned their major income from their art or writing. Of the 83 percent who earned anything at all from their artwork, only half of them earned enough to cover the expenses of their art materials.

What is it inside otherwise sensible people that leads them to participate in this constant financial and artistic high-wire act? Can it be that God's creative breath still lingers in the nostrils of human beings?

It is an amiable illusion, which the shape of our planet prompts, that every man is at the top of the world.

Emerson, *Uncollected Lectures: Table-talk*

3

HUMILITY IN A WORLD OF EGOMANIA

The world of art is a sea awash in a red tide of egomania. For pure, self-centered, soul-destroying, selfishness, nothing rivals the insecure, inward-looking *self* of the artist. Moviemakers, writers, musicians, painters, actors — petty tyrants all!

A child playing near his parents will often keep one eye on the game but the other on his audience. "Look at me, Mom!" Children reach a certain stage of maturity when they stop performing for an audience of parents or friends, become less self-aware, and begin to do things for their own sakes. Artists, however, never fully mature in this respect. We artists are, by definition, performers. "What do you think of it?" is the first question of most artists concerning his or her work. Because art is an expression of the human soul, the question really being asked is, "What do you think of me?" Art is a conscious expression of the Self. Even God, in the capacity of creator and artist, became His own audience and critic when He pronounced His creation "good."

Artists suffer constant rejection, and this can lead to unhealthy self-analysis and inward-looking selfishness. When allowed to flourish, this poisonous mixture produces towering, self-centered egos: egos that treat spouses and children badly — egos that drive people to endlessly ask themselves *Am I happy? Am I whole?* — egos that trample and use others. In history, perhaps only great military commanders, surgeons, and preachers have rivaled artists in their egos! While many people, perhaps with deplorable aesthetic taste, go unassumingly about their daily lives, many artists, actors, painters, composers, and writers behave like some mutant combination of Narcissus and Napoleon.

The fact that the particular hardships of the free-lance artistic life, to some extent, justify the self-protective reaction of developing a very thick skin, an ego only makes things worse. It gives us a mental room in which to hide when our conscience comes looking for us.

There is very little that we can do by our own efforts to address the sin of selfishness in our lives. Self-curing Self is only another form of egomania. Self-created humility is not genuine humility, expressed when we *stop* thinking about ourselves, stop looking inward, stop asking *Am I happy? Am I whole?* or *Who is to blame for my problems?*

Artists are, of course, not alone in their selfishness. We live in a self-centered age — an age whose political and economic necessities have spawned the practice of dumping babies and children into the living abandonment of day-care centers, while parents pursue money and careers at their children's expense. An age in which marriages and fetuses alike are murdered; for convenience's sake, children are destroyed and vows broken. An age in which some Christians have even developed a "theology" of selfishness disguised as a quest for "inner healing," "wholeness," and going on an "inner spiritual journey" or looking inward to find "spiritual gifts." Artists are not exempt from the selfishness of our times. The monstrous behavior of Picasso toward his wives, children, mistresses, and friends stands as a cautionary tale — wickedness he excused by the needs of his artistic life. One can be far less callous than Picasso and still very sinful toward God and one's family.

Professional Strawberries

Actors are professional strawberries; they spend their lives pathetically whimpering, "pick me, pick me." In one way or another, all of us in the arts are the same. To do anything well in the arts takes immense concentration and self-awareness. And to succeed requires self-promotion. Yet, if one is to live as a Christian, one must attempt to have godly priorities. It is better to fail at one's profession yet succeed as a human being, if that unhappy choice is forced upon us by circumstances. "Choose first the kingdom of God."

Naturally, our responsibilities differ toward different people. A dependent child or spouse has a very special claim on us, above that of other people. But virtuous behavior is not only a question of grinding, self-effacing duty. Joy and redemption are the result of realizing proper priorities in our lives.

Reading a positive review of a movie of mine (shown at the Cannes film festival in 1989) in *Variety* brought satisfaction. But reading a book to my little son, seeing him laugh, kissing him good night, kneeling next to him as he said his simple prayers—this gave me joy that is true, eternal, sharp, biting as good brandy on the tongue. By comparison, what *Variety* thought of my latest movie receded into the shadows of trivia.

"Success"

Failure can breed a graspingly desperate selfishness, but so can success. Ovid writes that, "Pride grows greater in prosperity, nor is it easy to bear good fortune with an undisturbed mind" (*Ars Amatoria*, Bk. 2, Line 438). In my own experience, the selfishness bred of success has been of a more virulent kind than that bred of failure. Failure has tended to send me crashing back into the presence of the Creator, my tail between my legs. My prayers may at such times take on the cringing servility of Uriah Heep, but at least I pray!

Success, however, is another matter. When I've been "on a roll," high on my horse, sure that for once I have got it right and that I have slipped through the border into the land of plenty, then I have often forgotten not only God, but the people He has given to me to love. Wife, children, friends, and piety become weak shadows cast by the reflected glory of *my brilliant career*. I remember my attitude of pride during the mix of my first feature film — strutting around like some puffed-up bantam rooster, assuming that air of jovial condescension toward the poor minions who were sweating away making *my* movie, pleased that "beautiful people" were dropping by to take a look at the maestro at work. I was breathing pure oxygen, snapping rudely at anyone who disturbed *my* concentration while I worked on *my* movie, and ready to conquer the world. "I'll show them!" I regarded people as friends only if they were helping *me* in *my* quest, on *my* epic — an epic *I* was writing and creating like a self-fulfilled prophesy.

Fortunately, the real world is a prickly place of sharp, jagged edges that puncture my little balloons of self-centered, self-indulgent *success*. Deflated, I crawl back to God. *Successes*, real or merely imagined, have, for me, usually ended in reenactments of the parable of the prodigal son. The morning after, all that is left is the flaccidity of a punctured ego. As Shakespeare wrote in *As You Like It*, "My pride fell with my fortunes" (Act 1 sc. 2).

Faith

The life of the artist *can* become a life of faith. The insecurities *can* lead to greater daily reliance upon God, to a sense of our total dependence on Him. Where other people have the false security of a "real job," the artist — as any actor waiting in line at an audition or any writer waiting to hear from a publisher will tell you — is daily reminded that destiny cannot be controlled. This knowledge can lead to faith, but often, sadly, in my life it has led to looking for security where there is none — in myself.

Modern psychology may tell us to "feel good about ourselves"; the Bible has no such comfortable instruction. Some Christians tell us to go on inward journeys of self-discovery, but we can search the Scriptures in vain for such pleasantly selfish commands. Christ told us to do many things but never to "seek a good self-image." Some people have tried to tell us that because we are to love our neighbors "as ourselves" that self-love is therefore justified; this is false. We are to care for the needs of our neighbors as we would our own, but this attitude bears no relationship to the kind of self-love and pseudo-spirituality we all indulge in — the kind of self-love that prevents us from even seeing that we do have neighbors because we are too busy seeking to "affirm" ourselves under the guise of living the life of faith.

As believing Christians, our security lies in the fact that God *knows* us, not in how we *feel* about ourselves. Our salvation is not measured by how we feel and whether we feel "whole" or "fulfilled," but by whether we obey Christ's clear instructions. How we "feel" about things is usually unimportant. Feelings are unreliable. "Worship experience" is not love of God; obeying His law is. It is what we *do* that counts. This is faith.

Suffering

Emerson wrote in his *Conduct of Life*: "Art is a jealous mistress, and if a man have a genius for painting, poetry, music, architecture or philosophy, he makes a bad husband and an ill provider." My wife, who has selflessly shared in bearing the burden of my perpetual anxieties, could endorse the veracity of Emerson's observation! As artists, our spouses and children bear a unique burden; therefore, it is important that they also be given special joy — not only the pleasure of seeing our artwork complete, but also the deeper satisfaction of living with a person whose *self* is growing slowly less while Christ is growing more; a person who is not on a selfish journey of inner self-discovery but instead is on a journey toward God.

There *is* great suffering, often bitterness and stress, because of the insecurity of the artist's life. Sadly, we often take revenge for our distress on the people we love most. This, as my wife and children can tell you, is wicked behavior. When we are humiliated by a gallery owner or a rejection letter, or when another actor gets the part, or when we are misunderstood by an ignorant church, all too often it is our longsuffering spouse or child who feels the lash of our tongue and the dark tide of our despondency. That artists in all fields tend to be driven to drink, to drugs, to use promiscuous sex as an autoerotic escape, or to become sickly, dependent, and even addicted to spiritual or psychological "counseling" is not a coincidence. The artist lives a hard life. Yet, as Christians, we need not be ruled by our weaknesses. We can choose God, fail, yet choose Him again.

"Blessed are they that hunger and thirst after righteousness." To Christians, this hunger and thirst must be expressed by declaring war on the ego, by turning the battle of the Self into godly war. Our aim must be to bring our sufferings to Jesus to receive His peace rather than take them out on our loved ones. It is a slow, daily struggle won only in increments and never fully achieved. However, the battle, as it rages, can be progressing toward the light. Pressure of work is no excuse for sin. Self-knowledge is not an adequate substitute for self-discipline.

No one may understand what we are doing and many may reject us. What better place to imitate Christ? Jesus, too, was criticized for keeping bad company. Jesus, too, broke the petty religious rules of His day. People misunderstood His stories, His parables. God Himself has seen His creation ruined, defiled, "recut," edited into oblivion. God understands artists. If we must storm, rage, argue, then we should do so in the presence of God; He knows us and can answer us. Our spouse, children, and friends cannot. They are not responsible for our feelings of failure. It is not their fault that we are pricked by jealousy of those who seem to be enjoying greater success or prosperity, or that we are depressed by constant rejection. But God does understand. He gave us our creative talents and He can multiply them. We should pray that He will give us the inner discipline needed to carry on our work, alone if necessary. We can attempt to adopt God's historical perspective and (hard as it may seem) to look for His lessons — His refining fire — in the countless setbacks, disappointments, and travails of the artistic life.

Humility

I have learned that God's timetable of success is not the same as mine. It has begun to dawn on me that perhaps His ambition for us is greater than our own. He sees our lives in the context of an eternal history. He is preparing us for eternity. He *will* bless us, but the trash in our spirits, artistic and personal, must be burned away first. For some of us, this purging will require a lifetime of failure. The hardships, loneliness, betrayal by other Christians, and our artistic failures become the fuel for a bonfire in which the rubbish in our lives can and should go up in smoke. We should pray that the fire of sorrow and failure would purify our talent and our souls: this is true success. Artistic or commercial success may be ours, or it may not, but the fire will have done its work: humility.

It seems to me that godly humility is the opposite of the concept of modern psychological self-awareness. It does not seek to unravel every tangled knot in our spirits or ascribe blame for our problems to people or past events. Instead, humility places us at

Jesus' feet where we ask for His forgiveness and move forward and outward, not backward and inward.

Humility, as illustrated in Jesus' life, is not some form of smarmy self-abasement, of hushed voice and "holy" tone, nor is humility the kind of false Christian piety that Robert Burton alluded to when he wrote, "They are proud in humility; proud that they are not proud" (*Anatomy of Melancholy,* pt. II, sec. II).

Humility is a vigorous state of being in which we have a sense of who we are and, more importantly, who we are not. It is not a self-conscious attitude of hand-wringing quietness in the face of evil nor an attitude of whining niceness. Humility provides us with a state of mind in which we no longer are overly conscious of ourselves. Instead, we are free to look *outward,* to enjoy those about us and know the goodness of God. Humility allows us to be free. The humble spirit gives thanks to God and rarely asks, *Am I happy? Am I fulfilled?* or *Am I whole?* But instead asks, *Am I doing the right thing?* Humility leads us towards the realization that our purpose here on earth is *not* that we come to know ourselves but that we might begin to know God. He knows us already; therefore, contrary to popular opinion, knowing ourselves need not be our life work. In this life we will never be whole, but God is and we can trust His goodness. Humility is the rejection of the self-pitying syndrome that perversely rejoices in being needy, wounded, and introspective. Humility is natural, warm, forgiving, and forthright. Humility has no hidden agendas.

The Bible contains many verses on the folly of pride. We are told in Proverbs that "the fear of the LORD is to hate evil; pride and arrogance and the evil way" and "a man's pride will bring him low, but the humble in spirit will retain honor" (Proverbs 8:13; 29:23). In Mark 7:21–22, the writer lists pride along with the grave sins of the flesh. "For from within, out of the heart of men, proceed evil thoughts, adulteries, fornications, murders, thefts, covetousness, wickedness, deceit, licentiousness, an evil eye, blasphemy, pride, foolishness."

I realize that what I have written above is more of a prayer for saintly behavior than a statement of action that I have carried out myself! But, to quote the inimitable Frank Zappa, "Jesus knows you're a jerk!" There is no need to attempt to fool ourselves, let alone God.

So full of artless jealousy is guilt,
It spills itself in fearing to be spilt.

Shakespeare, *Hamlet*, Act IV, Scene 5

4

FALSE GUILT—TRUE GUILT

I n the arts, there should be no segregation of secular and religious subject matter. Reality, like God, is one. This is not an unusual idea. It is, after all, a derivative of St. Augustine's foundational concept embodied in *The City of God*. Augustine saw the cosmos as one unit divinely infused and all mankind as one brotherhood. He saw reality, spiritual and physical, as moving toward an unfolding of God's purposes. Reality was a cumulative advancement of mankind, materially and spiritually, through time, as history taught God's lessons through experience. Augustine rejoiced in the goodness of the arts and extolled their virtue as part of God's creation. To him, all of reality was part of the divine unfolding of history.

False Guilt

Christian artists who agonize over *what* they should create, from the point of view of what is allegedly Christian subject matter, are engaged in an exercise in futility—an exercise usually motivated by false guilt bred of a bad theology that has divided reality into "secular" and "Christian" and that perceives art as only a useful propaganda tool for evangelization.

For the Christian, there is no taboo subject matter any more than there are evil or taboo colors. Though how we portray each subject is important, as is its context, *reality, as it is perceived, is the fit subject for the artist.* To tell the truth is our only artistic, moral imperative. To portray evil as good is sin. To portray evil *as* evil is to do right. To turn the whole world on its head and portray virtue as evil is sin. Often the context in which we portray a subject is as important as the subject itself. For instance, there is a vast difference between sexuality in art and pornography, just as there is a difference between sexual intercourse between married people and fornication and adultery. It is the context in which sexual relations take place that determines their morality, not sex itself. In artistic works, the context of events and the subject matter being portrayed determine the work's moral content and whether it is telling the truth. By truth I do not necessarily mean telling the truth about big or cosmic subjects much less theological ones. Truth can involve exploring color or texture in an abstract work. Integrity in materials, the weight and texture of an art work, or the resonance of music—all can ring true or false in a way that can be intelligently discussed and examined.

As an example of a movie telling the truth, in a figurative medium, in this case about sin and depravity, consider *Sid and Nancy,* a biographical film about the lives of Sid Vicious and his girlfriend, Nancy, made famous by the Sex Pistols, Sid Vicious' punk rock band. In the movie, the sorrow and decadence of Sid and Nancy's lives were not glamorized. The truth was told. The ugliness of the debased, anti-Christian philosophy they lived by was portrayed as producing ugly results, as death-causing, tragic. To make a truthful movie like *Sid and Nancy* that is consistent with reality is ideally the goal for the Christian and non-Christian filmmaker alike.

Compromise

Many of us who are artists are not yet in the position of being able to write or choose our own material, any more than most auto workers in Detroit are engaged in designing the cars they make or setting corporate policy. We are often engaged in the making of movies, books, music, plays, etc., that do *not* wholly reflect our point of view and do not wholly tell the truth as we see it. However, the need to compromise is not a problem peculiar to those in the arts. We have to interact every day with a world that is far from ideal. For example, we pay taxes to a government that, at present, allows and often pays for abortions and has failed miserably to address the problems of a poverty-stricken underclass. We live, work, and educate our children within the confines of a fallen world.

There are too few people in the church who comprehend the artistic struggle and encourage Christians to succeed in the arts. There are, however, many Christian guilt-mongers who place burdens on others that they themselves do not bear; their attitude is embodied in the what's-Christian-about-that? school of art critics, who do not understand the arts or the daily reality of the artist's struggle. In my life as a moviemaker, for instance, there are many forces at work, most beyond my control in terms of choosing the subject matter of the movies I direct. Therefore any artistic progress I make is incremental. As artists we have to pay our dues, to suffer, to look for long-term results, to be successful, *before* we have the artistic freedom to choose the subjects we wish to express. Success must be *earned* from within the movie business and from within other artistic fields, and cannot be bought; there are no shortcuts. Few seem to understand this. They expect quick, dramatic results from what is necessarily a slow, very imperfect process.

There are hundreds of small battles we fight daily in our work and life — undramatic victories, small progress over a lifetime of work. As artists, we yearn for sympathetic Christian critics with a knowledge of art and the historical perspective about art movements necessary to make an intelligent contribution to our work. Such understanding is, unfortunately, rare. Instead, we are often subjected to moralistic posturing on the part of Christians whose ignorance is only matched by their intransigence.

Most of us in the arts know we are fortunate to be working at all in our chosen field, much less being in command of that field! Since much of the Christian community has ignored the arts in our recent history, the Christian who wishes to learn about art must, by necessity, learn in the larger world, outside of the Christian ghetto — a ghetto that some Christians have created in a misbegotten attempt to find a sort of heaven on earth.

There is no heaven on earth. And those, like the millennialist puritans of the seventeenth century, who think we can create an earthly paradise are proven wrong in their assumptions, nor is there a place remote enough to run and hide from the world. We are called to be "in the world but not of it." We must at times create movies, television shows, books, art, music, theatre, and dance that does not mirror our worldview, while working to not be tainted in our inner being by the unbelief around us. We must not lie to ourselves about what we are doing but compromise bravely, keeping our eyes on our eventual goals. We must admit we need to walk before we can run. There will be shabby compromises aplenty necessitated by our work, not because we are artists, but because we live in a fallen world. Perhaps unfairly, artistic compromises are more misunderstood than the compromises routinely made by businessmen, teachers, lawyers, nurses, pastors, people in professions more familiar to middle America and the church.

If an actor who was a well-known evangelical Christian played the role of a homosexual in a movie, he could expect ritual condemnation for having "sold out" or worse. Yet it is no more reasonable to believe that an actor or director or dancer is expressing approval of homosexual behavior by working with a homosexual or portraying one in a film or play, than it is to accuse an insurance salesman of "underwriting sin" because some homosexual's lover is named as the beneficiary of a life insurance policy. Nor is the merit of an artistic statement's truth less if we discover that sinners were involved in its making. The star of *Chariots of Fire*, who played Christian athlete Eric Liddel, died of AIDS. Yet does his alleged homosexual behavior lessen the virtue of that movie? I think not.

The fates of the sinful and the saved are inextricably interwoven in our fallen world. The "wheat and the tares" will be sorted out on Judgment Day, but as Christ taught us, to attempt to do the sorting now is often an exercise in futility. Because the arts and media are so visible and yet so misunderstood, Christian artists are singled out for unjustified criticism from which other professions are less apt to suffer. This in no way abrogates a Christian's individual responsibility to live morally or to speak up against immorality. But in the case of the arts and other professions, it is foolish to expect people to be able to sort out every implied consequence, real or imagined, of how they must earn their living.

Steven Hawley

Even contemporary Christians in the arts who *have* achieved the success and skill necessary to choose their subjects and portray them exceedingly well have often been rejected by many people in the church. Thus, some excellent work that *does* reflect a Christian artist's worldview has been rejected by modern fundamentalist Christians. The brilliant novels of Walker Percy are a case in point, and there are many other examples. When the first edition of the serious Christian journal on the arts, *Image,* was printed in 1989, it had on the cover a reproduction of a painting by Steven Hawley, one of America's premier, post-modern, neo-realist painters and a believing evangelical Christian. The painting of a pear, a skeleton, and a fish has a small, painted photograph in the background of Hawley's pregnant and nude wife. *Image* received a number of vitriolic letters from outraged Christians furious over this nudity in a Christian publication. "In view of the nudity in your publication . . . take me off your mailing list." "Shocked," "horrified," and "dismayed" were typical of some of the sentiments expressed.

Yet the painting, which is now in a famous private collection, has (for any with eyes to see) a strong *Biblical symbolism*. For example, novelist Harold Fickett wrote in *Image* about Hawley's painting, *Black Glass Still Life with Pear, Fish and Skeleton:*

> The painting . . . asserts its character as an altar piece. . . . the symbolism is blatant. . . . The coordination of the iconography here presents a devastating interpretation of sacrifice that re-explains to us what an altar means. . . . The three central images . . . picture three separate stages in life. We see a pregnant [nude] woman in the Polaroid on the right nearing the end of her term, the baby almost the more present for being concealed in her flesh. On the left we see a young boy — Steve's second son, Vincent — standing in one corner of the studio, with a full-sized cross set up behind him. Beside the cross there is a ladder. In the middle of these two images we have a Polaroid of a man screaming out in agony. The triptych form directs our reading of these images. Because of their reference to the crucifixion we are going to be looking at life as it leads to death. Then, too, there are interior elements that tie the three together. The little boy continues the theme of growth and development enunciated in the pregnancy. The ladder leads us to connect the boy with the man in agony, for it suggests that the boy's ascent in life as he grows will simultaneously lead to the universal crucifixion of mortality. . . . The body of the fish lies on red and white tiles. The fish, since the beginning of the church, has symbolized the Christian faith, particularly in its sacramental aspects. Christ, as the fisher of men, calls us to the altar, where he breaks the loaves and fishes, supplying a meal that satisfies our eternal hunger. . . . The life that Christ extends to us, the painter seems

to be saying, He gives to creatures who in their mere flesh are nothing but bones that cannot live. (*Image* [Spring 1989])

Art historian and critic Charles Jenks, in his book *Post-Modernism*, says of Hawley's work that it "achieves the richest luminosity of surface and texture . . . [and] shows the virtuosic effects . . . Photo Realism can achieve" (New York: Rizzoli, 1987, 146–47).

To perceive the truth in Hawley's work, the angry, middle-class evangelical and fundamentalist Christians canceling subscriptions would need an artistic mental vocabulary and knowledge of art history similar to Fickett. Their outrage, a manifestation of gross ignorance in the face of transcendent beauty, highlights the uphill battle any talented Christian artist will endure in expecting any understanding or encouragement from some of his fellow Christians.

Cross-Purposes

As an illustration of the gulf separating pietistic fundamentalist Christianity and the arts, I remember an incident that took place some years ago and, at the time, left me speechless.

My book *Addicted to Mediocrity* had just been published. The cover featured a detail from Michelangelo's Sistine Chapel ceiling portraying God creating Adam. On the book cover, a painter with a roller brush is covering the famous fresco of the partially nude figures. He has a Christian fish symbol stitched onto his back pocket. The message is clear: Christians are so insensitive to the arts that they are metaphorically painting out art altogether.

A few days after the book came out, I was speaking at an evangelical gathering where a famous fundamentalist preacher was in attendance. He and his wife were leaders of a number of organizations that claimed to be "bringing God back into American life." This pastor congratulated me on the book. He said he had not read it yet but liked the cover, which, as he put it, expressed just what he had been saying about art. "It was about time," he said, "that someone said what needed saying about *getting rid of nudity in art!*" It slowly dawned on me that this man *assumed* that the cover of the book was *advocating* the exact attitude it was satirizing!

Oddly enough, a similar incident occurred in regard to another book of mine. A friend in the movie business had read *A Modest Proposal,* a Swiftian satire I had co-written examining the anti-life ideas embodied by the abortion industry and new eugenics movement. In one passage, we "advocated" using fetuses as a source of protein. This woman congratulated me on having the nerve to *propose* what she thought was a perfectly logical idea! My views were so far out of line with hers that what to me was a far-fetched, obviously satirical, even sick suggestion seemed to her a serious, logical proposal!

These two gross misunderstandings symbolize how very out-of-step Christians in the arts are with both fundamentalist Christianity *and* fundamentalist secularism.

In addition to being misunderstood, the Christian artist must contend with two other problems: first, the Christian community's reaction to the highly secularized media, and second, the effects of middle-class values on society — effects that have replaced the tough, raw, real, robust absolutes of Scripture with something akin to the saccharine anti-reality embodied in the "family entertainment" of some live-action Disney movies.

The artist's response to the first problem, fear of aggressive secularism by the church, should be love and understanding. Christians and Christian ideas have taken an ideological beating in this century — a beating often administered by a hostile media. However, in the case of the second point, offended false pietistic sensibilities, the artist cannot tell lies for the sake of appeasing Christians who have absorbed (by cultural osmosis) dainty, middle-class values. The world *is* a rough, violent, gritty, and fleshy place of immense joy *and* sorrow. That some people are offended by reflections of reality, even beautiful pro-life reflections as in

Hawley's painting of his nude pregnant wife, is not the fault of the artist. And it is not the artist who should change what he or she is expressing to accommodate such wrong-headed ideas. To do so would be to use his or her God-given talents to tell lies — perhaps nice, middle-class lies, but lies nevertheless.

Reality

Art is about truth. Art is not an expression of wishful thinking. Art is about beauty, inasmuch as beauty, too, is part of truth. But there are different kinds of beauty. There is beauty in the *way* something is done as well in the actual subject matter. For instance, one can have a beautiful photograph of an ugly incident. Conversely, one can have a silly, sentimental photograph or painting of a beautiful subject, the kind of an obscenity that typifies Playboy's soft-core porn; the decorative art of the "hotel-motel" variety that one sees displayed on countless sidewalks in tourist resorts; and the sort of "art" that some pastors delight in hanging in their "counseling" rooms.

Artistic questions are more complex than a list of "dos" and "don'ts." Artists will make mistakes. Most artwork is not fully resolved; it is only a way station on the path of learning which leads to more finished, more complete work. The artist is involved in a lifetime struggle to produce anything finished, complete, and valid in his or her art. And it is the lifetime work of the artist that should, in fairness, be judged, not his or her every halting step. Artists need time, a *lifetime,* to develop their skills and to perfect their work. Beyond the individual artist, art movements in history need many lifetimes, each building on the last to create any permanent cultural impact.

I have for years been nonplussed by the overserious ideological, "theological" response to my own artistic endeavors by some other Christians. I have felt that people have mistaken my own efforts, such as they are — first in painting, then film — for sermons, when in fact they were often only experimental works containing many flaws. I have learned from and progressed beyond these flaws only to discover that even more remains to be learned! By the manner in which some Christians have discussed, and even savaged, my work, I assume they thought that I was trying to "say" something in the same way as, for instance, I am "saying" something in this non-fiction book. However, a non-fiction book *on* the arts is a very different thing from art itself. Color, texture, poetic nuance, and mood cannot and should not be reduced to theological categories as if art work were no more than another means of carrying on a seminarial debate.

I have had people ask me what a certain scene in a "secular" movie I directed "meant." I have felt like replying that it was not in the original script but was invented to replace some other scene we were not able to shoot due to rain. All that it meant was that it had rained that day. More often than not such an apparently flippant explanation would be closer to the truth than a more considered, philosophical reply when it comes to the reality of making movies.

When the first ill-fated feature I directed opened in eighty theaters in the Los Angeles area in 1986, one Christian radio talk show took questions for three whole days from irate or supportive Christian listeners who related their "theological" reactions to the movie that Francis Schaeffer's son had made. *The Los Angeles Times,* noting this unusual manifestation of interest in and criticism of a movie by the normally complacent, evangelical fundamentalist Christians, ran a piece headlined "Flock Flails Flick." The sad truth was that *Wired to Kill,* a first and flawed directing effort, did not deserve any of this attention. Had evangelical fundamentalist filmgoers noted that as a first-time feature director I had much to learn, they would have been on the right track. As it was, my movie was criticized as if it were a failed "message" movie, when in fact it was just another ultra-low budget, action, sci-fi, "horror" film directed by a first-time feature director—a half-baked footnote in cinema history, at best, soon to be relegated to late night cable TV hell! In the midst of this tempest in a very small teapot, I received a great deal of personal condemnation because the "message" of my movie was not only not "Christian," but R-rated and violent. How could *this* be a "Christian" statement? Who could "get saved" watching this? This movie wasn't like a Billy Graham movie. It wasn't inspiring like *Chariots of Fire*. Why not? Had I "sold out"? Was I still a "Christian"? In this debate, I heard few encouraging voices. One or two people seemed to understand that a low-budget, genre movie made for the action-horror market cannot very well be held up for comparison with a ministry-generated, gospel movie or with larger budget films such as *Chariots of Fire*, made by men like David Putnam, a producer at the pinnacle of a long and exceptional career with abundant resources and experience.

The experience of being shot at, even by some friends, was hurtful for me and caused quite a lot of inner pain and soul searching at the time. Yet I was fortunate. I knew that there was a rational, compassionate Christian alternative to the witch-hunting mentality I was encountering. I had experienced this tolerant alternative in my own home from my parents and from a number of believing Christian friends who understood something of the necessities of trying to launch a movie-making career. I had had the privilege of having a father who knew, loved, and understood film, and with whom I had shared many movie ideas before he died in 1984, including early script ideas for *Wired to Kill,* which he had liked for what it was. We had had, over the years, many a long and encouraging talk about my dream of making movies.

Thus, I had enjoyed my share of encouragement. I was not completely at the mercy of the pious mob or professionally jealous, back-biting Christian "colleagues." Had I thought that the furious criticism I was facing represented the teachings of Scripture or of the wisdom of the historic, apostolic church on the arts, and had I never known of another way of looking at culture and art other than through a nervous, middle-class, propagandistic, fundamentalist set of spectacles, then I would have been in the desperate position of trying to choose between my faith and my movie-making.

Fortunately, this was not the case; I had the privilege of enjoying a wider perspective. Not everyone employed in the arts has been so fortunate. I have observed many creative people browbeaten and finally cowed and crushed into submission. They litter the path of the evangelical fundamentalist juggernaut, chewed up, then regurgitated, by the faithful. The absence of Christians in the movie business, indeed in the arts in general, bears mute testimony to the success of some of the Christian world in eliminating talent from its midst.

True Guilt

Just because many burdens of false guilt have been placed on Christian artists does not excuse us from heeding our consciences when pricked by the Holy Spirit. Adultery, divorce, abortion, fornication, lust for power and money, homosexual behavior, arrogance, and the other *real* temptations and sins which may beset us must be resisted with moral fortitude. These sins, which devour so many in our culture, including many Christian "leaders," produce death. In some instances, the church, in imitating the surrounding society, has begun to subtly surrender to these evils and even condone them. In these matters of spiritual and physical life and death, the Christian artist must, for the sake of his or her own soul, stand firm.

If we are to live as Christians obedient to Christ, we must, like Tolstoy, long for righteousness. And, unlike Tolstoy, who seems even in his declining years to have followed his sexual appetite more than his conscience, succeed in doing more than just wishing for sanctity! We must be sexually chaste, faithful to our spouses, good husbands and wives, good parents. We must renounce greed, divorce, and blind ambition. To even attempt to live by these normal, ageless virtues of Jewish-Christian teaching sets us apart from many nonbelievers and also from an increasingly compromised church that minimizes sin in the name of love. In today's climate of religious experience for experience sake, it is easy to forget that to love Christ is to obey Him. This love is not a feeling, experience, or a mere idea. Our love for Christ can be measured against our success in obeying His clear commands, His teaching.

Daniel

Pursuing righteousness will give us a measure of spiritual clarity of vision, the sort of wisdom Daniel possessed while in the court of Nebuchadnezzar. He participated in the court life of Babylon, yet he was not corrupted. Daniel kept himself holy, not by forming a religious ghetto or school separated from Babylonian culture, but by being a part of the pagan governmental system without being consumed by it.

Daniel was eventually able to speak for God because he was *in* the court, not outside of it, because he worked *within* the sinful structure of the recognized regime. He was deemed "ten times better" at what he did academically than his non-Jewish competition. He was measured by the academic standards of his day and not found wanting. He was in the right place at the right time. Babylon was no worse a challenge to personal morality than Hollywood. Daniel stood; we can too.

The Roman Soldier

In the New Testament, there is a similar example of someone called to remain in the world without surrendering to it. John the Baptist, in Luke 3:14, exhorts a soldier to moral conduct while remaining in the immoral Roman army. He told him to not extort

money, not to accuse people falsely, and to be content with his
pay. John the Baptist told him to be, in effect, in the world—in
this case the Roman army—but not of it. That John the Baptist
advised the Roman soldier to *remain* in the military may be surprising from our point of view. The Roman army served dictato-
rial, imperial Rome and was a violent, profane, pagan organization. Yet John did *not* order the soldier to leave the military and
be a missionary instead. John told him to be a moral person in the
midst of immorality.

It is a hard task to direct our lives and minds away from the
false burdens of spiritual guilt that call us to be out of the world
and out of life and toward the true call of God to be in the world
but not of it. It is an undertaking complicated by the fact that to
be a good artist and a faithful Christian is, by definition, to offend
the pietists who control the thought of much of the church today.

Christ deeply offended the Pharisees, and if we are to live as
good artists and good Christians, we will offend their modern descendants as well. But Christ also stood up to Satan and was loving to the "least of these." Unlike the simplistic rules of fundamentalism, the Christian life is a balancing high-wire act. We will
fall from time to time, but there is a net.

We can be sure that the Roman soldier had many problems
trying to follow John's instructions while also serving Caesar. But
John, like Christ and unlike today's pietistic Christian leadership,
was never in the facile business of making things easy for his
followers.

Issues

The artist must struggle through many issues. One is the question
of performing other peoples' works of art. Most art is performance art or its equivalent. A concert violinist, an actor, a movie
director, a book or magazine editor—all have a job to do. It is a

way of honorably earning a living; it is a way of obeying the Biblical command to use our talents.

If Christ is truly Lord of all life, then an artist who is part of an orchestra performing a symphony by Mahler is praising God just as much as a member of a church choir singing an excerpt from the *Messiah.* An actor with a part in a second-rate movie he does not even like is praising God by using his talent just as much as a missionary feeding the hungry in some flea-ridden hellhole.

What we make when we can freely choose our subject is important, but the *how* and the *why* are equally important. Our creative work may be on projects that will not reflect what we believe to be true. But the artist needs to learn, to work, to succeed enough to be given the opportunity to call his or her own shots. Like Daniel, who surely found Babylon less than ideal yet used his opportunity when given it, we must slog forward one step at a time and attempt to be good at what we do — "ten times better" — to succeed and be in the right place at the right time, to be moral people in the midst of immorality. Like Daniel, to be prepared is our job. And like the Roman soldier, we should attempt to pursue our careers honestly and well.

Bad Advice from Worse People

We as Christians need the help, guidance, and advice of other believers. But we must be careful, as artists, to have realistic expectations about this human advice. Just because someone is a believing, practicing Christian does not mean he or she will have the wisdom, knowledge, or sympathy to advise us knowledgeably about our artistic work. Just because someone *claims* that God has laid something on his heart does not mean God has! The pastor, teacher, friend, or family member may or may not know enough about a particular field of endeavor to give good advice.

We must be wise in choosing those from whom we seek personal and professional advice and to whom we present our fragile ideas. In their infancy, ideas can be aborted if handled by the insensitive hands of well-meaning but ignorant believers or nonbelievers.

As Christians in the arts, we should pray that God would give us one or two understanding colleagues to know as friends. Since all people are created in God's image, whether they acknowledge Him or not, there are many sensible and wise nonbelievers to whom one may look for good artistic, aesthetic, and career advice. Better the knowledgeable advice of a nonbelieving expert than the heavy yoke of false spiritual guilt imposed by an ignorant believer, however well-intentioned. Artistic talent is truly a gift and must be protected, especially against the onslaught of misguided saints.

In my own experience as a moviemaker, some of my greatest discouragements have come from contact with other Christians and their vitriolic criticism. However, to be candid, there are many areas about which I am ignorant and judgmental myself. I have often been less than kind in my own public critique of some fellow Christians. To receive harsh treatment at the hands of my fellow believers is, in my case, really no more than to get a dose of my own caustic medicine. However, my own comeuppance aside, it is a tragedy that so many Christians who seek to work in the arts and media receive so little *knowledgeable* encouragement. There are legions ready to critique the first stumbling efforts of someone like myself, and few to offer practical help or advice. Without wishing to judge individual motivations, there seems to be an uglier undercurrent to some of the criticism given to those who, like me, attempt to work in the "secular" world. As the old saw goes, misery loves company. And those who by choice or fate are imprisoned in the Christian ghetto and have settled for its small, creatively unsatisfying boundaries are sometimes resentful of people who attempt to escape, let alone who enjoy some small measure of success.

*Someone at Universal Pictures
found the best way to promote the
film,* The Last Temptation of Christ:
*to leak certain blasphemous por-
tions of the script to conservative
Christians. They reacted predictably to the bait.*

Cal Thomas, *Los Angeles Times Syndicate,*
August 14, 1989

5

THE MISUNDERSTOOD
MEDIUM

Today's Christians often mistrust and misunderstand visual media. An extreme example of the basic negative attitude toward movies that pervades the little world of evangelicalism, fundamentalism, and some Roman Catholicism can be found in the publication *Movie Guide: A Biblical Guide to Movies and Entertainment.* This earnest "Biblical" guide "morally" rates the content of movies as follows: acceptable, caution, extreme caution, bad/decadent, evil. Thus, according to *Movie Guide,* the beautiful children's film *The Adventures of Baron Munchhausen* should be approached with *caution.* It finds *The Dream Team,* a romp of a slapstick comedy, morally *bad.* Unbelievably, it advises that Walt Disney's *Peter Pan* be approached with *caution,* and that the luminously beautiful *Dead Poets' Society* is *bad! Parenthood,* a celebration of family life, is also rated as *bad,* as is the ethereal *Field of Dreams.* Of all the films it considers, the overwhelming majority receive a very negative "moral" rating of which the examples above are a fair sampling. (It would be disingenuous of me if I were not to mention that one of the writers for the *Movie Guide* savagely criticized one of my own movies as morally evil.)

Such a rating system is a perfect metaphor for many Christians' sorry record of understanding, let alone enjoyment, of our contemporary culture. That there are any willing readers of such sanctimonious absurdity underscores the paranoid and anti-intellectual climate now dominating parts of the church. That anyone would want his entertainment prescreened and effectively censored for him by such a publication and not feel that his intelligence had been insulted, is an example of how genuine Biblical values have been replaced with lazy middle-American niceties by many Christians. Pious sentimentality has replaced robust virtue. Some Christians look to such guides to provide them the means to evade the world around them and, I suspect, their own need to think things through for themselves. In avoiding the arts, including many movies, some Christians, sadly, cut themselves off from a great deal of truth and beauty.

A Christian young person, being raised in the atmosphere of cultural paranoia typified in the censorious *Movie Guide*, is not going to be encouraged to develop an understanding of, or interest in, movies or culture. Nor is such an unfortunate likely to develop a love of creativity or artistic expression. No future movie directors need apply for inspiration to the authors of the "Biblical" *Movie Guide* or those of like mind.

To rate movies as *evil* shows a lack of precise thinking. Abortion clinics are evil. Auschwitz and its gas chambers are evil. The television evangelists who have cynically stolen the widow's mite in the name of the "Lord's work" are evil. The actions of Pol Pot and the Khmer Rouge are evil. There is real evil in the world without squandering our moral outrage on a movie. With abortion clinics merrily liquidating one-and-a-half million babies a year in our country, it would seem wiser to concentrate whatever firepower Christians have on shutting these clinics rather than persecuting those who offend our sense of cinematic propriety. With runaway children being coerced into prostitution in our cities, surely the evangelical-fundamentalist Pharisees who find time to print trivial "Biblical" ratings of movies, could direct their pious energies toward issues of greater moment. However, it seems that Christians, having given up on an artistic culture that they have not participated in for decades, are now content to merely throw stones from the sidelines to, as they foolishly imagine, "pressure the system to change." The "system," at least in the case of the movie business, merely ignores such foolishness.

Cal Thomas, the *Los Angeles Times* syndicated columnist, wrote in response to the picketing of Universal Pictures by Christians protesting the distribution of the movie *The Last Temptation of Christ*.

> A strong case can be made that the very ones most vehement in their opposition ought to be held at least partially responsible for helping to create the type of climate that promotes the success of such films.
>
> In addition, the conservative Christian church in the 20th century has deliberately created its own artistic and intellectual subculture, while failing to take advantage of opportunities to use mainstream filmmaking to fulfill its mission.
>
> Instead, I have heard numerous sermons on the "evil" of Hollywood, and I have heard preachers condemn attendance at movie theaters. . . . Paul McGuire, an independent filmmaker, says that not only have Christians had no influence in film's 100-year history, "they have actively discouraged those who are artists, filmmakers and dancers from creative expression." (*L. A. Times Syndicate*, August 14, 1989)

Reform

If Christians want to encourage a renaissance in the arts and humanities, then what is needed is an informed, long-term, Augustinian view of history and art, and an intelligent, willing generation of Christians who will make movies and other artworks from *within* the system. Cal Thomas ends his column, "So, my fellow Christians, protest this film if you like, but then how about devoting some energy to fill the vacuum created by your retreat from popular culture."

We need to acknowledge that getting into the film industry, and all other branches of the arts, is a long, slow, *messy* process. Those who would do so must actually love their work in the arts and accept the fact that believing Christian artists will need to work *through the system*, making their own quota of *bad, evil,* or *caution* artworks, *before* they can acquire the skill and success to incrementally add their own perspective to their work. (Even then they may well be vilified by the keepers of the flame of fundamentalist ignorance.) To have an informed view of the arts, we Christians have to understand how art, culture, and, in the case of film, Hollywood actually work. We need the patience of St. Francis and the perception of St. Thomas Aquinas. We have to abandon quick, dramatic, evangelistic propaganda in favor of a lifetime of hard, undramatic work. We will have to read, watch, study, and *think*. We will have to go beyond middle American, post-Victorian niceties and take risks, keep bad company, be criticized from all sides, and be vulnerable. We will also have to abandon the respectability that many Christians, of the Biblical scorecard variety, seem to crave above all else.

All of this will be hard and complicated, like the Christian life itself—a battle. Simplistic lists of "dos" and "don'ts," which attempt to remove the need to struggle through issues, to work and live for Christ in the complicated and often ugly world, should not be labeled as "Biblical." Respectability should not be confused with godliness.

The example of the "Biblical" movie scorecard is only one of many attempts, concerning several areas of life, to reduce the Christian faith to a list of simplistic rules expressed in the religious how-to books, tapes, radio programs, and television programs which have recently multiplied like tumor cells. These pat teachings are simply Christianized imitations of the fashion for irrationality in the nonbelieving world, which is addicted to seeking easy solutions for complex problems and to reducing everything to the lowest common denominator. Any drive around Hollywood, with its well-advertised palmists, psychics, and "spiritual advisers," shows that the secular world, too, looks for instant solutions and easy, false advice. Christians and Jews should know better.

More Movies

Because of the level of ignorance about art in general and movies in particular within the evangelical-fundamentalist ghetto and because some Christians' aversion to modern cinema extends to not even seeing an R-rated movie, many movies are ignored — movies that *do* present ideas that are truthful about issues Christians *say* they care about. Consider a few random examples.

Fatal Attraction is a "pro-family" movie if there ever was one. The faithful wife, who stays at home to raise her child, is the heroine — a point that was not lost on the many irate feminist reviewers who excoriated the movie, in such publications as the *L. A. Weekly*, for presenting such a "traditional" female role in so positive a light. The philandering husband sets a series of events in motion that clearly shows the wages of sin to be death.

In a similar vein, *The War of the Roses*, a hilarious black comedy about divorce, could almost be an essay on the fact that a permanent, one man/one woman marriage for life is the only ideal for human sexual relationships. The movie poignantly shows that divorce is inherently unworkable. There is also a strong subtext in the film exposing the flimsiness of materialism as a basis for life, married or otherwise.

Crimes and Misdemeanors, a Woody Allen film, is a long discourse on the sanctity of life and a search for meaning through

God. The Socratic debate contained in the dialogue could have been lifted from a panel discussion between Malcolm Muggeridge, C. S. Lewis, and Thomas Acquinas.

The Terminator is a movie about the importance of individual heroic action and moral choices in history, and is directly pro-life in its implications concerning the uniqueness of each individual life, as well as antitotalitarian. There is even a dialogue line in the movie condemning the murderous intent of the Terminator as a "retroactive abortion."

Blade Runner has a deeply moral theme concerning the sanctity of human life infusing its text and subplot. It is a denunciation of human engineering on a par with *A Brave New World.*

The movie *River's Edge* reveals more about the results of godless secularism in the lives of young people—lives lived as if there is no transcendent meaning—than a month of sermons could. It is a virtual documentary on the results of the failure of "liberal" secular education policies and of the "values clarification" approach to moral education that has done so much to eviscerate our culture.

All That Jazz mirrors the book of Ecclesiastes. The movie expresses exactly the sentiments of "vanity, vanity, all is vanity." It is a film that rings true in an uncanny and almost absolute sense in regard to the problems of a creative life. It illustrates the idea that even while we are in life, yet we are in death. While clearly demonstrating the shallow inadequacies of a life lived only for temporal pleasure, it also expresses the poignancy of spiritual longing that is at the heart of even the most profane creative lifestyle.

Wish You Were Here, a serious and wonderfully made film, is about a young girl who chooses to keep her baby instead of having an abortion, as she is urged to do. It is an affirmation of life in spite of overwhelming odds and a touching essay on the vulnerable sexuality of a young person surrounded by the cynicism of older people who are jaded by their failures.

Rain Man expresses tenderness and compassion even for the unwanted and unloved in our society. It is a testimony against the idea that there is such a thing as a life unworthy of being lived. If the "right to die" (read, "right to kill") doctors, parents, and lawyers in Bloomington, Indiana, who starved the unwanted "Baby Doe" to death, had believed what the makers of *Rain Man* believed, Baby Doe would be alive today.

The implications of the story of the original *Dirty Harry* lead us to ask a valid moral question: What is the individual's responsibility to see justice done even in a society in which the criminal justice system has failed? This is the same question posed by Agatha Christie in her novel *Murder on the Orient Express*, in which she writes a mystery story about people taking the law into their own hands when a system of justice fails. It is also a theme that Sir Arthur Conan Doyle explored in a number of his Sherlock Holmes' stories, and it is a repeated Biblical theme.

Babette's Feast, one of the best movies of recent memory, actually takes place in a specifically theological context. It portrays a small, declining, nineteenth-century Danish Christian community into which a wonderful, irreverent French refugee woman comes. The story concerns the conflict between small-minded religiosity and the enjoyment of God's world to its fullest. The battleground is a banquet prepared by Babette (the refugee) and the Christians' shocked, ignorant reaction to what they regard as culinary waste and excess. It is a funny, moving, and deeply thought-provoking movie, and, to one as personally familiar with small Christian communities as I am, uncannily accurate as well as sympathetic in its subtleties.

Dead Poets' Society is a beautifully made movie about the nature of peoples' creative spirit—a film that captures, if somewhat romantically in a "Thoreauian" sense, the divine nature of the creative gift in each person. It is a film that strikes a blow for the importance of each individual and of art. (It is a movie that, as we have seen, irony of supreme ironies, the *Biblical Guide to*

Movies and Entertainment rates as morally *bad!*) This is a film that spans the generations in its appeal, as illustrated by the fact that my seventy-five-year-old mother, Edith Schaeffer, found it to be her favorite movie of the year in which it was released, as did my sixteen-year-old son.

The Boost and *Bright Lights, Big City* are both cautionary tales that warn of the personal cost of drug-taking as a way of life. Both movies follow a young man in a prodigal son-like story. *The Boost* follows an ambitious deal-maker as he ruins his career and marriage because of his drug use and his blind, materialistic ambition. *Bright Lights, Big City* is a similar story, exposing the ruin to which naked ambition and amorality lead.

Driving Miss Daisy is a movie that explores the tender qualities of human relationships and shows that they can transcend gender, race, and economic status.

Cinema Paradiso, the creation of the brilliant writer/director Giuseppe Tornatore, is a breathtakingly humane and beautiful film which profoundly explores the meaning of childhood. In it the local priest and other characters are portrayed as luminous and important people in spite of the humble lives which they live in a small Italian village. Perhaps no recent film has come so close to presenting the warmth and importance of ordinary life from such a clearly Biblical perspective.

The examples briefly mentioned above (and the list could have been much, much longer, especially if I included older film classics such as *Sunset Boulevard*) are not "Christian" movies, any more than a good dinner is a "Christian" dinner. They are not even all good movies. However, they are films that, inasmuch as they do reflect on the stories they portray, reveal their subjects to us in ways that reflect truthfully on issues about which thinking Christians at least *profess* to be concerned.

It is terribly unfortunate that many Christians needlessly avoid so many interesting movies because of what they wrong-headedly regard as illegitimate "sexual situations," "profanity," and "violence." As a result of such closed-minded, false piety, they cannot enjoy them or benefit from the useful discussions they would generate in families and amongst friends. Nor can they appreciate the creativity of the people who made them. Nor do they take advantage of the many thoughtful allies they have in the entertainment business who are at least raising questions that pinpoint certain realities in our society in a way that directs our attention towards eternal and transcendent themes.

No real movie is purely a "message movie" in the sense that Christians often seem to expect. Good movies must work on many levels. What movies "say," if anything, is only a part of the whole filmwork in question. However, there are quite a few movies that do tell the truth about their subjects, yet are unrecognized or, worse, actually vilified as *bad* or *evil* because they do not fit in with the false niceties of language etiquette or the behavioral norms relative to sex and violence which contemporary, middle-class American Christianity believes are suitable to express in the arts — norms that owe more to middle America than to Biblical understanding. Christians have enough real cultural enemies without ignoring or attacking their artistic allies, many of whom may not be believing Christians but nevertheless share a worldview often sympathetic to Jewish-Christian beliefs concerning some specific area or problem.

Religion and the Media

This is not to say that Hollywood has been particularly sympathetic to the Christian church and its doctrines, or even to Christian people. Michael Medved, movie critic and co-host of P.B.S.'s *Sneak Previews*, wrote concerning Hollywood's often hostile posture toward religion:

> As the world's most visible religious institution, the Roman Catholic Church has become a particularly popular target for

contemporary filmmakers. *Agnes of God* offers us the elevating image of young nun Meg Tilly murdering her own baby and attempting to flush the tiny body down the toilet of her convent room. . . .

Protestant pastors suffer the same rough treatment at the hands of Hollywood. . . . Independent feature films like *Pass the Ammo, Salvation* and *Riders of the Storm* have savagely satirized greedy and greasy evangelists lusting after sex and money. . . .

In explaining the hostility to our Judeo-Christian heritage that characterizes so many of these films, industry insiders firmly deny any deep-seated anti-religious bias. They insist that moviemakers are merely responding to the beliefs and prejudices of the film-going public. According to this argument, they are merely following the honorable capitalist practice of giving the customers what they want.

There is, however, one gigantic flaw in that line of reasoning: . . . the movies I've mentioned above . . . flopped resoundingly at the box office. . . .

[The producers'] mysterious behavior becomes even more difficult to understand when one takes a brief look at the public reception for those exceedingly rare films of recent years that have taken a more sympathetic view of organized faith. . . .

Like *Chariots of Fire, Tender Mercies* confounded the experts with its strong audience appeal. Robert Duvall won an Oscar as a washed-up, alcoholic country-and-western singer whose life is transformed by religious faith. In one of the most artfully underplayed scenes in recent films, he is baptized on screen and most convincingly born again.

Why hasn't Hollywood gotten the message? The one thing this industry is supposed to be able to do is to read the bottom line. Why, then, do savvy producers continue to authorize scores of projects that portray religious leaders as crazed, conspiratorial charlatans, when similar films have failed so conspicuously and consistently in the past?

It is hard to escape the conclusion that there is a perverse sort of idealism at work here. For many of the most powerful people in the entertainment business, hostility to traditional religion goes so deep and burns so intensely that they insist on expressing that hostility, even at the risk of commercial disaster. (*Imprimis*, a publication of Hillsdale College, Hillsdale, Michigan, [December 1989, Vol. 18, No. 12])

Though Medved does not attempt to analyze *why* there is such hostility toward Christianity in some quarters in Hollywood, the fact is that Christians have often brought much of it down on their own heads. First, by ignoring the medium, we are voluntarily conspicuous by our absence. There is no "plot" to keep Christians out of the film business. And second, Christian misunderstanding of art, culture, and film is so rampant that it would be hard to prove that the seeds of Hollywood's hostility toward what it understands as Christianity is not simply a reciprocation of the hostility many Christians and Christian institutions have shown toward those in the film business for many years. Moreover, those wishing to expose the greed, lust, and malfeasance of some "Christians" in their movies may choose from all too many glaring public examples.

Jim and Tammy

Because today the visual media is so little understood by Christians, when we have ventured into making movies and television, our work has generally been mediocre and the results poor. This is the complete and tragic reversal of the practice enjoyed in former centuries when believing Christians and Jews dominated the arts. Christian TV has become an object of ridicule to much of the Christian community as well as to the larger world, where, for all the claims by TV evangelists that they have seen "millions saved and thousands healed," tens of thousands of individuals have been permanently turned off to Christ by the ridiculous and crass posturing of televised preachers.

P. J. O'Rourke, an entertaining writer published in *Rolling Stone* and *The American Spectator,* paid a visit to the hellish fiasco that was Jim and Tammy Bakker's Heritage USA just before it closed and Jim Bakker was arrested, prosecuted, and sentenced for fraud. For Christians who wonder what the "world" thinks of our efforts to "reach" them, the following excerpt from P. J. O'Rourke's book, *Holidays in Hell* (New York: Atlantic Press, 1988), should provide some insight.

> My friend Dorothy and I spent a weekend at Heritage USA. . . .
> The architects must have been touched by the Holy Spirit because they were definitely speaking the language of design in tongues when they did this. At one end there's the Heritage Grand Hotel — Georgian on steroids, Monticello mated with a Ramada Inn and finished in Wendy's Old Fashioned Hamburgers Gothic. This is attached to a two-hundred-yard stretch of bogus Victorian house fronts, which screen the shopping mall. . . . The Christmas decorations were still up at Heritage. From the entrance gate all the way to the water slide, the place was festooned with Yule lights and other pagan symbols of the season — tinseled evergreens, holly wreaths, snowmen, candy canes. But no Santa Claus. His elves were there, stuffing stockings and wrapping presents, but Santa himself was nowhere to be found. When we walked into the hotel lobby, carolers were singing:
>
> > You'd better not frown,
> > You'd better not cry,
> > You'd better not pout,
> > I'm telling you why.
> > Jesus Christ is coming real soon.

And I thought Heritage USA was going to be dumb. But I'd only been there fifteen minutes and I was already confronted by enough serious theological questions to send St. Thomas Aquinas back to Bible college. Did Santa die on the cross? Will he be resurrected at Macy's? Were Christ's disciples really elves? When the second coming happens, will Jesus bring toy trains?

While I puzzled over these mysteries Dorothy went shopping. She's normally as good at this as any human female. But she was back in minutes with no bags or packages and a dazed, perplexed expression, like a starved Ethiopian given a piece of wax fruit. What could be the matter?

We went into the bookstore and I found out. There on the shelves were personal affirmations of faith by Roy Rogers and Dale Evans, a born-again diet plan, a transcription of the horrible (though rather unimaginative) things you can hear if you play rock-and-roll records backward, and a weighty tome arguing that every time the New Testament says "wine" it really means "grape juice." But I couldn't find anything you'd actually call a book. . . .

Then we went into the music store. It was the same thing. There were racks of tapes and records by Christian pop groups, Christian folk groups, Christian heavy-metal groups, Christian reggae groups, all of them singing original compositions about the Lord. No album was actually titled *I Found God and Lost My Talent*, but I'm sure that was just an oversight. . . .

I looked at the people crowding the Heritage "Main Street" mall. They didn't seem to be having much fun. Many of them were old, none looked very well-off. There was a dullness in their movements and expressions. Even the little kids looked somber and thick. Heal them, Oh Lord, for they are injured in the taste buds. . . .

And that was when it dawned on me. There's only one explanation for Heritage USA. Jim and Tammy were working for the other side. Their own recent behavior seems to make that obvious. And consider the other evidence: a bookstore without books, a record shop without music — what else could these be but the vain and empty works of the devil? (pp. 91–98)

These are not the biased ramblings of a person who hates Christianity, but are true, if wickedly funny, observations. Many a chintzy Roman Catholic trinket shop (not to mention the idle guitar-strumming that passes for a "people's mass") and many of the evangelical and fundamentalist churches in America, their bookstores, schools, and congregations, are miniature Heritage USAs. The problem of crass, tasteless commercialism did not go away with Jim and Tammy. Heritage USA was not an aberration but simply the evangelical, fundamentalist, charismatic norm on a scale of vulgarity that was finally noticed.

"Christian" TV

Nowhere has Christians' lack of knowledge about art and media or its effect on the culture at large been more appallingly apparent than in our gross misuse of television. Christian TV, as it evolved in the 1970s, became simply televised sermons heavy on fundraising, with a few mundane talk shows, also heavy on fund-raising, thrown in for good measure.

The unintended comedy of Christian television and its "evangelists" aside, it was left to the so-called secular world to use television creatively. For example, in the 1970s and 1980s, the makers of P.B.S.'s *Nova* series, the *MacNeil-Lehrer News Hour,* the B.B.C's series on Winston Churchill entitled *The Wilderness Years,* the B.B.C.'s Shakespeare's drama series, the anti-television anarchic *Late Night with David Letterman Show,* some of HBO's comedy specials, the second and third seasons of *Saturday Night Live,* and the *Buffalo Bill* series all went to great lengths to expand television's creative possibilities. These shows were mainly the intellectual descendants of American television's one original genius, Ernie Kovaks, or pre-television British theatrical expertise translated for television use by B.B.C. or other British producers. Yet nary a trace of creativity is to be found in that barren wilderness that encompasses the notorious National Religious Broadcasters Association.

Neil Postman, professor of communications at New York University, has written one of the best analysis of television and its impact on our society. His book *Amusing Ourselves to Death* (New York: Penguin Books, 1985) traces the effects on our culture of moving from a print culture into an age of television information.

Postman brings up many intriguing questions regarding what the technology of television is doing to the *way* we think, how we educate our children, and how we perceive the world and worship. He argues forcefully that television is an altogether inappropriate medium through which to express profound religious content. (See Appendix B for further information.) In a chapter of his book entitled "Shuffle Off to Bethlehem," Postman writes,

> On television, religion, like everything else, is presented, quite simply and without apology, as an entertainment. Everything that makes religion an historic, profound and sacred human activity is stripped away; there is no ritual, no dogma, no tradition, no theology, and above all, no sense of spiritual transcendence. On these shows, the preacher is tops. God comes out as second banana. . . .

> This fact has more to do with the bias of [i.e. the technology of] television than with the deficiencies of these electronic preachers, as they are called. It is true enough that some of these men are uneducated, provincial and even bigoted. They certainly do not compare favorably with well-known evangelicals of an earlier period, such as Jonathan Edwards, George Whitefield and Charles Finney, who were men of great learning, theological subtlety and powerful expositional skills. Nonetheless, today's television preachers are probably not greatly different in their limitations from most earlier evangelicals or from many ministers today whose activities are confined to churches and synagogues. What makes these television preachers the enemy of re-

ligious experience is not so much *their* weaknesses but the
weaknesses of the medium in which they work. . . .

The preachers are forthright about how they control the content
of their preaching to maximize their ratings. You shall wait a
very long time indeed if you wish to hear an electronic preacher
refer to the difficulties a rich man will have in gaining access to
heaven. The executive director of the National Religious Broadcasters Association sums up what he calls the unwritten law of
all television preachers: "You can get your share of the audience
only by offering people something they want."

You will note, I am sure, that this is an unusual religious
credo. . . . As a consequence, what is preached on television is
not anything like the Sermon on the Mount. Religious programs
are filled with good cheer. They celebrate affluence. Their featured players become celebrities. Though their messages are
trivial, the shows have high ratings, or rather, *because* their messages are trivial, the shows have high ratings.

I believe I am not mistaken in saying that Christianity is a de-
manding and serious religion. When it is delivered as easy and
amusing, it is another kind of religion altogether. (pp. 116-124)

Not all Christians may agree with Postman's blanket condem-
nations of religious television, but to me he seems to be on track.
Moreover, the idea that television *must* be used to spread the gospel if the church is to compete in our society is false. The max-
ims, *If it's there, use it,* or *If it can be done, do it,* should not be
the guiding rules of the church. The thriving, growing churches in
countries that were until recently dominated by Communism had
no access to television with which to express their faith or
through which to seek new converts. Yet, if anything, the
churches behind the once "iron curtain," for instance the Ukrai-
nian Catholics or East German Lutherans, are more orthodox,
lively, and faithful, and are growing faster than many of the
churches here in the free West with all our access to the "miracle"
of mass communication. Many a self-serving study has been con-

ducted to determine all the "good" Christian TV has done. But who has quantified the irreparable damage it has done to the cause of Christ?

"Christian" Movies

Christians sometimes band together to make a "Christian movie." The result of such propaganda attempts has been the sorry spectacle of pictures like *Born Again* or the nearly endless and expensive absurdity of the "Genesis Project" *Media Bible* in which the makers claim the whole Bible is being filmed. When pastors, churches, and other Christians have tried to back "Christian movies," they have often been preyed upon by has-beens claiming to be "Christian" or "inspirational" or recently converted producers, who descend upon the foolish like vultures smelling rotten flesh. A great deal of money has been spent in the name of "reforming Hollywood," but little film produced.

The movie business cannot be reformed from the outside any more than the church. In addition to which, Hollywood is in no more need of "reforming" than the church is itself. Having lived in both communities, I can honestly say I have found as much integrity, or as little, in Hollywood as in the evangelical world of radio, TV, and publishing media in which for some years I had the misfortune to lanquish.

Christians unwilling to do the long-term work from *within* the system fail when they capriciously decide to dabble in film or television for "evangelistic" or political purposes. For a career in the arts and media to be successful, it must be a life work motivated by a love of the medium itself. The movie business is a tough business even for those who understand it and are in it full-time. Imagine the results when the unwary, green, Christian propagandist, however well-intentioned, ventures into it. No wounded cow crossing a piranha-infested river has ever been more vulnerable!

If one wanted to produce a top athletic team of Christians to compete at world-class levels, one would need more than money or a desire to "reclaim sports for Christ." One would need to seek out and then train *generations* of children, young people, and adults to first *enjoy* the sport in question. For instance, the United States will need years of its children kicking a soccer ball around for *pleasure* before it produces an effective World Cup team. So it is in the arts and media. When *generations* of believing evangelical, Catholic, Orthodox, and fundamentalist Christian children and young people grow up appreciating and understanding film and the arts for what they are, and are encouraged to pursue professional careers in artistic mediums *for the love of media, art, and film itself,* then and only then will the presence of believing, informed, and talented Christians be felt in the film industry. You cannot buy nor criticize your way into the arts and media. You can only *work* your way in, *and* you must love what you are doing for its own sake. You cannot see the arts and media as mere propaganda tools to be used for your cause or through which "America will be turned around."

Christians are conspicuous by their absence as filmmakers. Except when protesting some movie like Martin Scorsese's *The Last Temptation of Christ* or the Monty Python production of the *Life of Brian,* or rating some movie like *The Dead Poets' Society* as *bad, evil,* or *unbiblical,* the church hardly has taken notice of that most figurative of all forms of modern communication: cinema. People of the Book have seen celluloid and not liked it. Those few filmmakers with evangelical Christian backgrounds, like writer-director Paul Schrader (*Hardcore, Patty* and many other fine films), are often sensitive people who, after one dose of fundamentalist religion — in Schrader's case, the narrow Reformed theology of Grand Rapids, Michigan, and Calvin College — have never stopped running away from what was presented to them as "Christianity."

Yet, having abandoned their personal faith, many filmmakers have not lost their interest in religion. Schrader's movie *Hardcore* is a great commentary on the pathetic, ineffectual inability of contemporary Christians to come to grips with the real world. Schrader's movies show much more understanding of evangelical Christian norms and reformed theology, however unsympathetically, than evangelicals in general show in understanding his films.

What Is a Good Movie?

The better the movie, then the closer to reality, of its subject and to life as we know it, it will be. A good movie will reflect upon reality in the spirit that Amy Lowell defines as "the desire of a man to express himself, to record the reactions of his personality to the world he lives in" (*Tendencies in Modern American Poetry,* 7).

Science fiction movies like *Blade Runner* or movies about life in small villages, as portrayed in *Jean De Florette, Cinema Paradiso, Le Grand Chemin,* or *La Strada,* may be about very different subjects; nevertheless, all these movies have something in common. They tell the truth about their subject matter. For instance, in *Blade Runner* we see the inhuman trends in our pro-abortion, pro-genetic engineering culture projected into the future to their logical conclusion and examined minutely and truthfully from the Jewish-Christian moral perspective. In *Jean De Florette, Cinema Paradiso, Le Grand Chemin,* and *La Strada,* the villages and country life portrayed ring true to one who, like me, grew up in a small European village where I spent my childhood in and around peasant communities of simple farm people. The universality and humanity of their stories strike one's heart.

Film Basics

A movie has a story to tell and tells it with pictures, borrowing from painting, words, theater, and music—borrowing from God.

There are as many potentially satisfying movies as there are stories, fables, parables, and biographies worth exploring. Movies have a special power over their audiences because they engage more senses simultaneously than most other art forms. The musical score plays on the emotions. The dialogue can tell the story and develop the characters, involving the audience in an intimate way. The photography — its composition, its movement, and the art direction — shows the audience the highly personal,. visual point of view of the director.

Most movies are not "Art" with a capital *A*. Movies belong in neighborhood theaters or at home on one's television, not in museums. Movies are part of the fabric of daily modern life in the same way that theater was part of ordinary life in seventeenth-century England.

The best movies are the ones that achieve their artistic results in ways only available to film. They are not merely plays or paintings on film, but expressions unique to the medium and which take the medium to its limits. *Lawrence of Arabia, Satyricon, The Godfather, Blade Runner, A Clockwork Orange,* and *Citizen Kane*, among others, are movies that tell a story in this uniquely filmic way. In other words, they push reality to limits that only film can reach. For instance, the photographic spectacle and pacing of action in *Lawrence of Arabia* is purely cinematic; it is impossible to conceive of this movie being a play. The devastatingly effective combination of a musical score with the somber photography and close-up performances in *The Godfather* is uniquely filmic in its density. The complex, alternative worlds created by the directors of *Blade Runner* and *A Clockwork Orange* are unthinkable in any other medium but film. The stark narrative use of camera movement developed in *Citizen Kane* is unthinkable in any other medium. In these movies, the atmosphere and art direction, sets, acting, lighting, and sound effects conjure up a totally engrossing imagery and sensory experience. These all achieve what only a film can in a way that a play, painting, or novel cannot. In other words, they all attempt to use the unique qualities of the medium to the fullest extent possible.

Movies are a form of entertainment that, at their most successful, at least border on art. For the time being, I do not believe that there are any movies that clearly can be seen to have the timeless, artistic merit of the art of the high Middle Ages or later Renaissance or other accomplished periods of art in our Western history. That is because the medium of film is extremely young, being invented even as we speak. It has not even begun to define itself. A long time must pass before movies can be placed with accurate perspective in a historical context. The Renaissance began with explorations in perspective and proportion by painters like Giotto and Masaccio. Then, several hundred years later, it came to its fruition in the works of Michelangelo, Raphael, and Leonardo da Vinci. Movies, as we know them, are barely seventy years old, hardly a blink of an eye in terms of art history.

Whatever movies are now or will become, to be a moviemaker today is to be part inventor, part vaudevillian, part artist, part promoter, part playwright, part magician, and part painter — and all negotiator. Some movies are merely business deals on film, others only extensions of the traditional circus and magic act (nowadays called "special effects"). Movies can be a window on the world and a mirror all at once. The worst movies tell pretentious lies about the kind of world in which we live — either cynical, cruel lies that would twist good and sublime things to show them as frauds, or misleading, optimistic lies that make us feel good for no reason. The latter being the kind of mindless pablum that middle America loves and the church often hails as "acceptable family entertainment." The best films challenge, and leave us entertained, amused, uncomfortable, sometimes sad, never bored, perhaps angry.

Many "movies" are not even real or complete films. Many are what magazines are to books, what pulp is to great fiction. They exist on film in a technical sense, but they are, like almost all television programs, merely entertainment formulas; they are the cotton candy of the movie industry. They are not evil; they simply exist, just as McDonald's hamburgers exist in a gastronomical limbo. It is a mistake to take the content, such as it is, of these exercises in commerce too seriously. This over-seriousness in judging movies' "morality" often leads people to deplore the state of Hollywood and the moral or intellectual climate of contemporary filmmaking. This is as silly as it would be for the *New York Times* food critic to endlessly review McDonald's various restaurants in the New York area, and then to rant and rave about the decline of cuisine in America. It is foolish to invest a mere money-changing operation with intellectual weight and then criticize it for being less than brilliant! Most horror, action, and science fiction movies fall into this mundane, often artistically meaningless category. A great deal of Christian criticism of movies comes from people who are not able to discern between real films and mere deals, people who invariably take things too seriously and give everything an inappropriately serious theological examination. People who cannot even distinguish between bland, often silly, tongue-in-cheek *imitations* of evil, for instance in horror movies, and evil itself are in no position to pronounce judgment on films in general.

Overly ideologically exercised people misunderstand film. Thus it is that the worst film reviews routinely appear in some religious journals and political publications of the Right and Left. Many political ideologues share, with fundamentalist Christians, an overserious view of film. The Left and Right each have a political "theology" by which they judge the "right thinking" of everything. Like many believing Christians, those on the Left and Right take everything they do very seriously. Thus they imagine that everyone else does, too. They do not realize or believe that most people, including most moviemakers and other artists, are not engaged in some sort of ideological conspiracy, but rather are just earning a living as best they can.

Propaganda

Ideology often destroys films. The best films are the most carefully made, yet ones where the final result is the *least self-conscious*. The worst films are the most ideologically pretentious. Often this is because their makers have a hidden or overt political or religious agenda. For instance, people like director Oliver Stone (*Platoon, Wall Street, Born on the Fourth of July*, etc.), Billy Graham (a great and inspired evangelist but an indifferent film producer), and Jane Fonda (of Hanoi and the People's Republic of Santa Monica and L.A., CA) specialize in making politically, socially, or religiously "relevant" propaganda. Their zealous efforts may succeed as a form of preaching but often fail as movies. Propaganda is a poor excuse for art or even cinema.

In the case of Oliver Stone, his efforts to propagandize, in his case from the far Left, have begun to grate on the nerves of people who might even agree with his politics, but, nevertheless, see that he is prostituting his use of film. For instance, David Ansen (*Newsweek's* film critic) in the context of a review of Stone's film, *Born on the Fourth of July* (Oscar nominations notwithstanding), described Stone's politicized drum beating as "his own brand of emotional authoritarianism. . . . Stone is conversant only with the politics of emotionalism. . . . There's no denying that Oliver Stone has a vision; his conviction, his anger, and his talent are for real. . . . But Stone's aesthetics of hysteria can take you only so far; it's the cinematic equivalent of heavy metal, awesome fragments buried in a whole lot of bombast" (*Newsweek*, December 25, 1989). As some of Oliver Stone's films illustrate, propaganda is too small a use for film; it is a waste of the medium. The film critic of *The New Yorker* had this to say of *Born on the Fourth of July*, . . . "[The film] is presented in a nostalgic aesthetically reactionary way: . . . The director . . . plays bumper cars with the camera and uses cutting to jam you into the action, and you can't enjoy his uncouthness, because it's put at the service of sanctimony" (January 1990).

Why Make a Movie?

Why breathe? Why procreate? Why eat? Why love? Why pray? Human beings have insatiable needs, and one is the need to create. Thus a moviemaker is driven to make movies. This creative drive is similar for painters, musicians, writers, dancers, designers — each moved to create by a deeper impulse than merely a rational choice of career.

Roaming Hollywood, licking the crumbs from the movie industry's table, is an arid business. I have been reduced at times to taking the opportunity to "do lunch" with a prospective producer, not only because there was a chance of getting a job, but because the free lunch itself figured importantly to my nutritional needs in my impoverished condition. For months, feeling like some salesman at rest stops on Italian highways — a salesman of stolen watches, the kind that opens his coat to show you fifty or so hanging inside — I have pounded the pavement, tempted in desperation to offer even a casual passerby a selection of moldering scripts.

But I have not been alone; the blind lead the blind in Hollywood. I have arrived at a meeting to pitch an idea and found myself, instead, listening to a producer tell me about *his* idea. It has dawned on me more than once that the people I have been looking to for help are often in worse career trouble than me. They, under some misapprehension as to my status in the business, have been looking to me for help with their project while I was looking to them for assistance.

Hollywood, that valley in the shadow of ambition, is full of lost souls, each, like some apostle of Robert Schuller, assuming that enough positive thinking will induce others to share their secrets of success. There is as much money made in Hollywood by selling the hope of success, by acting coaches and "managers" for instance, as by success itself. Most hopefuls are mere peons floating in a noxious broth of disappointment, far from the real "powers that be" that run the movie industry, far from the people like superagent Michael Ovitz, who guides the powerful Creative Artists Agency as it packages movie deals for the high and mighty.

Occasionally a mere streetwalker like me catches a glimpse of the Ovitzes of the world. Standing in a pay phone on the corner of Sunset and La Cienega, I spot a pale blue Rolls sighing past the intersection. I am tempted to run after it, begging its well-dressed occupant to stop and help me. But reality beckons. The operator wants twenty-five more cents. The parking meter is showing red. The meter maid is only two cars away. "Boy, have we got a deal for you!" Why don't *I* ever hear those words? The Rolls is gone and my party hung up on me. "Your call cannot be completed as dialed; please try again."

Making a movie is like carving Mount Rushmore with your bare hands — an impossible undertaking. All movies are impossible. That is why there are no perfect movies, not even many good ones, and perhaps no great movies at all. There is just too much going on at any one time, too much money pressure, too short a time, too many people with egomaniacal tendencies involved, to do more than paint in broad strokes. But, like mountain-climbing, the satisfaction comes from the attempt, even if the summit remains indistinct, surrounded by brown smog.

Very few movies are good. Very few directors or actors get an opportunity to choose good material. For many reasons, most directors will never know what they could achieve; they will never have the success necessary to give them the freedom to make what they want. Money and business play a huge part in moviemaking, as do egos and greed. When these elements exert themselves like so many powerful currents, it is hard to swim up river. Thus it is, as anyone knows in the film business or in other branches of the arts, a triumph to get *anything* made at all. To even have a job remotely related to your eventual goals in the arts is a victory. To have the necessary control over the various elements to make a good movie is a matter of timing and good fortune as much as talent. What that is like, I have yet to learn.

Suddenly the pale blue Rolls pulls over. The tinted glass window slides down with an electric purr. "Say, you must be that brilliant young movie director who has made all those lousy but promising 'B' movies," calls a friendly voice. "Well my name's Ovitz, Michael Ovitz. I'm putting together a little project and I thought . . ." As Jimmy Hendrix said, "Dream on!"

Lessons

Any human event can change history in large or small ways, so can movies and other works of art. But the reason most people make movies, aside from money, is to express their humanity, to employ their creativity. With a few exceptions, they do not set out to make "statements."

However, the result of a particularly powerful film can be dramatic, usually in changing the *way* people look at the subject of the movie. A movie can affect the social consciousness of an elite or even the general public. For instance, the entertaining and well-made films of Woody Allen have been important to developing the worldview of a whole generation. The brilliant and glittering movies of Steven Spielberg and George Lucas have helped create the "be happy" generation and spiritually sustained them in their "yuppie" comas as surely as the drug *Somma* placated the mob in *A Brave, New World.*

Some of the movies of Ridley Scott — for instance, *Alien, Blade Runner,* and *Someone to Watch Over Me* — have combined an artistic sense of visual beauty with a clear prophetic Jewish-Christian moral vision of our world, a world in which transcendent meaning and moral absolutes are being squandered but where moral heroism still is portrayed as having ultimate value.

As a movie director, I despair at the shortcomings of my own work; I learn from many people; I admire anyone with the audacity to even try to succeed in the film business or other branches of the arts. I have a new respect for all entrepreneurial individuals because of my own hard journey into film.

I now realize that there is no one way to get into the film business or succeed in it. Everyone has a very individual, unique story to tell who has "made it." There is no easy formula, no "inside information" on how to succeed. No savior will arrive in a Rolls to magically provide for my needs as a director! It is all hard work, setbacks, and then more hard work.

When I am not in production, I watch about three movies and read two scripts a week. I struggle to get past the gatekeepers into the inner sanctum of filmdom so that I can initiate projects that I would like to direct. I have directed more than twenty-five hours of documentary films and, as of now, three feature films, yet I feel I know very little about making movies. Learning is slow. I am grateful for the work I do have as a director, even if it is not on the kind of movies I like. I learn; I stumble. I attempt to infuse my movies with more truth and life than they would have had if I had not been there; and I never fully succeed in realizing even this modest ambition.

In a recurring waking nightmare, I have just completed my twenty-ninth schlock-action-horror "B" movie, another piece of film destined for direct release into video twilight. In this dream I am older now, much older — so old it's getting hard to concentrate on that *great project* just around the corner. If only I could get a meeting with, with, now who was it? . . .

As a director, I appreciate what it takes to make a movie, and therefore have sympathy for those who attempt to be painters or pianists or work for advertising agencies. There is a brotherhood in creative struggle. I work to be good at what I do, and to improve, I must work. I direct every movie I can, whatever its problems, however bad the result, however furiously I am denounced by my "brothers" in Christ, and, within reason, however much I dislike the project in question. I pray for the day that I can choose between scripts and not just count myself fortunate to direct *any* script.

I have found that if I want everything I will get nothing. If I wait for the perfect project, the right conditions, the approval of the Pharisees, the correct circumstances, the right "message," a script I like, I will never make any films.

Hope

There are some very good film directors: Francis Ford Coppola, Martin Scorsese, Ridley Scott, Woody Allen, Frederico Fellini, and Giuseppe Tornatore, to name but a few. These people all have individual styles and unique personal stories as to how they succeeded in their profession. Because they are successful, they are therefore able to choose scripts and initiate projects worthy of their talent. That directors of this caliber exist and work at all gives hope to those of us who, like me, struggle forward as we make our low-budget movies while hoping for better opportunities.

art. (art), n. 1. The production or expression of what is beautiful, appealing, or of more than ordinary significance. 2. An illustration. 3. A department of skilled performance. 4. (pl.) Liberal arts. 5. Skilled workmanship. 6. Cunning. 7. Artificiality in behavior. 8. An artifice.

6

ART VERSUS MESSAGE: WHAT IS ART?

I s art propaganda? Is it entertainment? What *is* art? To understand a work of art, one needs knowledge of the technique employed, the artist, or at least its historical context. Art, contrary to today's ideas of "enlightened" egalitarianism, is rarely for the masses, though there have been periods in history when the general public has been unusually well informed—the High Middle Ages and the Florentine Renaissance, for example, or Elizabethan England, when theater was appreciated by the general public much as film is today. At one time the working class represented by the craftsmen's guilds supported some of the greatest artistic achievements in the Florentine Renaissance. For instance, the armorers guild commissioned Donatello in 1416 to sculpt his famous St. George, a revolutionary statue that, for the first time since the art of the Roman Empire, portrayed a hero as real, not just a symbol.

As an example of the common people's awareness of the great artistic achievements of the Florentine Renaissance and their appreciation of the arts, take this quote of Benedetto Dei, a Florentine merchant who wrote to a friend in Venice in 1472: "Go through all the cities of the world and nowhere will you ever be

able to find artists . . . equal to those we now have in Florence"
(*Art of the Western World* [New York: Summit Books, 1989], 90).

In Holland, during the "golden age" of painting in the seventeenth century, the common people, in contrast to the nobility and the church, supported the work of the painters who proliferated in that era. Peter Jansz, Jan Vermeer, Pieter De Hooch, Jan Steen, Willem Kalf, Jacob Van Ruisdael, Frans Hals, and Rembrandt were only some of the many painters that produced the portraits, landscapes, and still lifes that were purchased by Holland's merchants, craftsmen, and laborers. Some of the greatest pieces of art produced in that period were purchased by blacksmiths, cobblers, tailors, and bakers. Their interest in a pictorial examination of everyday life led them to support the greatest artists of northern Europe.

However, art is rarely casual. Art is a form of human expression pursued professionally and vocationally, full-time for a lifetime. Michelangelo is said to have joked about his cradle-to-grave dedication to his art: "With my wet-nurse's milk, I sucked in the hammer and chisel I use for my statues."

All of an artist's works are not of equal value. Artists reach an artistic peak, recognized later in time. His or her progress — like all human history — is linear, from less experience to more experience and accomplishment. The artist, at some point, achieves maximum productivity combined with maximum skill, and this height of effort intersects the highest level of his or her technical experience, producing at that time the artist's masterpieces — the millennial golden age of one life, if you will.

All human expression has intrinsic value, but not all is equal. Art is the highest form of human expression when the artist expresses truth about his or her chosen subject through accomplished, professional ability, natural talent, hard work, and discipline. Through history, art styles have changed, but the basic nature of the vocational, lifelong effort of the artist remains the constant, necessary ingredient for producing great art. Hard work and lonely pilgrimage have been the common lot of artists throughout history. Rejection by other people remains the basic fact of life to most artists.

What Is Art?

Art is different from craft. The crafts tend to serve some literal function, for instance, as furniture or pottery. Art is *pure* expression in the sense that art is not useful or practical in the same way as crafts might be.

People make art because we, as humans, respond to the deep calling of our creative, heavenly Father. The capacity to produce and enjoy art is one of the abilities that makes humans uniquely different from other creatures. Art is the expression of the divine *uselessness* of beauty, truth, and reality.

To help understand what art is, let us look at another area of divinely inspired human expression: prayer. Sometimes we pray because we want some specific things: a home, a wife, money, political change, whatever. This is the spiritual equivalent to the physical craft — useful and for a specific purpose. Sometimes, however, we pray to worship, to express our love for God, to express a nameless sense of fullness in our spirit, sorrow, or anxiety beyond words. This is equivalent to what art is in relationship to craft.

Art is useless but far from meaningless. Our capacity to be sustained by useless beauty, meaning, and truth — for instance, the comfort of home and hearth — is one of the reasons why we can be certain that we are created creatures of infinite value. Theories of the evolution of the species may explain biological complexities and changes; however, they stand mute in offering an explanation of Beethoven's Ninth Symphony or why we love it.

Our enjoyment of crafts can always be explained by ulterior motives; for example, the need to use them in some way to better our daily lives. However, our enjoyment of the useless beauty of art and worship can only be explained by the fact that we are responding to a larger call than the mere needs of survival. Man does *not* live by bread alone. The arts are for sustaining human life just as much as food, worship, water, air, and love.

The existence of the arts mirrors God's own extravagant creativity, His creation of useless beauty, His abundant expression of variety, and His attention to aesthetic detail. God has a commitment to beauty — beauty which is real and not merely in the eye of the beholder, beauty that exists in a quantifiable, abstract sense.

I believe that beauty exists independent of the personal taste of the observer. In this sense aesthetics are as absolute as physics. This does not mean that we, in our fallen state, can ever achieve an absolute understanding of what is beautiful. However, we can perceive abstract beauty as the divine signature on nature. In this fallen world our sense of beauty is also fallen; therefore, tastes vary and people will disagree. However, God will show us what is beautiful and what is not by creative example in the new heaven and the new earth. Created nature already points the aesthetic way. God said His creation was "good." This was an absolute statement covering all aspects of reality, including aesthetics.

Even in the fallen world, nature and the highly developed, God-given skills in the arts help us define *aesthetics*. There is a reason why sensitive and tasteful people react negatively to synthetic, highly processed materials. Tweed *is* absolutely preferable to polyester. (How's that for an absolutist claim for which I have no supporting evidence!)

When art is deliberately corrupted to become "useful," it is as repugnant as it would be to ban worship from the Christian life to be replaced only with "utilitarian" social work. There is a place for practical charity, but also, as the sinful woman who perfumed Christ's hair and washed His feet with her tears understood, a place for worship, for its own sake, for the love of God Himself. Much of our lives is spent pursuing tangible, measurable goals, but life soon becomes gray and pointless if our souls cannot explore beyond the pragmatic. In this sense all art is abstract. All art is a language of the spirit, even if words, as in theater, are its medium.

Art is all at once one of the most pointless of human luxuries and one of the basic necessities of life. All cultures, even those that are materially poverty stricken, produce art. This should tell us something concerning the nature of people and their need to express themselves. The appreciation and creation of art is a manifestation of the love of God for people, manifested by His willingness to share that most rare of all gifts with His mere creatures: creativity.

Propaganda v. Art

To use art as propaganda, even for good causes, is a waste. This is not to say that art does not at times legitimately express a particular viewpoint; because art is human expression, it will often express an opinion. But in genuine art, the expression of a particular religious, political, or human viewpoint is unselfconscious and is submerged in favor of expressing truths, common to the experiences of all mankind. A particular viewpoint may emerge along with many other elements that make up the integrated totality of the artwork in question. Just as gratuitous violence and sex are justly condemned in some artworks, we should be equally suspicious of gratuitous "good" messages and obviously intrusive statements that do not belong in an artwork beyond the artist's desire to push a certain politico-religious point of view.

The expression of political, cultural, sociological, or theological viewpoints, should not be the motivating force behind the artist's work. Art soon slides toward propaganda if the motivation for it is too utilitarian and immediate. It ceases to be art and is less honest than forthright proselytizing. Picasso's painting protesting the brutality of the destruction of Guernica by the Nazi's bombs is a good political poster but, I suspect, not his best art-work. Oliver Stone's movies will be forgotten as soon as the po-litical climate changes, thus rendering them unintelligible and ob-solete. When his movies are forgotten, a film like *Moonstruck* will always have an audience. That is because the narcissistic politics of the post-Vietnam generation will someday be unintelligible, but the human race will always understand a love story.

The existence of art is a manifestation of *who* people are, a witness to the character of God in people. Art is not to be prosti-tuted, even for good causes. Art is not to be tampered with for a message's sake or for expediency's sake, any more than mother love should be manipulated as a tool of the state or church, to serve something "better," "higher." It *is* already the better thing in itself. Watching a mother breast-feeding her baby does not teach us about love; it *is* love in action. The purpose of art is not to teach us about God; it *is* God's love for us in action. Jesus did not only come to earth to teach us about goodness, He *is* goodness. Art is not a means to an end; it *is* an end in itself, a reflection of the name of God, *I Am*. Therefore, the idea of producing "Chris-tian" art, music, novels, plays, etc., as it is commonly understood by many earnest but misguided fundamentalist and evangelicals, is wrong.

Dr. Hans Rookmaaker addressed this point when he wrote in his book *Modern Art and the Death of a Culture* (Downers Grove, IL: Inter-Varsity, 1970, 228–230):

> In a way there is no specifically Christian art. One can distin-guish only good and bad art, art which is sound and good from art which is false. . . . A work of art is not good when we know that the artist was a Christian: it is good when we perceive it to be good. Nor is a work bad if we know that the artist was a hater of God. It would be possible to make an exhibition of beautiful Picassos. The exhibition would possibly not do justice to the spirit that drove Picasso on in his creativity, yet it would show us that the man is human. . . . Art needs no justification.

The mistake of many art theorists, (and not only of Christian ones), is to try to give art a meaning or a sense by showing that it "does something." . . . Art needs no such excuse. It has its own meaning.

Craft v. Propaganda v. Art

Naturally the divisions between art and craft consist of many shades of gray. Classical Greek vases, Gothic cathedrals, the jewel-like modernist architectural creations of I. M. Pei come to mind as functional creations defying easy categories. For instance, Pei's buildings and Gothic cathedrals serve a function, are "useful," but the creative genius of their makers transcends the merely functional. The Dallas Symphony Center, The Bank of China in Hong Kong, the breathtakingly beautiful National Gallery extension in Washington, D.C., with its razor-thin angles in stone, and Pei's other buildings have the weight and permanence of masterpieces on a par with Michelangelo's architectural artwork, for instance, the Medici library in Florence. The mastery of architectural geometry and light in Pei's work surely transcends the division between what is art and what is architectural craft. Genius confounds simple definitions. The creators of Chartres Cathedral cannot be labeled mere artisans. In fact, Gothic architecture is an expression of that uniquely Christian mind-set found in the Europe of St. Thomas Aquinas and St. Francis. Gothic architecture was a heroic departure from the Romanesque past. In a way, it was the real new beginning or "renaissance" in European art looking forward not backward. The Renaissance was less radical of a new beginning than was the explosion of Gothic creativity.

G. K. Chesterton captures its advent well. In his 1933 book *Saint Thomas Aquinas*, ([Doubleday, 1956] 41, 91), we read:

> Nobody can understand the greatness of the thirteenth century, who does not realise that it was a great growth of new things produced by a living thing. In that sense it was really bolder and

freer than what we call the Renaissance, which was a resurrection of old things discovered in a dead thing. [Roman culture] in that sense medievalism was not a Renascence, but rather a Nascence. It did not model its temples upon the tombs, or call up dead gods from Hades. It made an architecture as new as modern engineering: indeed it still remains the most modern architecture. . . . gleaming into the northern skies, partly picked out with gold and bright colours; a new flight of architecture, as startling as flying-ships.

Some craft becomes art. Some art becomes propaganda. Some art entertains without becoming mere entertainment. These lines are real but not fixed. Yet, special exceptions aside, there is a definite difference between craft and art. Craft is immensely worthwhile and often adds as much beauty to our lives as does artwork. To distinguish art from craft is not an attempt either to aggrandize art or belittle craft, but simply to recognize each for what it is.

Eternal Meanings in Art

As the fathers of the West from Augustine to Jefferson to Martin Luther King understood, reality comes from God. All reality, therefore, even fallen reality, is worth exploring. Art, like science, explores this fallen reality and also creates new realities. Art continues God's creative process and even enlarges on it. By recombining materials God created and using His creative gift to make unique works of art, people create objects and ideas that exist as distinct entities apart from the artist and God.

God endowed us with the capacity to make moral choices. Remarkably, He also has given us the ability, through art, to create *beyond* His own creation, to make our own worlds and universes, for good or ill. Yet within His will, we fulfill our creative destinies by exercising our God-given free will.

All art serves God's purposes by its very existence. As Leonardo da Vinci wrote of the artistic mind, it is "a copy of the divine mind, since it operates freely." By responding to art, we make choices, expressed by our reactions. In this way there is a dialogue between the artist and the audience, a dialogue that bridges the centuries and binds all humanity together in a common experience. We can know Leonardo da Vinci as well as our neighbor across the street, perhaps better.

The love of art guards us from returning to the lumpish masses of clay from which we were taken. Sadly, the words that Robert Bolt wrote concerning Henry the VIII's wife, ill-starred Catherine, and Henry's reason for wanting to divorce her could also well be a description of the lumpish fundamentalist and evangelical Protestant church. She "had grown increasingly plain and intensely religious" (*A Man For All Seasons* [New York: Vantage Press, 1960], 2). Not too endearing a quality in a wife or church!

Transcendence

From the pre-historic scratchings on a cave wall in southern France to the ceiling of the Sistine Chapel, art speaks with one voice: Mankind is special; mankind is transcendent in his spirit; mankind's existence has eternal meaning. Art communicates in universal terms from one generation to the next.

Observing and enjoying art gives deeper meaning to our love of God and God's creation, humanity. Art thus leads us toward God.

Art can be full of comedy, wit, and humor, and be a dazzling experience that wakens the spirit. Art is the stone against which we sharpen our wit and intellect, and also our emotions and senses. Sexuality, humor, fear, worship, sense of weight and texture, love, enjoyment of beauty, and terror are only some of the emotions and senses that art stimulates. Our senses were created by a God who gave us bodies, minds, and souls; our senses need not be at war with our spirits but are one with them when we submit to the lordship of Christ. Thus, to enjoy art, we need not abandon our intellect and merely *feel*. Art communicates in concrete terms, expressing ideas, ways of seeing, and content as well as human emotion. Contrary to popular, modern critical scholarship, we *can* look at art and know the intent of the artist or author. As fellow human beings, we have more in common with them than distinctives that keep us apart. Gender and race and cultural experience pale in contrast to the common human bond between all of God's children.

Great art is often explosive; it defines and gives meaning to whole peoples, periods of history, and nations. It has the capacity to show us what is important in life and to define our perceptions of reality. It shows us ourselves. "Art," said Henry James, "is nothing more than the shadow of humanity."

The gentle events of daily life portrayed in Vermeer's paintings infuse the ordinary with dignity. For instance, in one work, *Young Women With a Water Jug* (1665), we see a mother at home, at peace with God and her neighbor. By painting her, the artist has made her life an event, part of the fabric of the important things in life worth celebrating. The translucent beauty of Botticelli's *Primavera* reinforces the Thomast idea that nature is good in itself, that our world is a world informed by rare, symbolic, divine beauty, and that the graces are just as important as commerce to man's existence. It also shows us a sexuality in which base lust is absent. Botticelli's work speaks in universal human terms, as relevant today as the day he finished it.

Great art, while challenging our ideas, nevertheless often restrains man's rapacity and sinful tendency toward chaos and destruction; it assists in creating societies that know their worth. In that sense, the art of Shakespeare *is* Elizabethan England. The art of the Renaissance *is* Florence. And, conversely, the "art" of the subway graffiti artists in New York *is* New York today.

It is no accident that tyrants have hesitated to destroy artistically rich cities like Florence and Paris. Or at least, as in the case of Hitler, the tyrant's minions have disobeyed destructive orders, thus saving those cities for posterity. The drastic measures taken by some Protestants during the social upheavals following the Reformation, the smashing of statuary and other artwork in Roman Catholic churches, has rightly earned condemnation by civilized people. This outrage was only partially mitigated in later years by the vast contribution to the arts by Protestant Christians that came out of Reformation northern Europe.

The existence of the arts is the most tangible evidence of the existence of the soul. When a person stands quietly looking at a painting, he is bearing witness, consciously or unconsciously, to the vast difference between people and the rest of nature. The arts create a climate in which ideas concerning mankind's meaning can be discussed.

Freedom for Art

When artists are given freedom of expression, they contribute to a climate of intellectual and political freedom for the whole culture. It is no coincidence that the ugliest, grayest, and dullest parts of the world today are places where people have been persecuted for their ideas. The listless grime that is, or was, the Communist bloc owes some of its haplessness to its imprisonment of the arts. Communism has censored and coerced art until it has become mere propaganda. The visual ugliness of Communist society, or societies recently dominated by Communists, is a result of communism's ideological misunderstanding of the human soul.

It is not by chance that the independent, relatively free republics of Tuscan, Italy, which came into being in the twelfth and thirteenth centuries, produced the climate of tolerance which in turn led to the creative explosion that was the Renaissance. Freedom, as it nourishes people's souls, produces creative results.

The truncated, dwarfish theology of American twentieth-century evangelical fundamentalism has ignored the arts and produced many cultic groups who have succeeded, even in a free society, in erecting their own miniature Soviet Gulags of the mind. Petty, Gray, Lumpish, Stupid, Small, Sterile, and Sad could be the names of the seven fundamentalist dwarves who have labored to produce the current pietistic prison in which so many Christians apparently live!

Some people regard art as *elitist* because they have confused specialization with elitism. We do not object to the specialization of a skilled surgeon. We do not call him "elitist" because he can cure his patient.

The lowest common denominator is *not* the right standard to set either in medicine or the arts or any other field of endeavor. As the black conservative American economists Thomas Sowell and Glenn C. Loury have so amply demonstrated in their writings, a purely egalitarian view of life produces dreadful results because it is not a reflection of the reality of human existence but merely a wishful, utopian idea. There is nothing wrong with high and even exclusive standards of complexity in medicine, sports, statecraft, business, and the arts. There is nothing wrong with the high degree of sophistication needed to make a great work of art, or the study or knowledge necessary to appreciate it. In our society, all people may have equality under the law, but it is absurd to pretend that all people are equal in skills or talents. That everything is not instantly accessible to everyone is a fact of life, not a condemnation or a put-down of any particular people who are less talented or knowledgeable in some areas than others.

The arts and humanities can be enjoyed on many levels. No one need feel left out because no one is totally included. The appreciation of art, like life and spirituality, is a journey. We never reach our goal completely, but there is meaning in the effort.

Religion in Art

A great deal of art in Western history has had religious subject matter. Sometimes this has been mere church-inspired propaganda; sometimes, as with the frescoes of Fra Angelico (or contemporary artists like Edward Knippers), a genuine artistic declaration of faith and an exercise in religious contemplation by the artist—what John Brown alluded to as an "Art . . . quickened from above and from within" (*Horoe Subsecivoe: Notes on Art*).

Fra Angelico, a monk in the monastery of San Marco in Florence, was an artist to whom the expression of religious content in his frescoes was a very personal and natural declaration of his belief and interest in Biblical themes. Vasari, the first biographer of the artists of the Renaissance, wrote of him: "Fra Angelico was a man of simplicity, and most holy in his ways. . . . [He] would never have taken his brushes in hand without first offering a prayer. He never painted a crucifix without tears streaming down his cheeks." (*Artists of the Renaissance.* First published in 1568, London: Allen Lane, 1965)

One of his principal paintings, *Descent from the Cross*, is described by Michael Wood.

> Within a pristine Tuscan landscape, Christ is lowered from the cross. As Mary Magdalene reverently kisses Christ's feet, John the Evangelist assists Nicodemus in lowering the sacred body. Cosimo's [Cosimo de' Medici was Fra Angelico's supporter and patron] namesake, Saint Cosmos, shows the crown of thorns and the nails, while a host of mourners crowds around the Virgin. . . . Hushed, respectful, and completely devout, the assembled figures present a scene that equates clarity of form, purity of color, and rationally conceived properties with transcendent spirituality. The mode of expression is dignified, rational, and human. (*Art of the Western World*, 102)

Art has often been commissioned by the church and religious institutions, the subject matter often chosen for the artist by the patron. Some artists have made the subject matter of commissions, religious or otherwise, their own, as with the intensely spiritual Michelangelo and his Sistine Chapel, thus going beyond the limits of the commission while faithfully fulfilling it.

Michelangelo's relationship to his patrons in the church is instructive and proves that even though it was fraught with difficulties, in the end it was a mutually beneficial arrangement typical of the stimulation the church often provided for the arts in his period of history. *David* was commissioned by the directors of the Duomo, Florence's cathedral. Thus it was the church that commissioned this most famous and sublime monumental nude sculpture of the human figure. The tempestuous friendship between Pope Julius II and Michelangelo resulted in the pope summoning Michelangelo to Rome to produce a variety of works—the Sistine Chapel frescoes and the figures for an unfinished, monumental tomb for Julius, among them. These and other commissions were almost completely in the control of the artist. Michelangelo even forbade the pope from setting foot inside the Sistine Chapel until he had finished the great work—a work that nearly killed him as he worked against almost insurmountable odds of heat, cold, sickness, and a dislocated neck (from bending back to paint above him for four years). He thus appropriated the commission.

Michelangelo was a deeply spiritual, Christian man. His religious works, especially late in his life, were a personal expression of faith. His many poems express a deep Christian faith and contemplation. Thus his religious works for the church were much more than mere commissions. Just before his death he wrote,

> My course of life already has attained,
> Through stormy seas, and in a flimsy vessel,
> The common port, at which we land to tell,
> All conduct's cause and warrant, good or bad.
> (*The Complete Work of Michelangelo* [New York:
> Artabras Books, 1964], 541)

Here the great artist speaks of facing judgment and of heaven: "The common port." His last work was an evocative unfinished pietà.

Others less skilled, or with less opportunity, have collided with the restrictions of commissions and been stunted by them. For instance, many a baroque Madonna, however beautiful it is in its craftsmanship, seems to have come off some assembly line of church-sponsored propaganda, rather than from the soul of an artist.

Yet many a believing artist, composer, writer, and architect have found that as they acquire experience, prestige, and opportunity their works have been naturely infused by the love of God. This has not come about out of some urge to propagandize but rather out of the artist's natural conversation through his art with his God. Then, like the first light of morning, the darkness flees, and the horizon for a moment becomes a seamless sphere touching the sky. Art, prayer, and confession merge into a cry from the heart of a man to the heart of his God.

It is a revealing symptom of our cultural malaise that for two decades our academic institutions have been shaken by spasms of radical reevaluation of what to do with [art and literature] ranging from uneasy self doubt to incipient panic to the exhilaration of an intellectual witch's sabbath.

Robert Alter, *Commentary Magazine,*
(March 1990)

7

THE ART KILLERS

A t some crossroads of insincerity, art degenerates into mere craft — illustrations on a wall, altarpiece, or book. Illustration, unlike art, serves a definable commercial, social, political, or religious purpose. Illustration is often good, but it is not usually to be confused with the divine uselessness of art. Illustration is a craft. Religious crafts can be beautiful and, as many a fine old hymn demonstrates, as personally meaningful to the participant as art. But what art *is* must be jealously guarded, as should the meaning of all human activities and the words that describe them. Words such as *art, god, worship, love, genius*, and *evil* have special meanings and are debased by overuse or misuse. Our perception of the meanings of things makes a difference in the way we look at the world around us. Thus, for example, for fundamentalists to label diverse activities and artworks that don't suit them as *evil* or *sinful* is a way of trivializing the concept of *real* evil.

Standards of Excellence

Truth is important, and one way to defend truth is to uphold academic, cultural, artistic, political, linguistic, historical, and theological standards to the best of our ability. The debate should be over which standards to uphold, and not, as is often the case today, over whether we should have any fixed cultural standards at all or whether we can perceive any universal meaning in art or history.

A curse of our own time is that there has been an unwitting collusion between the unlikely bedfellows of middle America and the politicized leftist academic elite to do away with standards of excellence in the arts and humanities. Middle America tends to resent anything that has not sufficiently been "dumbed down" to accommodate it. The egalitarian left, for its part, is reflexively against anything that is not part of its great leveling of all society into a gray "equality." Witness the destruction of the public school system or the abandonment of standards in many academic and artistic fields as utopian dreams of "affirmative action," "equality," or "learning from other non-Western cultural traditions" have taken hold. These are pursued in spite of the resultant lowered standards of academic excellence.

The well-known black professor of political economy at Harvard's Kennedy School of Government, Glenn C. Loury, in describing one aspect of this phenomena as it has effected the black community in America, writes:

> So widespread has such practice become that, especially in the elite levels of employment, all blacks must now deal with the perception that without a quota, they would not have their jobs. All blacks, some of our "leaders" seem proud to say, owe their accomplishments to political pressures for diversity. And the effects of such thinking may be seen in our response to almost every instance of racially differential performance. When blacks cannot pass a high school proficiency test as a condition of obtaining a diploma—throw out the test. When black teachers cannot exhibit skills at the same level as whites, the very idea of testing teachers' skills is attacked. If black athletes less frequently achieve the minimal academic standards set for those participating in inter-collegiate sports, then let us promulgate for them a separate, lower standard, even as we accuse of racism

those suggesting the need for a standard in the first place. ("Achieving the 'Dream,'" A paper delivered February 12, 1990 at the Heritage Foundation, Washington, DC.)

Ideology has proven stronger than fact, let alone common sense, as the "Knowledge" elite has labored to destroy our educational system while it "saves it." The humanities and the arts are also suffering.

The results of this unwitting, Left-Right back-scratching have been many. For example, in the universities the *great books*, books that were once regarded by generations of Western scholars as being indisputably the classic foundational works of Western thought, have been abandoned as required reading.

Consider the actions of the present-day heir of the American Left, perpetual candidate and media creation, the Rev. Jesse Jackson. History will record the day he led a march at Stanford University chanting, "Ho, Ho, Western culture has got to go!" This was an effort to "reform" curriculum and to get rid of the great books, the classics, as required reading, to be replaced by less "elitist" — read, less *Western* — works. In an article in *Newsweek* (October 16, 1989), Jackson was quoted as saying, "Wherever I focus, others follow. I can bring the light." Yet one wonders what "light" Jackson and those of like mind will use to replace the light of Jewish-Christian civilization. If it is time to bid Western civilization good-bye, which models of social and artistic behavior are we now to follow? Who will be our heroes? Idi Amin? Yassar Arafat? Stalin? Castro? The Visigoths? Who?

Allan Bloom made the following observation about the American university landscape, where those who disparage Western culture have triumphed in removing the classics from the curriculum and in destroying any sense of the permanent achievements of Western thought in human history. He writes:

Such education is little more than propaganda, and propaganda that does not work. . . . This gradual stilling of the old political and religious echoes in the soul of the young accounts for the difference between the students I knew at the beginning of my teaching career [in the 1950s], and those I face now. The loss of the [great] books has made them narrower and flatter. Narrower because they lack what is most necessary, a real basis for discontent with the present and awareness that there are alternatives to it. . . . The very models . . . have vanished. Flatter, because without interpretation of things, without the poetry or the imagination's activity, their souls are like mirrors, not of nature, but of what is around. The refinement of the mind's eye that permits it to see the delicate distinctions among men, among their deeds and motives, and constitutes real taste, is impossible without the assistance of literature in the grand style. (*The Closing of the American Mind* [New York: Simon and Schuster, 1987], 61)

Middle America may not think it has much in common with the Rev. Jesse Jackson and those other latter Vandals who would banish the light of Western culture in favor of third-world folklore, but in its own way, God-fearing middle America also wants Western culture to go. Meat-and-potatoes middle America resents intellectual and artistic complexity, anything that takes a little thought to approach. Witness the miserable addiction to TV programming in our nation, some evangelical sermons, the level of "teaching" many parents accept for their children, and the majority of "Christian" books, including certain recent best-selling "Christian novels." The "moron factor" that dominates intellectual life in middle America is not the result of an accident; it is a choice which reflects the market response to the high-calorie/low-protein taste of the public. And the market does not lie—popular culture exists at this level because rubbish now sells.

Yet while Christians have been absent from the cultural arena, others have been hard at work. Middle American Christendom may have slumbered, but a whole cavalry of termites have been awake and hard at their destructive labors. Typical of these labors have been those of the practitioners of feminist witchery.

Artistic Whores

Who will answer the politically radical feminists masquerading as scholars who have reduced "literary criticism" to their war against "patriarchal tyranny" hand-in-glove with "capitalism?" Who will offer an alternative, transcendent vision of literature to university students confronted by strident feminists who *seriously* debate the "literary" merits of "vaginal criticism" versus "clitoral hermeneutics"? Those confronted by the state of the arts and humanities today are likely to be inquiring into a monstrous spectacle, one in which the prevailing trends in literary artistic theory run to deconstructionism, Marxism, "third worldism," and feminism. Today, literary criticism is dominated by claims that all meanings in art are only created by the audience, that there are no universal meanings, that art and words are nothing more than the subjective playthings of the critic, that the original intent of the artist-author cannot be understood. In other words, we as humans are really all islands, unable to communicate with each other, and with no common human bonds that can transcend gender, race, religion, and politics. In other words, art is dead.

As George Steiner has recently written in his book, *Real Presence* (Chicago: University of Chicago Press, 1989), the new literary criticism ridicules the search for truth in art. It even calls into doubt the basic idea that language is able to communicate meaning from one person to another, let alone through art or literature. This form of artistic suicide pretending to the throne of literary criticism also denies the existence of God. Thus, this *deconstructionism* teaches that one can discern no eternal meaning in human communication. This once obscure French theory is now dominant on American campuses.

Steiner, a long-time fellow of Churchill College at Cambridge and a professor of literature at Geneva University in Switzerland, has concluded that ultimately it is impossible to really believe in principles of understanding, in the arts or in aesthetics, unless one believes in God and the meaning His existence gives to our lives and our attempts to communicate. He goes so far as to argue that the repudiation of God rules out all possibilities of real artistic creation. Just as there can be no criticism without a work of art to criticize, so there can be no art without Creation itself standing at the root of all creativity.

Sadly, though well qualified, Steiner seems to be one of the lone voices from the academic establishment even willing to challenge the prevailing deconstructionist, anti-art mood.

The arts are in as much of a predicament as the humanities are in the universities which Steiner discusses. Here, too, Christians are conspicuous by their absence. As we have seen, many Christians who should know better either misunderstand the arts in general, or worse, like many so-called Christian publishers and musicians, think of themselves only in regard to their evangelical, fundamentalist propaganda potential as they attempt to "reach the world, through their art."

Peter Shaw, literary scholar and journalist, has written one of the best, most readable and most provocative books concerning the plight of the humanities. In *The War Against the Intellect* (Iowa City: University of Iowa Press, 1989), Shaw argues in a series of essays that the humanities have been brought to the edge of a new Dark Age. (I have excerpted a substantial portion of his remarkable book in Appendix A.)

It is as if the deconstructionists, the feminists, and the other modern critics in the fields of literature, art, and the humanities resent the fact that there was ever an age of moral certainty when people knew who they were, what they meant to say, and, above all, in what they *believed*. To the modern critic, people of moral or artistic certainty are suspect. Because the modern relativist cannot imagine herself feeling any moral certainty, she is sure no one else can either, now or ever! Thus, modern criticism seeks to turn even pre-nineteenth-century art and literature into "modern" art, drama, and literature by investing it with the motivations of our lost modernity. By divesting the past of its meaning, today's scholars rob future generations of their common human heritage. With the humanities and arts being guarded by friends like these in our universities, they need no enemies!

Ironically, today's critics and academics no longer believe in the ability of art to communicate ordinary *human* meanings, but they certainly *do* believe that art can communicate *political* meanings. Thus, many people besides fundamentalist Christians now also view art as a mere propaganda vehicle. We have feminist, Afro-American, leftist, homosexual, and other special interest "art" and "literature." Art exhibits and films are sponsored by various gay/lesbian task forces. Leftist propaganda "art" exhibits and films are sponsored by various "revolutionary" groups and their friends amongst the intelligentsia. At this point in time, much to its detriment, art has been thoroughly confused with craft, the craft of political propaganda — not even a very transcendent or uplifting craft at that. It is a craft more useful to drum-beating cranks than to thoughtful individuals. Art has been prostituted and put to the service of equal rights, evangelicalism, affirmative action, African-American studies, and every *ism* which abounds in our now fractured, special-interest society.

Art needs its practitioners, its defenders, its lovers, and its friends as never before. Lorenzo de' Medici, call your office!

Nothing is so chaste as nudity.
Venus herself, as she drops her gar-
ments and steps on to the model-
throne, leaves behind her on the
floor every weapon in her armory
by which she can pierce to the
grosser passion of man.

George Du Maurier, *Trilby*, 90

8

NAKED AGAIN

I n our time, the question of the use of nudity and violence in art has divided Christians of goodwill, not to mention countless Christians of ill will who, like the poor, seem to always be with us.

The Bible

The Bible is not only the Word of God, divinely inspired to give people understanding of the way of salvation, but is also a literary work, a work of art. Descriptions of nudity as well as extreme violence are found in profusion in the Bible. From the story of the Garden of Eden to such instances as Noah's youngest son looking on his nakedness, to the Levite's concubine who was cut in twelve pieces and distributed to the twelve tribes of Israel at God's command, to the account of David cutting off two hundred Philistine foreskins, to the graphic sexuality of the Song of Songs, to Christ's often violent imagery in His parables, we find realistic, factual, literary descriptions of sex, nudity, and violence in the Bible. We also learn that God has used violence and people's sexual behavior, even immoral behavior, to shape history, to punish the wicked, to chastise, and to build up His people.

God, evidently, is not worried by any ratings board, not to mention the maintaining of polite niceties. When it comes to His own literary work, even His action in history, God's attitude seems to be, let the chips fall where they may. The Bible is many things, but it is certainly *not* suitable family entertainment. The Bible would probably not be sold in any "Christian bookstores" if it was perceived as merely a book to be thoroughly read rather than as a *religious* devotional work.

As Christians we look to the Scriptures for moral teaching. From their study we can conclude that the Bible seems unafraid of flesh and deals openly with nudity and violence. Historically, the church has not always been as unfriendly toward flesh as some fundamentalists are in our own times. Historian and scholar Etienne Gilson shows there was not a lack of awareness of the physical aspects of the individual in the church of the Middle Ages.

> One of the surprises in store for the historian of Christian thought lies in its insistence on the value, dignity, and perpetuity of the human body. The Christian conception of man is almost universally taken to be a more or less thoroughgoing spiritualism. . . . But to the no small scandal of a goodly number of historians and philosophers the contrary turns out to be the fact. St. Bonaventura, St. Thomas Aquinas, Duns Scotus, I will even say St. Francis of Assisi himself—one and all were men who looked benignly on matter, respected their bodies, extolled its dignity, and would never have wished a separate destiny for body and soul. (As cited by Robert Nisbet in *History of the Ideas of Progress* [New York: Basic Books, 1979], 80-81)

The Historic Vacuum

Pascal wrote: "Men never do evil so completely and cheerfully as when they do it from religious conviction" (*Pensées*, Sec. XIV, no. 895). Fundamentalist mischief to the arts by pious men and women has been great. "I fear this iron yoke of outward conformity hath left a slavish print upon our necks" (Milton, *Prose Works*, Vol. II, 97).

It is the exercise of a peculiarly Protestant arrogance that ignores church history and tradition and assumes that as we look for answers to moral problems, we are alone before God, armed only with our own reading of Scripture and our puny consciences. The fact that in their wisdom, countless faithful churchmen through generations before and after the Reformation found nothing intrinsically offensive about nudity and violence in art is instructive, at least to those who regard themselves as part of the historic church.

Unfortunately, in addition to ignoring church history, few Christians seem to understand the importance of the *context* in which something appears. Thus they are left with a few, inadequate, simplistic rules, which are not necessarily Biblical or aesthetic, by which to judge art.

There is no single rule that covers the question of aesthetics in art, including violence and nudity. Each work must be judged individually and in its context. The situations portrayed by a Christian in the arts are of merit if they accurately portray the truth of a subject honestly and properly in its context. Reality *is* tragic, violent, bloody, and evil, not to mention sublime and beautiful.

Those seeking to work as Christians in the arts will explore their own way haltingly and with little absolute certainty in these areas. They will get almost no help from today's evangelical let alone fundamentalist Christians. If they seek guidance, they will have to look elsewhere. The historic church beckons.

Nudity in Art

By consulting various sources (including James Hall's most helpful *Dictionary of Subjects and Symbols in Art* [New York: Harper and Row, 1974]), we learn that the response to nudity in art by people in all periods of Western history has varied from time to time. Yet the nude human figure has always been a dominant, if not the dominant, subject in the visual arts. Both in pre-Christian Western history and the Jewish-Christian era, nudity in art has been common.

Catholic and Protestant teaching and tradition has approved some nudity in art at some times and disapproved of it in some contexts at others. The context in which nudity was used and the subject being portrayed have been the determining factors in judging its appropriateness. Usually when objections to nudity have arisen, our own fundamentalistic, pietistic times being the exception, it has been over its perceived misuse, not over nudity itself.

Pliny, in his *Natural History* (36:20-22), writes that a nude statue of Venus was eagerly purchased by the islanders of Cnidus, having been rejected by the islanders of Kos. From this example we learn that some Greeks of the classical period accepted nudity in art and some did not. To the Romans nudity, symbolized various things: shame in some cases, poverty in others, and beauty in yet others.

In the Old Testament, the graphic eulogy of the female body and its sexuality in the Song of Songs seems to contradict another sentiment of Hebrew modesty expressed, for instance, in Jeremiah 13:26: "So I myself have stripped off your skirts and laid bare your shame!" (NEB).

However, descriptions of nakedness and nudity run through the Scripture, sometimes as a description of fact, such as the nakedness of Adam and Eve, other times as a metaphor for vulnerability. There are one hundred and four verses in the Old and New Testaments in which the subject of nakedness is a central theme. In addition to which, there are countless other frank allusions to sexuality, nudity, and violence as part of Biblical history.

To the Christian church of the Middle Ages, nudity in art presented four different aspects. The first, *nuditas naturalis*, was personified in nude paintings of Adam and Eve before the Fall or the nakedness of the many martyrs such as St. Sebastian — graphic nudity and extreme violence combined to illustrate his bloody and painful death. Nudity was also used in portraying the resurrected at the Last Judgment. Nude bodies were often used in a purely decorative way, for example consider a personal favorite of mine, the many nude figures carved into the marble pulpit in Orvieto's cathedral. These were all seen as worthy and good uses of nudity by churchmen and laymen alike. Far from frowning on such artworks, the church itself commissioned and displayed them.

The second category of nudity, as accepted by the church of the Middle Ages, was *nuditas temporalis* — nakedness understood in a figurative or allegorical sense. It symbolized the absence of worldly goods, either as a result of a misfortune, as with Job, or by saintly choice, exemplified by St. Francis of Assisi and the penitent Mary Magdalene. The same idea of naked purity is expressed by Milton in his descriptive line, "In naked beauty more adorned" (*Paradise Lost*, Bk. IV, l. 713).

The church understood nudity in art to also be *nuditas virtualis* — the third aspect of nudity that represented a quality of sinlessness in daily life, as in the nakedness of Truth. Finally, there was *nuditas criminalis*. This represented, in art, the ancient sins condemned by the prophets and was embodied by representations of the pagan gods and goddesses as well as the devil himself.

In the late thirteenth and fourteenth centuries, the church began to commission nude figures of the virtues, such as naked Truth painted standing next to robed Mercy, illustrating Psalms 85:10. The church also sponsored art containing nudity in scriptural themes to which it properly belonged — Massaccio's *Adam and Eve* in the Carmen Chapel in Florence or the figures in Giotto's *Last Judgment*, for example.

The human figure, naked and robed, was the keystone to Renaissance art in Catholic Italy *and* northern Protestant painting as well. From the first works of the Renaissance by painters like Cimabue, Giotto's teacher, to Leonardo da Vinci's anatomical studies in the late Renaissance, the human body was perceived as good, *the* fit subject for study, portrayal, and enjoyment. The human body was the basic model for all drawing, draftsmanship, and sculpture. To remove the nude figure from art of that, or indeed any period, would be to remove the very basis of all figurative artwork in Western art history.

The Florentine philosophers and theologians during the Renaissance taught that of the two aspects of love, divine and earthly, divine love was superior. To express contempt for the things of this world, they believed that divine love should be symbolized by a naked woman. Earthly love was portrayed as a clothed woman, richly dressed and bejeweled.

During the Renaissance in Italy, the church's stated attitude toward nudity in *secular art* — art not commissioned by the church itself — was ambivalent. However, we see in Cosimo de' Medici — the greatest patron of the church *and* the arts of the fifteenth century — a man who, as well as supporting San Marco and the religious works of Fra Angelico, also commissioned in 1440 the nude sculpture of *David* by Donatello. This was the first sculpture since Roman times made to be seen "in the round," from all sides. It was unashamedly nude, with no implication of sin or disgrace in its Biblical narrative portrayal of a young, innocent male body.

Later, the portrayal of nudity in religious art, not other art, was condemned by the Council of Trent except for religious subjects that specifically demanded it — Adam and Eve, the Last Judgment, and so on. The Council of Trent notwithstanding, many individual churchmen continued to commission art containing nudity in nonsanctioned subjects, for instance, in Carreggio's frescoes in the Camera di San Paolo at Parma, Italy (1518), which were the apartments of the abbess of a convent, or the decoration of the Farnese Palace in Rome by the Carvacci brothers for Cardinal Odoardo Farnese at the turn of the sixteenth century.

In Spanish art, redolent of a lingering Islamic repression, nudity is more rare. Goya, of course, painted beautiful nudes such as his *Maja nue*, as well as religious subjects, portraits of royalty, and so forth. He also portrayed the sins of *nuditas criminalis* in his etchings and paintings of nightmares, witchcraft, and other horrors.

In the Protestant north of Europe, nudity was not perceived as wrong *per se* by most churchmen until the post-Victorian pietistic times which foreshadow our own. And even in the era of Queen Victoria, we find a great deal of nudity in ninteenth-century British art. Though the prudish Ruskin, as the executor of Turner's estate, is said to have burnt a whole portfolio of Turner's "indecent" drawings!

Long before the advent of the Victorian era, Lucas Cranach, the German painter and a devotee, friend, and follower of Martin Luther (even the godfather to Luther's children), painted various nude subjects including his famous *Adam and Eve.* Luther was very fond of Cranach and his paintings and commissioned him to paint various portraits of himself and his wife. In this context it is also worth noting that Luther was unashamed of his own sexuality. We have his letters to a friend describing, in what would be seen by today's timid Christians as unhealthy and ribald terms, the pleasures of his marriage bed, complete with allusions to the pleasure he took in penetrating his wife and other robust, earthy sexual references.

Albrecht Dürer, a devout believer and an early follower of Luther, portrayed nude subjects in his etchings, including his Biblical illustrations such as *Adam und Eva,* as well as many other works. For instance, his strong pen-and-ink drawings, including *Ein Frauenbad* (The Women's Bath), *Der Mann mit dem Lowen* (Man with a Lion), and his *Das Grobe Gluck* (Nemesis), all portray nude men or women. Dürer also used mythological figures in his work — his nude *Apollo,* for example — thus echoing the Italian Renaissance interest in the classics. His anatomical studies in human proportion also mirror a scientific-artistic interest similar to Leonardo da Vinci's. In fact, his female nude study of *Figur aus der Proportionslehrer* (female proportions) uses the same configuration as Leonardo's famous male proportion study that has since become a worldwide symbol of humanity.

In his own writing, faith, and work, Dürer seems to have seen no conflict between his nude studies, his classical mythological studies, his Biblical subjects, and the various portraits he did of religious figures of his day, including one of Erasmus in 1521. Like most believing Christian artists throughout history, Dürer felt no tension between his deep, personal faith in Christ and his artwork. The wide-ranging choice of subject matter also tells us that Dürer fully understood all of life to be God's and rejected the division of life into *secular* and *sacred,* as if the *sacred* were more important. Dürer pays as much loving attention to a painting of a rabbit crouching next to a dandelion as he does to his portrayal of Christ at the *Last Supper.*

Rembrandt and the other Dutch seventeenth-century masters painted nudes fairly frequently. Rembrandt's nudes include those of his wife, who, like all artists' wives, often served as his model. Rembrandt, as a devout Reformation Protestant Christian, is typical of his time in his use of nudity. Rembrandt's paintings mirror reality in a down-to-earth way that speaks of an artist at peace with who he is and with a knowledge of the world and its fullness. His interests, like Dürer's, ranged beyond Biblical themes to the ancient classics, for example, in his red chalk drawing of *Cleopatra* as she seductively presents her breast to the serpent. In *The Anatomy Lesson of Professor Tulp,* Rembrandt paints not only the portrait of the students and the professor but a very dead cadaver, the tendons of its left arm dispassionately dissected. In *The Rape of Ganymede,* a child is plucked aloft by an eagle. The fearful infant is urinating as he looks desperately for help. In *The Holy Family* we see Mary in a darkened interior. She holds her breast out for the infant Jesus to suck. An old woman looks on tenderly. Joseph, in the background, goes about his day's work as a carpenter. The total, unromantic realism of the scene speaks of the historicity of the Christ child as Rembrandt saw Him. In *Susanna and the Two Elders*, all the voyeuristic lust of the ages is written on the faces of the two "dirty old men." One is tugging at the drape of a young, naked, and vulnerable girl where innocence contrasts sharply with the jaded elders as they use their status and respectability to try and coerce her into giving them sexual favors. Using a wide choice of subject matter, Rembrandt and Dürer are typical of the artists of the Reformation era who were devout Protestant believers.

In our own times, Christian artists, such as the Roman Catholic mystic Rouault, have painted nudity, and Jewish artists like Marc Chagall, have also used the nude figure delightfully. Today, thoughtful evangelical Christian artists, like Steven Hawley and Edward Knippers, continue to use the nude figure, male and female, as a central part of their work.

In retrospect, we can see in church history that an outright ban on all nudity is extremely rare. And a ban on violence in art, or even the idea that portraying violence could be morally bad in itself, is almost totally unknown in church history outside of our own time. The questions discussed by serious and informed men and women have always been about what nudity is appropriate to what subject in what context. Classical Greece and Rome, the Roman Catholic Church, and later the Protestant reformers seem not to have shared the attitude of modern pietists that nudity or violence in art is itself wrong in *any* context. Thus the evangelicals and fundamentalists of today are out-of-step with the traditions of the church, Catholic and Protestant, on the one hand, and with the explicitly descriptive passages of Scripture, such as the Song of Songs or the crucifixion of Jesus, on the other hand. (In this light, one wonders what an art department at some evangelical or fundamentalist Christian college that forces its students to draw models in bathing suits is doing, other than making an unintended joke at the expense of both art and Christianity.)

The Christian artist who wants to proceed with his or her painting, writing, sculpture, film, drama, and photography can therefore feel secure that present-day fundamentalist-evangelical hostility in some quarters concerning nudity and violence in art does not represent the wisdom of the ages, the Bible itself as a work of literature, or for the most part, church history and tradition. The precedent set by the great Christian artists who once dominated Western art history tells a very different story, one of freedom of expression.

Christian artists today must be as courageously creative in pursuing their work in the face of evangelical, fundamentalist opposition as was Michelangelo, who got around the problems of a temporary church ban on anatomical studies by striking a deal with the prior of Santo Spirito in Florence. He was secretly allowed to dissect corpses in the cloister in exchange for carving a crucifix for the canny prior!

Pornography

Pornography, like the poor, will always be with us. In the pre-photographic age, the Romans sometimes used their fresco paintings to portray pornographic images. For instance, in one fresco in Pompeii, one can see a man with a huge penis masturbating into a cornucopia of fruit—pretty obvious stuff, even if excused as a homage to fertility! Yet no one in his right mind confuses this crudely fashioned "art" with the serious and sublime classical sculpture of Greece and Rome. In our own times, we can see a vast difference between sexuality being sold as sinful pornographic titillation in some so called "adult" magazines and serious works of art. Common sense *should* tell us this.

Of course all nudity, even of the Virgin Mary's breast in an icon, has some sexual content, but then so does all of human life. But such portrayals are not selling sexuality for sexuality's sake, divorced from a loving human relationship, as is pornography. Sexuality itself, in a proper context as a subject matter for art, is not always wrong. There will be many gray areas in between licit nudity and pornography. But that fact, too, is typical of life in general, most of which is a balancing act. Not everything can be reduced to an easy formula.

There is a clear difference apparent to many people, though perhaps not to many A.C.L.U. lawyers or fundamentalists, between voyeurism and aesthetic nudity in art. Some modern Christians have called all nudity in art *pornography*. An unintended consequence of such overstatement has been the fact that by such absurd conjecture they have made it virtually impossible to stand against *real* pornography in any meaningful and effective way. Those who cannot see the difference between Michelangelo's *David* and an X-rated video tape in which two women are copulating with one man and an animal cannot really be taken too seriously. Crude, sexually abusive images produced for people to masturbate on are of an entirely different kind than those of art works. This may be a difficult concept to write into law in a free society, but, I believe, it is one that is not impossible to grasp for the average person.

False Piety

Typical of the fundamentalists' attitude toward nudity in art is a passage from a famous "Spirit-filled" television evangelist's biography in which he speaks passionately of the changes he made in his domestic life after his conversion to the Christian faith from "secular humanism." In one passage he explains to the reader how he and his wife removed all traces of *secular* and *evil* things from their lives. The list of "sins" they renounced in favor of a closer walk with God included a reproduction of a certain nude painting he had in his house. The painting was a Modigliani, the beautiful if over-reproduced *Nu Assis* (seated nude) painted in 1914 by the famous Italian artist. Modigliani is one of the greatest painters of the early twentieth century, a painter whose work was limited exclusively to the human figure, which he painted in very expressive works distinguished by their purity of line. Modigliani's lifetime of work was thus dismissed as "sinful" by an evangelist whose personal, "sanctified" taste, as exhibited in his multimillion dollar university and television studio complex, runs to neo-colonial, Williamsburg-type structures on the scale of airplane hangars — buildings that look as if the Daughters of the American Revolution had commissioned Albert Speer to design a funeral home!

Conclusion

It is no accident that Christians throughout history have been drawn toward portraying the human figure. God's most complete and beautiful earthly creation has, by Jews and Christians, been understood to be men and women — men and women with beautiful, ugly, lumpish, or sublime, but always interesting, souls and bodies. Besides Jews and Christians, others, like the ancient Greeks, also understood man's unique qualities. Sophocles, in his *Antigone,* writes the famous line for the chorus, "Many a wonder lives and moves, but the wonder of all is man."

Men and women are worth painting, sculpting, *and* telling the way of salvation. We are told that we bear God's image in and on us. We are told that God Himself came to us in Christ through the flesh. God made man. We are told that our bodies are precious to God and will even be raised from the dead. In this context, is it any wonder that Christian artists and non-Christian artists, simply responding to who they are as human beings, have loved the human form even as God loves it? As St. Augustine wrote in Book 22 of *The City of God,* "Assuredly no part of the body has been created for the sake of utility that does not also contribute something to the beauty."

"And the LORD God formed man of the dust of the ground, and breathed into his nostrils the breath of life. . . . And the LORD God caused a deep sleep to fall on Adam, and he slept; and He took one of his ribs, and closed up the flesh in its place. Then the rib which the LORD God had taken from man He made into a women, and He brought her to the man" (Genesis 2:7, 21–22). God, who could simply speak a word and create matter from nothing, chose instead to *sculpt* the human form from clay and bone. Is it any wonder that His image-bearers, His children, have inherited His love of sculpting the human form?

There have been a few evangelical Christian thinkers of our own time who have had a love of art, a love of the gospel, and informed opinions about art. My late father was one such person. Here is a quotation from his book *How Should We Then Live?* (Westchester, IL: Crossway Books, 1983, 99-100). In the chapter from which the passage is drawn, Francis Schaeffer is making the argument for the positive results of the Reformation in the area of art. Would that all Christian commentators approached art with such sympathy and depth.

> We can think of Rembrandt's painting *Danae* (1636) in the museum in Leningrad. This is a picture of Rembrandt's nude wife waiting in bed for him. . . . There is love and gentleness here. Rembrandt understood that Christ is the Lord of all of life. As a Christian, he lived in the midst of God's world and did not need to make himself God. Rather, he could use God's world and its form in his painting. . . . This was the right direction, a proper view of nature.

*Persecution may shield itself under
the guise of a mistaken and over-
zealous piety.*

Edmund Burke, *Impeachment of Warren
Hastings,* February 17, 1788

9

FREEDOM VERSUS CENSORSHIP

The book *Huckleberry Finn* was banned in some circles when first published in 1885 because it seemed to be dangerously *against* the common racism of the day. Today there are calls by some black civil rights activists to ban *Huckleberry Finn* because the word *nigger* is used in the text. Some have called it racist.

Some fundamentalist Christian educators also wish to drop *Huckleberry Finn* from school reading lists — or worse, actually change and edit the text — to tone down what they regard as Mark Twain's antichurch, antireligious "offensive" worldview. It seems today that Mark Twain has trouble pleasing anyone.

People agree that Mark Twain was a great writer and that *Huckleberry Finn* is deserving of its place in the pantheon of American fiction. Everyone, that is, except today's censors, including some who claim to be "liberal," for instance, the feminist literati. Women who would rather ignore nonfeminist literature, except when condemning it, have an aversion to prefeminist literature of all kinds, unless of course it comes from some obscure non-Western source, perhaps a Sri Lankan lesbian describing her spiritual exaltation as she contemplates her menstrual cycle!

The black leaders who want to ban *Huck*, the feminists who want to reinterpret *Huck* and all other literature, the deconstructionist critics who say it is impossible to understand Twain at all, the fundamentalist Christians who want more sympathy for religion from Twain — all have one thing in common: they want to rearrange reality and history to suit their political, theological, or ideological tastes. Unfortunately, *Huckleberry Finn* is but one of hundreds of volumes of literature under attack by the ideologues in our country, from the political Left and Right and, judging by the deconstructionists' interpretations, from the lunatic asylums as well.

The New Censors

In our times, various ideologically dedicated groups increasingly use, in one way or another, censorship, coercion, or propaganda to limit access to ideas, literature, and the arts that they consider threatening.

African Americans

Black civil rights activists have not been subtle in putting censorious pressure on the educational system. For instance, activists pressured the Toronto, Canada, Board of Education to rule on June 23, 1988, that the novel *Lord of the Flies* was "racist and . . . that it be removed from all schools." Members of the black community complained that it denigrated blacks because the word *niggers* appeared in the text.

A number of American black Muslim leaders joined with the late Ayatollah Khomeini in calling for a ban on Salman Rushdie's *Satanic Verses*. Black groups challenged the Salem school system in Virginia Beach, Virginia, over the use of *The Actor's Book of Contemporary Stage Monologues* because some of the dialogue in the monologues contained *racial* slurs.

Black activists also forced the removal of a painting from public display in Chicago, in 1988, that offended the then black mayor of the city by portraying him in an "offensive" manner. The work was attacked as *racist* and then removed by force. Black leftists, the majority of black leaders, have also gone about quietly suppressing the views of black conservative scholars like Thomas Sowell and Glenn C. Loury, whose ideas they oppose as not reflecting their own views on racism and welfare*ism*.

Feminists

Feminists have concentrated their censorship activities on pressuring textbook companies to remove all "sexist" and "traditional" female role models from textbooks, including reading books. They have insinuated a picture of personally approved women's roles into many textbooks at the expense of all other visions of womanhood. Feminists have also been active in a quiet, informal, hidden censorship campaign. For instance, the action of individual women editors of like mind at various major publishing companies has effectively prevented authors and scholars critical of feminism, such as Michael Levin, from publishing scholarly works that take an informed but critical view of feminist achievements. Levin, who is professor of philosophy at CCNY, found it impossible to find a major publishing house for his book *Feminism and Freedom* due to the individual actions of an informal sisterhood of feminists who guard the gates of access to public discourse in many of America's leading publishing houses.

When Carol Felsenthal wrote a sympathetic biography of Phyllis Schafly, *The Sweetheart of the Silent Majority,* she experienced consistent hostility leveled at her by this sisterhood, resulting in the book being notable by its absence from many large bookstore chains, public libraries, and a whole range of magazines that would normally have reviewed a book on an important political female figure. Libraries and bookstores have many "sisters" guarding their gates. Anti-abortion literature has often met with informal banning.

That many well-educated women tend to think the same way and exhibit a herd mentality regarding issues of the day is not surprising when one is aware of the aggressive, almost unopposed dominance that feminist theology now enjoys in academia. Typical of the results of this sort of "scholarship" is a course offered at Duke University called Interdisciplinary Studies 140, "The Great Mother: Archetype or Stereo-Type?" This course of "study" is described in the school's prospectus of course offerings (1989) as follows:

> The Jungian archetype of the Great Mother and the emerging feminist critique of the Jungian model. The dual symbolism of the Feminine as nurturing and devouring Mother, the ambivalent nature of the mother-daughter relations, the identification of woman with Eros, and alternatives to the patriarchal myth of the Mother. Readings include Jungian and feminist theories; Asian, Egyptian, and Greek mythologies; and modern fiction.

With four years of such intensive feminist indoctrination (at $18,000 to $20,000 per year!), imagine how traditional Western ideas of truth and aesthetics, and artistic universality fare with the graduates of Duke and other schools. Unknown to them, the students in question are participating in a mammoth anti-historical, anti-Western experiment that will, like the Communist experiment in Eastern Europe, eventually crash in the inevitable ruins of all extremist, ideologically authoritarian excursions. But in the meantime, this indoctrination is destroying the students' chance to enjoy a genuine education. What today's students are *not* studying is also a form of censorship. Points of view they are *not* hearing is a form of intellectual coercion practiced by those who should be encouraging them to explore their diverse Western intellectual cultural heritage.

Being introduced to literature and art by the feminists and deconstructionist critics is like being introduced to sex via rape. It takes a long time to recover; literature will never be quite what it could have been for their unfortunate protégés.

To illustrate the massive revisionist campaign by feminist ideologues against the arts in general and literature in particular, Carol Iannone, in an article called "Feminism vs. Literature" (*Commentary,* July 1988), reviewed a number of works by feminist literary critics: Sandra Gilbert, who teaches at Princeton, and Susan Gubar of Indiana University. Iannone teaches writing and literature at New York University and is editor of *Academic Questions.* In her article she notes the deliberate destruction of the concept of the transcendent universality of the arts by the radical feminists who now dominate the literary university landscape, and who, by their theories of criticism, have managed to subvert the meaning of literature. Iannone writes:

> Scarcely a single scholarly discipline now stands without its corrective feminist insurgency, and the profession of English literature is no exception. In fact, in literary studies feminism is no longer an insurgency but an ascendancy. In the words of Peter Brooks, director of Yale's Whitney Humanities Center, "Anyone worth his salt in literary criticism today has to become something of a feminist." . . .
>
> Professors Gilbert and Gubar's first joint work, *The Madwoman in the Attic: The Woman Writer in the Nineteenth Century Literary Imagination* (1979) was one of a number of book-length efforts to appear in the 70s aimed at analyzing literature by women as a separate category. *Madwoman* begins with a question that might seem ironic coming from a feminist perspective, namely, how did 19th-century female authors meet the monumental challenge of being both women and writers? According to Professors Gilbert and Gubar, literary "assertion" is necessarily incompatible with the habits of feminine submission demanded by "patriarchy." Therefore, the "difficult task" faced by British and American writers was to achieve "true female liter-

ary authority by simultaneously conforming to and subverting patriarchal literary standards."

Jane Austen, for example, masks beneath the serene surface of her art "a subversive critique of the forms of self-expression available to her both as an artist and as a woman." How so? By, among other things, identifying herself in her novels "not only with her model heroines but also with less obvious, nastier, more resilient and energetic female characters who enact her rebellious dissent from her culture. . . . " Similarly, in Emily Bronte's *Wuthering Heights,* Catherine's "masochistic self-starvation" during pregnancy is not the exacerbated willfulness most readers have taken it for but a protest against female fate, an "obvious response to the pregnant woman's fear of being monstrously inhabited as well as to her own horror of being enslaved to the species and reduced to a tool of the life process."

What distinguished *The Madwoman in the Attic* from previous works on the subject of literature by women was its authors' willingness to suspend normal literary standards entirely and employ a so-called "female" or "feminist" aesthetic instead. Before *Madwoman,* many would-be feminist critics had found themselves bound by the traditional criteria that they either still respected or did not yet know how to be rid of . . .

Professors Gilbert and Gubar's second major effort, the *Norton Anthology of Literature by Women* (1985), collected writings from the Middle Ages through the 20th century. Unlike *Madwoman,* this anthology did arouse an open controversy over its methods when a living, breathing "woman writer" actually laid critical eyes upon it. Writing in the *New York Times Book Review,* the novelist Gail Godwin asserted that "the values of feminist interpretation are elevated to a *summa* at the expense of literary art and individual talents. . . ."

Miss Godwin's review provoked a flurry of angry responses. There was, predictably, no substantive disagreement with her contentions. Instead, in a letter signed by five prominent feminist critics, she was accused of "political bias" and lectured on the "illusion" of universality. "There is no universal literature," these respondents insisted, and "all of it arises from beliefs that are no less ideological for being unexamined or widely accepted as 'normal.' " Another feminist decried Miss Godwin's denial of a female literary tradition "in the face of massive and growing evidence to the contrary"; for still another, Miss Godwin's views could only be ascribed to "the resistance of a woman who is herself at odds concerning her relationship to a tradition of other women."

Of course, what specific "ideological" beliefs Miss Godwin had illegitimately propounded were not spelled out by her critics, nor was any of the "massive and growing evidence" of the female tradition actually adduced. But this did not matter. By 1985, the indignant insistence on a chimerical female tradition had obviously become a useful tool for wielding threats and subduing opponents.

Unfortunately, Professors Gilbert and Gubar are not unique in this reflection on the meaning of literature. They are part of a fashionable legion of feminist ideologues, literary critics all bent on rewriting, or should I say eliminating, the history of Western literature. Elaine Showalter, Ann Douglas, Elizabeth Hardwick, Nina Baym, and a gaggle of others have been at the forefront of the assault.

Feminists have borrowed a page from the Marxists when it comes to the manipulation of history, theology, the arts, and literature for their own political causes. The deadly sterility of Socialist Realism that typified Stalinist art has in common with feminist literary criticism a character that is at once propagandistic, manipulative, belittling to the human spirit, and is technically incompetent though ideologically "correct."

Fundamentalist Christians

Christian fundamentalist groups and individuals have also used the meat-cleaver approach to literary criticism as they have embarked on their own programs of censorship.

Aldous Huxley's *Brave New World* was challenged as required reading in the Yukon, Oklahoma, High School in 1988 because of the book's "language and moral content." (Thus, ironically, was dispatched by these "God-fearers" the greatest prophetic warning against a godless super-state ever penned!) *Catcher in the Rye* met the same fate at the Linton-Stockton, Indiana, High School in 1988 because the book was said to be "blasphemous and undermines morality." John Steinbeck's work fared no better. *Of Mice and Men* was challenged in the Marian County, West Virginia, schools and the Wheaton-Warrenville, Illinois, high schools, both in 1988, because the book contains "profanity." So much for great American literature.

The list of literary works under attack is unfortunately long. In 1988 alone there were more than five hundred attempts to ban books from libraries and schools across the United States. An anti-intellectual tradition in America runs deep in some quarters and is not a new phenomenon. For instance, in the Boston area in which I live, *Leaves of Grass* was banned in 1881, *Elmer Gantry* in 1929, *Strange Interlude* and *All Quiet on the Western Front* in 1930, *An American Tragedy* and *The Sun Also Rises* in 1941, and in 1950, *Strange Fruit* and *God's Little Acre.*

One common thread binds all the censors of our time: they all claim their actions are for the "good of society," or at least to liberate or protect us. Yet those who love and cherish the arts and humanities, not to mention truth, should be the first to reject claims by those who would limit human expression for some "greater good." What greater good can a society enjoy than freedom and truth? And how can freedom of expression exist in a pale, bloodless culture where not being offensive is seen as the first civic duty?

Hypocrisy abounds in the ranks of the modern puritans. Fundamentalist Christians, who claim to worship the God who endowed men and women with creative expression, can be seen vying with each other as they jockey for position on some school board to be the first in line to ban a book or boycott an "offensive" film, book, or television program. "Liberal" educators censor speech they find distasteful in the bosom of institutions committed to the free flow of ideas.

G. K. Chesterton once said (in an interview with the *New York Times*, November 21, 1930) that, "A puritan is a person who pours righteous indignation into the wrong things." He could well have been describing today's puritan leaders who compete in the stifling of freedom of expression.

In fairness to the actual puritans of the seventeenth century, I hasten to add that they, in reality, were far more open-minded than their contemporary namesakes. Both the puritans of England and those in the New World were devoutly open-minded in their appreciation of learning and science. In fact, puritan thinking was the foundation for the philosophy of secular progress in both Europe and the United States. Cotton Mather thought that the three greatest achievements of modern history were the discovery of America, the revival of the arts and sciences, and the Reformation. And Jonathan Edwards, father of the "Great Awakening" (the last bloom of puritan thought before Unitarian night closed in), had a keen interest in issues of psychological, sociological, economical, and political character.

Censorship Methods

Banned

Veronese, the great Italian painter, had a taste of censorship in his time. He had painted an enormous fresco of the *Last Supper*. Veronese peopled his painting with the Biblical figures one would expect: Christ and the disciples. However, in addition he used the enormous wall space available, filling it with contemporary figures, including German soldiers dressed in the style of his time.

Germany was a Reformation country and no friend to Catholic Italy or the Venetian patrons who had commissioned the fresco.

Veronese was hauled before the Inquisition for questioning as to why he had included German soldiers in a sacred work. His answer was that he had wanted to make full use of the wall space and that he had run out of Biblical figures! He was ordered to paint out the offending figures — an order he ignored, saying that it would ruin his work. Instead, he simply changed the title of his *Last Supper* to *The Feast at the House of Levi.*

At the height of the Counter Reformation, one expects such intolerance from the Inquisition. What is odd is to see twentieth-century "liberals" carrying out similar witch hunts. Today the sheer magnitude of the feminist assault on the arts may be un-matched in its brashness, even by Christian fundamentalists who have traditionally attacked freedom of speech, art, and literature, but this is not for want of trying. Mel and Norma Gabler, the founders of Educational Research Analysts of Longview, Texas, have been typical of a not very successful and crude attempt by some Christian fundamentalists to limit what some Americans can and cannot read and see. As Donald Rogers writes in his book *Banned* (Julian Messner, 1988), "These people wanted to safe-guard students from what they considered dangerous ideas about sex, race, religion . . . and patriotism."

In doing so, what many students were to be safeguarded from were merely ideas at odds with fundamentalist ideology in middle class taste. In other words, the students were being protected from a broad view of Western culture that, ironically, had been origi-nally informed by Jewish-Christian values concerning freedom. The fundamentalist's attempted banning of *A Brave New World* serves as a good example of this outworking of a house divided against itself.

Today's ideologues are like today's corporate leaders. Corpo-rate America complains about government restraint of business unless it is in *its* favor. Today's ideologues want freedom of speech as long as it is speech approved by *them*. They even want history rewritten to suit their taste. The earnest zealots are a legion who would ban, censor, revise, or otherwise interfere with or reinterpret ideas, culture, and history. We seem to be in a society that is descending to the level of a competition between intolerant special interest groups who all regard art and the humanities as dispensable and politics as sacrosanct.

Ironically, Christians and Jews are sometimes taking part in censorship, whether this is overt or inward guilt-ridden self-censorship. The freedom the Bible brought to the men and women of the West is a direct result of the practice of Biblical principles. It is no coincidence that Western society has, with some regrettable exceptions, given the greatest freedom to the arts ever known in the world. This historic treasure of freedom of expression should be cherished, not squandered by allowing people with coercive or extreme views to trash art and literature, forcing it to serve their puny ideologies.

The first duty of the artist is not to be socially conscious or to express "correct thinking." The duty of the artist is to express truth as he or she sees it. The duty of a free society is to demand, then preserve, this right.

Politics

Sometimes the battle over censorship takes on overtly political dimensions. This was the case in the well-publicized debate in 1989 over the N.E.A. (National Endowment for the Arts) funding of artworks by such artists as Andres Sarrano and Robert Mapplethorpe. Both artists had produced artwork that was offensive to a large proportion of the population, including myself. Both artists' work came under attack from right wing politicians, such as Jesse Helms, and conservative commentators such as Patrick Buchanan. Mapplethorpe was attacked for his photographs of vulgarly explicit homosexual subjects and Sarrano for his *Piss*

Christ, a photograph of a crucifix submerged in a bottle of urine that many people, myself included, regarded as blasphemous and a very second-rate work of art, if *art* at all. Neither artists' works are particularly good, and in the case of Mapplethorpe, are often prurient.

However, be that as it may, my own view is that there is *no place for censorship of art or ideas in a free society.* I also feel that because of the necessity to preserve freedom of expression, it is a mistake to involve the taxpayer in underwriting *any* art, good or otherwise.

Attorney John Whitehead, president and founder of the Rutherford Institute (a religious civil rights organization), writes concerning government funding of art.

> Funding art places the government in the untenable position of placing its financial weight behind ideological propaganda. A free government must in principle be evenhanded and nondiscriminatory in what it supports. If a free government, then, funds one form of art, it cannot logically deny another form. (Private correspondence with the author, February 9, 1990)

As Whitehead points out, the government has no business in the art business at all. But as long as the government *is* in the misbegotten business of underwriting artwork, then the government should not censor artwork based on what it interprets as morally good or bad. To do so means that it is drawn unwittingly into the censoring ideas in a free society.

Censorship invites reciprocity in public discourse by those who resent the censorship of what they would otherwise approve or tolerate. For example, Nicols Fox writes in *The New Art Examiner* (Summer 1989) in an article entitled "NEA under Siege":

> Irony abounds in this affair. In the current supermarket atmosphere that characterizes Christianity, an extraordinary diversity of beliefs is not only tolerated but supported by those who call themselves Christians. Those who rise in outrage against the

Piss Christ raised not a whimper of protest against the long-running Praise the Lord Club (PTL) heresy. Jim and Tammy Bakker were allowed to preach and practice, in the name of Christianity, a doctrine of pure materialism, a gospel of goods and getting and an eternal life in the hot tub — the antitheses, to be precise, of Christ's Sermon on the Mount.

Freedom of expression does not imply that everyone must approve all that is said or done. It is, I think, legitimate to boycott an artwork or a media presentation as our exercise of freedom. As a believing Christian, I am careful about what images I wish to absorb. For instance, I did not see *The Last Temptation of Christ.* To me, my image of the Lord Jesus Christ is too precious to risk by seeing images of Him that are detrimental to an orthodox understanding of His life and work. However, the fact that I did not want to subject myself to such images is not to say I wished to deprive Martin Scorsese of the right to make his movie or that it was a badly made movie much as I might have hated the experience of watching it.

In a free society, there is a legitimate role for protesting things, including art, that we find distasteful. There is a difference between *boycotting* something and *censoring* it. That is why it is inappropriate for the government to spend the tax dollars of its diverse citizens to underwrite art that its citizens will find distasteful. However piecemeal, censorship is not the answer. Freedom is — freedom from government censorship or support, and freedom to make moral-artistic choices in a free market of free ideas.

Methods vary when art is censored: It can be banned outright, as Jesse Helms suggested as he attacked the funding of certain kinds of artwork, or it can be censored by giving it a false, antihistorical interpretation that imposes a present-day ideology in the minds of the young and impressionable, as feminist scholars are doing when they indoctrinate the semiliterate and inexperienced with their political ideas. I believe both methods to be inappropriate, in fact and in spirit, within a free society.

Labeling

Besides naked attempts to ban books, art, and films, there are other ways in which artistic and intellectual expression is being systematically intimidated in our society. There are unspoken but clearly understood parameters now effectively limiting what can or cannot be said in "right-thinking" company. Black civil rights advocates have become experts in using the label of *racist* to intimidate any person, even a fellow African American, who offends them, however legitimate their point of view. Some Jewish groups use the label *anti-Semitic* as a bludgeon with which to silence all adverse opinions concerning the state of Israel or other questions of particular interest to Jews. Feminists have become past masters at condemning as *sexist* those who dare to oppose them in their political machinations. And in some circles, the fear of being labeled *homophobic,* is enough to silence those who challenge the orthodoxy of belief of some gay rights' task force.

Many speakers whose views are not congenial to the "right-thinking" leftists who dominate American campuses, have been literally driven from the podium by the vicious behavior of those bent on denying them the right to be heard. Supposedly liberal institutions, such as Harvard, have specialized in accommodating the rantings of these latter-day Brown Shirts in the very heart of educational institutions once dedicated to free speech.

Islands of Repression

Chester E. Finn, Jr., who served as Assistant Secretary of Education from 1985 to 1988 and is now professor of education and public policy at Vanderbilt University, writes in an article entitled "The Campus: An Island of Repression in a Sea of Freedom" (*Commentary,* September 1989) about the rising tide of "liberal" intolerance in our universities:

Two weeks before the Supreme Court held that the First Amendment protects one's right to burn the flag, the regents of the University of Wisconsin decreed that students on their twelve campuses no longer possess the right to say anything ugly to or about one another.

Several months earlier, the University of Michigan adopted a six-page "anti-bias code" that provides for punishment of students who engage in conduct that "stigmatizes or victimizes an individual on the basis of race, ethnicity, religion, sex, sexual orientation, creed, national origin, ancestry, age, marital status, handicap, or Vietnam-era veteran status." (Presumably this last bizarre provision applies whether the "victim" is labeled a war hero or a draft dodger.)

Not to be outdone by the huge state schools, a number of private universities, like Emory in Atlanta and Stanford in California, have also made efforts to regulate unpleasant discourse and what the National Education Association terms "ethno-violence," a comprehensive neologism that includes "acts of insensitivity. . . ."

Constraints on free expression and open inquiry do not, of course, depend on the adoption of a formal code of conduct. Guest speakers with controversial views have for some years now risked being harassed, heckled, even shouted down by hostile campus audiences, just as scholars engaging in certain forms of research, treading into sensitive topics, or reaching unwelcome conclusions have risked calumny from academic "colleagues." More recently, students have begun to monitor their professors and to take action if what is said in class irks or offends them.

[The] additions to the formal and informal curricula of American colleges and universities, like the behavior codes and anti-harassment policies the institutions are embracing, are invariably promulgated in the name of enhancing "diversity" on campus. That has become the chief purpose of present-day affirmative-action hiring and admissions policies, too . . . In recent months,

I have run into several outstanding young (white male) political scientists who are finding it impossible to land tenure-track teaching posts at medium- and high-status colleges because, as one of them wryly explained to me, their scholarly strengths lie in the study of "DWEMs." When I confessed ignorance of the acronym, he patiently explained that it stands for "Dead White European Males." Had they specialized in revolutionary ideologies, the politics of feminism and racism, or trendy quantitative social-science methodologies, they could perhaps have transcended their inconvenient gender and mundane color and have a reasonable shot at academic employment. But to spend one's hours with the likes of Aristotle, Machiavelli, Hobbes, and Burke is to have nothing very important to offer a political-science department today, whatever one's intellectual and pedagogical accomplishments. . . .

Diversity and tolerance, evenhandedly applied, are estimable precepts. But that is not how they are construed in the academy today. Nor do the narrowing limits on free expression lead only to penalties for individuals who engage in "biased" talk or "hostile" behavior. They also leave little room for opinion that deviates from campus political norms or for grievances from unexpected directions.

Literature

Great literature comes from the desire to write and write well and expresses the artist's love of life and interest in his or her fellow creatures. Politics, in contrast to art, serves a worthy but distinctly different purpose. Its power to move human action is directed to often more temporary questions.

The "politics" of the artist's work in question is often more in the eye of the beholder than in the artwork itself. Thus by one generation, *Huckleberry Finn* is labeled as scandalously anti-slavery, by another as scandalously anti-black. Perhaps tomorrow someone will say it is anti-Jewish, homophobic, or anti-environmental! But what was Mark Twain writing about? And how do we honor his efforts? First, I believe we study his life and the context in which he wrote. Deconstructionists and feminists aside, it is not beyond the realm of possibility that we can, through a little research, place Twain and other authors' intentions in rather clear perspective. We should also be humble enough to recognize that we are not so uniquely "enlightened" in our day as to be altogether different from our forbears. We share with them a universal human experience of life that *transcends* time, space, race, *and* gender.

So what was Twain up to? It seems to me that he was writing a book about the adventures of a boy; a story he infused with the timeless warmth of human companionship that never changes. Huck's sense of morality, his tenderness towards those in distress; Jim, the runaway slave's loyalty and compassion; the tawdry scenes about the exploits of the Duke and the King, punctuated by moments of Huck's unexpected virtue: these are attributes universal to the human character. These are the themes of all people's lives. These are the attributes of humanity that interest Twain, Dante, and Homer. These are the *common* bonds that span *all* time, history, races, and the sexes. That is not to say that there is no subtle, social satire in *Huckleberry Finn*; there is. But real art transcends mere politics.

The very fact that people *do* have common bonds holding them together alarms the special interest "scholars" of today. Those, such as feminists, marxists, some black activists, and fundamentalist Christians, who wish to segregate themselves from the rest of humanity have a vested, if unconscious, interest in destroying our common artistic and human heritage. They all have the same agenda: to separate little segments of the human race from the rest of humanity and to claim these unfortunates as their own, to be "led" whither the particular demagogues in question wish to lead them for their own political, sociological, or theological purposes. Integration, of the kind that Martin Luther King advocated, is the concept furthest from their minds. Today's ideologues work tirelessly to erect new barriers between races, creeds, and the sexes. This new racism and sexism is alive and well in the bosom of the "liberal" establishment and of the church.

Art is one part of the glue that binds people together. Is it any wonder that in this fractured age of special interest politics that art has been under attack or prostituted to become mere propaganda? Those who politicize art and historical interpretation are, I believe, the enemies of humanity — a humanity that St. Augustine understood to be unified into one body, progressing from darkness toward the light of progress under God's hand of divine providence.

Re-Editing — Even Babar!

Every imaginable artistic expression is now threatened by the new censors and their "correct thinking." One might think that a children's literary classic would be safe. Not so. In the 1981 edition of Random House publisher's *Babar's Anniversary Album,* six Babar stories from the 1935 edition of *Babar's Travels* have been edited in order to omit stories and illustrations which might offend some contemporary tastes. In this case, an episode was edited in which Babar and the queen of the elephants, Celeste, are attacked by a tribe of cannibals while stranded on an island. No doubt this hatchet-editing was done in service of some hypothetical standard of what black America, or at least its self-proclaimed leaders, is supposed to want children to read. As a result of this kind of tampering multiplied in hundreds of incidents, we find a sort of United Nations blandness creeping into even children's books and textbooks, in which "right thinking" is seen as more important than literary integrity, personal opinions of the author, history, or truth. It amounts to little more than censorship by the bland, for the bland, of the bland, and produces books that offend and interest no one. And since reality is deliberately distorted, the reedited books tell lies about the intent of the author or history.

This is a tragedy, and in the case of the Babar books and other children's books, ridiculous as well. We are becoming a nation of pale "equal opportunity" bureaucrats when it comes to our ideas of what is appropriate in art.

By Default

There is another form of censorship rampant in our culture — the trivialization of knowledge through television.

In *Amusing Ourselves to Death*, Neil Postman points out that as we moved from the rational linear thought promoted by the typographical age into the television age of irrational emotionalism fed by images, we have unwittingly rendered information trivial. Thus our access to knowledge is, in a way, censored by the trivialization of information presented via television. Postman writes:

> Television clearly does impair the student's freedom to read, and it does so with innocent hands, so to speak. Television does not ban books, it simply displaces them. . . .

> There could not have been a safer bet when it began in 1969 than that "Sesame Street" would be embraced by children, parents and educators. Children loved it because they were raised on television commercials, which they intuitively knew were the most carefully crafted entertainments on television. To those who had not yet been to school, even to those who had just started, the idea of being *taught* by a series of commercials did not seem peculiar. And that television should entertain them was taken as a matter of course. . . .

> We now know that "Sesame Street" encourages children to love school only if school is like "Sesame Street." Which is to say, we now know that "Sesame Street" undermines what the traditional idea of schooling represents. Whereas a classroom is a place of social interaction, the space in front of a television set is a private preserve. Whereas in a classroom, one may ask a teacher questions, one can ask nothing of a television screen.

Whereas school is centered on the development of language, television demands attention to images. Whereas attending school is a legal requirement, watching television is an act of choice. Whereas in school, one fails to attend to the teacher at the risk of punishment, no penalties exist for failing to attend to the television screen. Whereas to behave oneself in school means to observe rules of public decorum, television watching requires no such observances, has no concept of public decorum. Whereas in a classroom, fun is never more than a means to an end, on television it is the end in itself. . . .

Television is a nongraded curriculum and excludes no viewer for any reason, at any time. In other words, in doing away with the idea of sequence and continuity in education, television undermines the idea that sequence and continuity have anything to do with thought itself. . . .

And, in the end, what will the students have learned? . . . Mainly, they will have learned that learning is a form of entertainment. . . .

When a population becomes distracted by trivia, when cultural life is redefined as a perpetual round of entertainments, when serious public conversation becomes a form of baby-talk, when, in short, a people become an audience and their public business a vaudeville act, then a nation finds itself at risk; culture-death is a clear possibility. (pp 142-144)

While there are many who would debate some of Postman's conclusions, I, for one, find his argument convincing. How else can we explain the trance-like stupidity which stamps the faces and actions of a legion of "teenagers" (people ranging from age twelve through fifty!), who populate the nether world which is the product of so much of our media age? (See Appendix B for more from Postman on the subject of television.)

The M.P.A.A.

At times, attempts to censor lead to ridiculous hair-splitting. I became aware of just how silly trying to "rate" art or media for public consumption can become when I first encountered the ratings board of the Motion Picture Association of America. The M.P.A.A. are the people who rate movies as G, PG, PG13, R, and X for the American film-going public.

One of my movies was once threatened with an X for "violence" until I agreed to cut a scene by three seconds to eliminate a slap that the villain, a man, gave a girl, the heroine in the movie. That year, 1985, the fashion was to ban "violence against women" in movies (at the same time feminists were actively pushing for women to assume combat roles in the military). The M.P.A.A. had no problem with the many remaining scenes in which men were killed. Having cut the offending slap, I was rewarded with an R, thus the picture was then "releasable." (Major studio pictures routinely are awarded PG ratings for movies that have a great deal more violence in them than many a small, independent movie like mine. In status-conscious Hollywood, studios carry clout that small, independent producers do not possess.)

To give a movie an X for whatever reason is to effectively ban a film. An X-rated picture is automatically considered a *porno movie* whether it even has any sexual content or not. (Mine had none.) An unrated or X-rated movie cannot get a good general release. Many newspapers will not carry advertising for X-rated movies, no matter what the film's actual content. The M.P.A.A. forces almost half of the independently produced movies to make some content changes to get the rating needed to have a chance at a successful release. Depending on what's "in" and what's "out," the "suggested" changes can range from the trivially absurd, as in the case of my movie's offending slap, to the substantial, in which case whole scenes are cut, often rendering the story of the movie unintelligible.

Sometimes, as in our AIDS-conscious times, *sex*, at least of the "unsafe" variety, is out, sometimes it is *violence*, sometimes *language*, sometimes simply material that is considered *offensive*. This offensiveness can be anything that the M.P.A.A. expects will generate heat from groups ranging from homosexual lobbyists (no homophobic humor) to feminists (no girls to be slapped — unless in combat roles, I suppose) to fundamentalist preachers (no anything) to African-Americans (no black stereotypes).

Yet no one is satisfied by this system. Some find it permissive; others, like me, find it silly. Yet perhaps the capricious nature of the M.P.A.A. serves useful notice to us about the nature of censorship. Imagine the chaos in other fields of the arts that more heavy-handed censorship would cause, if the resulting confusion among moviemakers, because of the rather mild coercion of the M.P.A.A., is any indication. Certain things do not lend themselves to legislated regulation. Art is one of them. Politics is not the solution to all human problems. Recourse to the law is not the only or the best way to settle differences of opinion.

Self-Censorship

Extreme self-imposed censorship because of false guilt feelings is just as much a tragedy among some believing Christians as official censorship. Self-censorship based on false guilt retards and shrinks life in an anti-human, anti-Christian way.

Those who wish in our present day to interpret reality for us, whether they are right-wing fundamentalist preachers, television executives as mindless as their victims, feminists, or leftist ideologues, are miserable misers of life's experiences who would starve our spirits and give us a ration of thin ideological gruel, "right thinking," and trivial nonsense for subsistence.

The impulse to censor the arts and humanities on the part of so many men and women of modest personal achievements is suspect. As G. J. Nathan wrote, "Criticism is the art wherewith a critic tries to guess himself into a share of the artist's fame" (*The House of Satan*, 98).

Life is far bigger, far more diverse, glorious, dangerous, and complex than today's various censors would have us believe.

In the first century A.D., Seneca wrote that "the times will come when our successors will wonder how we could have been ignorant of things so obvious." One only hopes that these words will not be fulfilled by our own grandchildren looking at what we did as we passively abandoned the arts and humanities to the cranks. And one also hopes that one day soon the arts and humanities will be restored to their rightful place, and that they will once again be treated with deference, even love.

The Offense of Truth

The greatest works of art are often offensive to someone. They are not made to suit the tastes of blacks, whites, males, and females as if the human race were no more than a collection of political action committees. Nor is art made to please a multiracial panel of experts. Instead, it is created to express one person's vision of reality—the artist's! To force the art of the past into the straitjacket of contemporary, interpretive, ideological crusades is to squander the birthright of all human beings, male and female, black and white. The glory of art is that it can and does transcend passing fads, political squalls, and ideologies. The glory of freedom of speech is that people, even artists and authors, have the right to be wrong.

Art is the language of the soul, not the servant of political action committees, "right-thinking" ideologues, or trendy editors. To revise history in general and art in particular from an exclusively modern point of view is the height of arrogance. Such a revision attempts to put words in people's mouths and attribute thoughts and motivations to them from our perspective rather than from their own.

The feminist, deconstructionist, and Marxist interpretations of the arts and humanities, as discussed by Peter Shaw (see Appendix A), are arrogant attempts to steal from the people of the past their legitimate place in history and their voice. This rewriting of history is a censorship of ideas, just as surely as book-burning. Fundamentalist book burners use matches and gasoline; feminists, et al., use symposia and journals. Both forms of censorship are motivated by a desire to control, even legislate reality. Not satisfied with ruining the present, these people also want to destroy the past, like worms boring into some irreplaceable, priceless illuminated manuscript. They are parasites, living off the very culture they are destroying.

Christians should realize that censorship is a two-edged sword. As the deliberate mischievous misuse of the concept of the separation of church and state (that has been abused to sometimes keep evangelical and fundamentalist Christians out of the political arena or social debate) should demonstrate, we should be wary of giving a government or other semiofficial bodies, like the A.C.L.U. or the M.P.A.A., the power to censor ideas, art, or political debate. As Robert Brustein wrote in an article entitled "The First Amendment and the N.E.A." (*New Republic,* September 11, 1989), "If you are not prepared to protect bad speech, you are in a poor position to protect the good." The law that can stop the expression of ideas or art we find offensive can also, and probably will at some point, be used to prohibit *religious* expression that many people now find *offensive, sexist, homophobic, obscene, anti-Semitic,* or a perversion of the separation of church and state.

This is not to say that *all* human expression of *any* idea or *all* visual content is sacrosanct. There is no reason that child pornography should be legal. There is no reason that prostitutes should be coerced into being sodomized while pictures are taken to sell in "adult" bookstores. There is no reason that in a free country standards of behavior cannot be set down in law to prohibit the victimization of those used in the manufacture of pornography. This is not censorship; this is simply the application of the ancient common laws against pedophilia, homosexual acts, and sexual coercion that amounts to rape. Such laws to protect the innocent, even the quilty, should be vigorously enforced.

Nevertheless, there will be gray areas. There always are. Yet a great deal of the *production* of pornography clearly involves the victimization of people, which is not a gray area. Civilization has the right to protect itself from the criminal abuse of sexuality. And sensible men and women of good will should work hard to see that this legitimate protection of innocence does not then overstep its bounds and become a form of coercion. Sadly, by the very extremism that so many Christians have embraced in denouncing *all* nudity, violence and "language" in legitimate art and media, they have unfortunately disqualified themselves in this debate at the very time when their voices might be very usefully raised in the defense of virtue.

Censorship, in contrast to protecting the victims used in the pornography trade, is a pandora's box of unintended consequences that in the end affects everyone with something to say. The recent trend, by those who dislike someone's free speech, to resort to sueing them under R.I.C.O. statutes (Racketeer Influenced and Corrupt Organization act), which were designed to curb mob activities (not free speech), show the level to which some malicious people with an ax to grind will sink. The call for censorship, on the part of some people, is the result of well-intended, utopian, romantic notions of how we can "do good" to people by protecting them from some ideas. On the part of others, as the illegitimate use of R.I.C.O. tactics illustrates, it is a deliberate attempt to silence free speech by pro-life groups and others and to circumvent the right to assembly.

A Tradition of Freedom

Turgot, the eighteenth-century statesman and economist, is some-times considered the father of modern secularism. Yet even he, in his famous first address at the Sorbonne University in Paris in 1750, lauded Christianity above all else for its unique role in giving freedom to slaves, serfs, bondsmen, and others, including women, who, prior to Judaism and Christianity, had been in pagan bondage. Turgot, building on this idea of Jewish-Christian freedom, went on to extol the virtues of progress in science and the arts as *dependent* on that freedom. He frequently commented on the indispensability of individual freedom to inspire progress in art and science.

Edward Gibbon, author of *The Decline and Fall of the Roman Empire,* also recognized in the Christian West "the system of arts and laws and manners which so advantageously distinguished . . . the Europeans and their colonies."

Adam Smith was a believer in freedom and, as is less known today, in Christian altruism of the kind taught him by his great Glasgow professor, Francis Hutcheson, who himself was a devout follower of Shaftesbury. It was Shaftesbury's compassionate work to regulate child labor that began to humanize the harsh face of the early industrial revolution. Smith, contrary to the misinformed belief of our times, was deeply sensitive to the needs of the poor. Yet he believed that *freedom* was the answer to their needs; it would liberate economic resources chained by regulations and custom and enrich the whole of society. Smith's point of view has been largely vindicated as noted by historian Paul Johnson (also a believer in freedom) in an article entitled "The Capitalism and Morality Debate" (*First Things,* March 1990).

Thomas Jefferson's writings are steeped in the idea of human progress based on an idea of the basic goodness of freedom. The freedom given to Americans because of the ideas of Jefferson and others resulted in Turgot even going so far as to declare that "America is the hope of the human race."

Voltaire, another French thinker not known for his sympathy to Christianity, in his *Philosophical Letters* asserted that America was an improvement over free, merry old England and that the Quakers of Pennsylvania had created "that golden age of which men talk." In the writings of all these men, we see the reiterated fact that the West in general and America in particular has a great tradition of freedom — a tradition being eroded by the new censors and the trivialization of knowledge by the media.

Censorship, the twin brother of propaganda, is the tool of despots, of ideologues, of ayatollahs, of fanatics. However, there are more subtle forces at work hindering our ability to reason freely. For instance, television, the drug of a profoundly stupid society, creates a climate of silliness which becomes a form of self censorship. It is insecure people who reach for the censor's pen and people of flaccid intellect who reach for their television remote controls. Censorship of ideas, direct or indirect, should have no place in the community of Jews and Christians who have the truth as their spiritual foundation.

Christians and Jews should stand against propaganda, even religious propaganda. We should uphold the image of God in people; the image that is creative and free to choose, even free to make wrong artistic choices. We should stand against censorship in all its various and subtle forms, including that of amusing ourselves to death. The culture may be moving away from rationality, but there is no reason we should follow.

Legislating Reality

Restricting the freedom to communicate through art and media produces the same bad results as restricting economic freedom. Socialism is a failure because government cannot legislate economics successfully. By arranging an economy ideologically from the top down, a government stifles productivity and creativity, hurting rather than helping people's economic prospects. The gross failure of every redistributive, socialist-communist economy proves this. In this respect, art is similar to commerce. You cannot edit artistic impulses through censorship and the whims of elites — whether they be black leaders, feminists, fundamentalists, or communist governments — and get good results. Stagnation of the human spirit is the bitter fruit of all forms of censorship. It is true that people do, at times, abuse their freedoms economically and artistically. The existence of pornography shows this to be true in the media, as do shady business dealings on Wall Street in commerce. However, censorship of the economy or art is not ultimately the answer to sin: Truth is. As history has demonstrated, it is worth the risk of abuse to have the massive benefits of freedom — freedom that Christians can use as they speak the truth as they understand it.

*Again you shall take up your
    tambourines,
And go forth to the dances of the
    merrymakers.
Again you shall plant vineyards.*

Jeremiah 31:4–5 NAS

10

A WORD
OF ENCOURAGEMENT:
A CAUTIONARY TALE

B elieving Christians in the arts tend to become discouraged,
usually with good reason. One of the reasons for discouragement, personal failures aside, is the apparent disinterest many
other Christians have in the arts — or worse, the overt hostility of
some fundamentalist, evangelical, and Roman Catholic Christians
toward what they regard as a worldly pursuit.

When discouragement sets in, we should remind ourselves that
the church is a living church. For the believing, practicing Christian or Jew, there is no eternal death, only life in the present and
life in the future. C. S. Lewis, Bach, Rembrandt, Leonardo da
Vinci, and King Oliver (of New Orleans jazz fame) are not dead
but alive and well in the cloud of witnesses.

Because of the arts, we are not limited exclusively to our present period of history. We can stand in the Florence of Dante and
Vasari. We can listen to the music of Scarlatti. We can read the
words of Homer or Winston Churchill. We can listen to the music
of Mahalia Jackson. We can live, through the arts and humanities,
in all time at once, even in the enlightened High Middle Ages.

Evangelical-fundamentalist parameters of behavior and secular-pagan belief, two extremes that complement each other, need not determine our mental and spiritual boundaries. Our friends can be those we choose, past and present: Walker Percy, Cole Porter, Paul Johnson, Vasari, Degas, Toulouse-Lautrec, Charlie Chaplin, Francis Ford Coppola, Shakespeare (or even Shakespeare's children — Banquo, Rosencrantz or Juliet).

We are free to embrace friends from the past, artists like Giotto, and can thank their patrons and our brothers in the various merchants' guilds of Florence who sponsored the art that has become part of our souls. We can look at the wisdom and magnanimity of the devoutly Christian Cosimo de' Medici and his brilliant son, Lorenzo, and learn from them. As members of the first family of Florence, they exerted immense influence on the culture around them — influence that contributed toward creating what we call the Renaissance. In our own dispirited time, it is to the titans of Christendom like Thomas Aquinas or the Medicis that we can look for cultural as well as theological inspiration.

The High Middle Ages and the Italian Renaissance should serve as a practical example to us today. Our brothers of Florentine, Italy were facing a similar situation to ours. Moslem barbarism and general European chaos surrounded them. From out of the ashes of civilization, medieval, then Renaissance Christians resurrected the arts and humanities.

In Florence, men like Cosimo and Lorenzo de' Medici made a *conscious* choice to affect history, the humanities, and culture in particular. They saved rare books, even whole libraries that would have been lost forever. They became great patrons of the arts and expanded on the classical knowledge and learning of Rome. They sought out talented artists, sculptors, musicians, and scholars, and encouraged them. They were also Christians of deep personal piety who loved and served God. (This last is illustrated by many facts, not least of which is the pious correspondence between Lorenzo de' Medici and Marsilio Ficino, Lorenzo's old tutor and canon of the Florance cathedral.) They did all this while being far from perfect, handicapped like us by sin. The venerable Ficino was fascinated by astrology and witchcraft; he believed in the fates (La Fortuna) as much as divine guidance. He, like us, had blind spots related to his time and place in history. Yet, Ficino led a reawakening in Platonic scholarship. He was a devout Christian, a leading theologian, full of wit, humor, and compassion. His achievements *in spite* of his shortcomings, encourage us.

At the same time, these leading figures were not simply art-conscious. They were also men of commerce, banking, and international trade. They understood that prosperity comes from creative ideas that create wealth and enhance culture. (A point well-illustrated in the book, *The Medici* by C. F. Young [New York: Random House, 1930]). Let us look, however briefly, at the character of the two most famous Christrian patrons of the arts of all time.

Cosimo de' Medici

"Discreet, perceptive, and learned, Cosimo controlled the largest fortune then in private hands and used it to elevate the Medici to the first family of Florence. His patronage [of the arts] was legendary" (*Art of the Western World,* 93).

Cosimo de' Medici gave enormous amounts of money to the church and in patronage to the arts. His ledgers show that from 1434 to 1471 he gave 663,755 florins (today the equivalent of about 10 million 1990 dollars). A huge portion went to the church of San Marco. He gave so generously that the prior protested that he would ruin himself, to which Cosimo replied, "Never shall I be able to give God enough to set him down in my book as a debtor."

Cosimo exercised an almost fatherly influence over his artist friends to whom he was patron. On one occasion he even took to locking the young Filippo Lippi in a room to paint so that he would not be distracted from his work by his habit of chasing women! However, this precaution notwithstanding, the rascally Lippi, a friar no less, slipped out and visited the local convent. As a result Cosimo also arranged for a special dispensation for the nun whom Lippi impregnated. They were married and their son later grew to be a famous artist himself, Filippino Lippi.

Lorenzo de' Medici

E. Armstrong, in his *Lorenzo de' Medici,* writes of Cosimo's son, Lorenzo, "The Magnificent":

> Lorenzo was equally natural and unaffected whether he [was] planning a comic novelty for the Carnival, or critically examining the last new manuscript that his agents had brought or forwarded from Greece or elsewhere. At table he would give grave advice to young Michelangelo, throw a rhyme or epigram across the board to Pulci, or discuss the problem of unity in plurality with Marsilio Ficino. He would give audience to an ambassador, or a horse trainer, or a popular preacher; hold a party *caucus* in the Via Larga, attend a critical meeting of the Government, and then ride off to Careggi or Caiano to play with his children, and rise with the lark to ride to hounds, or fly his favorite falcons. Lorenzo's versatility is the frequent theme even of his contemporary countrymen. . . . A lover of the country rather than of the town, whenever he could he would escape to Poggio a Caiano or more distant villas. He was fond of the country people, their manners, their songs, and their pleasures. . . . His family life was extremely simple; he romped with his children, joined in their music, wrote a religious play for them to act. . . . In Lorenzo's career it is impossible to draw a hard and fast line between diplomacy and politics, art and literature, religion and philosophy, domesticity and public life, country sports and city functions. It is difficult to analyze so manifold a character. (As cited by C. F. Young, *The Medici,* 150)

Machiavelli wrote of Lorenzo in his *History of Florence* (1513):

> He governed the Republic with great judgment, and was recognized as an equal by various crowned heads of other countries. . . . He was the greatest patron of Literature and Art that any prince has ever been, and he won the people by his liberality and other popular qualities. By his political talents he made Florence the leading state in Italy, and by his other qualities he made her the intellectual, artistic and fashionable centre of Italy. (As cited by C. F. Young, *The Medici*, 151)

And yet, as C. F. Young writes of Lorenzo: "Though he had the capacity to do all this; and was in ability head and shoulders above the men about him, yet never throughout his life did he show any arrogance" (*The Medici*, 152).

It is instructive to note that the Medici family was also liberally tolerant of the Jewish population within their sphere of influence. In contrast to the sad and wicked anti-Semitic practice in much of Europe, the Medici's encouraged Jewish life and full Jewish participation in the life of the Florentine community. For instance, the famous Renaissance author of various learned works, including his well-known and well-loved dance manual, Guglielmo da Pesaro was one of many Jewish artists and schools attached to the Medici court. Jewish learning was often sought by Christian Hebraists, including Lorenzo de' Medici's friend and confidant Marsilio Ficino, as well as by the famed scholar-poet Pico and others.

Lorenzo used his influence for the good, the noble, and the beautiful, without taking to himself the formal reins of power or titles. We can draw inspirational sustenance from the Medicis' love for the arts, even if those surrounding us today are lumpish or worse. We belong to the human race and not only to our short period of history. Thankfully, the deconstructionists, feminists, et al., can only destroy the idea of the past and not the past itself.

We can leapfrog over them and go to the source, understand and learn from it, with or without the blessing of our "knowledge elite."

Heroes

Lorenzo de' Medici is not alone in that panoply of Jewish and Christian heroes, men and women of intellectual substance who once led the Jewish-Christian West. We have not always been "dwarfs standing on the shoulders of giants," to quote Bernard of Chartres. Other Renaissance men and women also pointed the way — Queen Elizabeth I, for instance, as well as Sir Thomas More. Robert Bolt, in the introduction to his play *A Man for All Seasons*, describes More, a devout Christian, thus:

> He . . . distinguished himself as a scholar, then as a lawyer, was made an Ambassador, finally Lord Chancellor. A visitors' book at his house in Chelsea would have looked like a sixteenth-century *Who's Who*: Holbein, Erasmus, Colet, everybody. He corresponded with the greatest minds in Europe as the representative and acknowledged champion of the New Learning [the Renaissance learning] in England. . . . He adored and was adored by his own large family. He parted with more than most men when he parted with his life. ([New York: Vantage, 1960], 13)

At the Frick Collection in New York one may see the portrait of Sir Thomas More that Holbein painted during his stay with the More family in 1526. From the canvas looks a powerful face, one who is indeed a hero of the faith, a model for us to emulate in our times of puny moral conviction and the zealous pursuit of ignorance.

We, as believing Christians, do have genuine heroes to emulate if we would trouble ourselves to turn off our television sets, ignore the academic termites, and acquaint ourselves with them. Discouragement comes from the self-imposed limits of our perspective. Our world has become too small. Like some unfortunate people who have a phobia of going out of their houses, we are afraid to go beyond what we can touch and feel, and not imaginative enough to go beyond the current foolishness of modern interpretation and closed-minded fundamentalist Christianity.

We can take hope in the fact that the church of the ages has not always been narrow, anticultural, and middle American. Polyester pietism has not been the norm in Christendom. Nor has the pseudoscience of revisionist, deconstructionist, leftist, and hysterical middle class feminist literary, theological, and historical criticism always dominated Western scholarship. There are other ways, better ways.

Men like Marsilio Ficino exemplify those better ways. A Christian, a Renaissance man, Lorenzo de' Medici's tutor and founder of the Platonic Institute was also a brilliant lutist, composer, singer, and poet, a man of letters, *and* the canon of the Cathedral of Florence, where he served faithfully for many years. Now there's a churchman for you!

His letters, which have been published in numerous volumes, bear witness to his profound spirituality and learning — simple, humane Christian charity and wisdom. His wit and humor transcend time and gender. He was a son of the church and of his artistically enlightened times. Also, he was a son of the ageless wisdom of the philosophers, he recognized that wisdom and truth are one. He, like Thomas Aquinas before him, understood that all men, whether Christian or not, are created in God's image. Ficino knew that a wise pagan, such as Plato, could tell him more than a foolish Christian could, at least about matters unrelated to salvation through Christ. He also searched the Hebrew Scriptures for wisdom and truth and was fascinated by Jewish tradition, which he loved and studied.

The West

The spiritual and intellectual depth of men like Aquinas and Ficino—and many others including Alenin, Augustine, Edwards, Faraday, Giotto—created a West worth defending from the barbarians—whether they were the infidel Moslem, scourge of the Middle Ages; or Hitler and Stalin, scourge of the democracies; or middle-American feminists, some Afro-American activists, fundamentalists, leftists, and Christian barbarians, who today are the scourge of art and culture.

The well-traveled P. J. O'Rourke writes in his introduction to *Holidays in Hell*:

> Civilization is an enormous improvement on the lack thereof. . . . So-called Western Civilization, as practiced in half of Europe, some of Asia, and a few parts of North America, is better than anything else available. Western Civilization not only provides a bit of life, a pinch of liberty and the occasional pursuance of a happiness, it's also the only thing that's ever tried to. Our civilization is the first in history to show even the slightest concern for average, undistinguished, none-too-commendable people like us.

> We are fools when we fail to defend civilization. The ancient Romans might as well have said, "Oh, the Germanic tribes have valid nationalistic and cultural aspirations. Let's pull the legions off the Rhine, submit our differences to a multi-lateral peace conference chaired by the Pathan Empire and start a Vandal Studies Program at the Academy in Athens." (Pp. 3-4)

O'Rourke may not acknowledge it, but what he is defending as worthwhile are the fruits of faith in the God of the Jewish Old Testament and Christian New Testament.

We can be thankful to God for the achievements of the Jewish-Christian West in which it is our good fortune to reside. And we should unashamedly defend our cultural inheritance whether or not we are accused of "chauvinism," "Catholicism," "racism," "sexism," "Zionism," "imperialism," or "anti-environmentalism."

Many have gone before us in defending the West in its many battles to survive. Individuals such as St. John of Damascus, who powerfully defended the church against attacks from those iconoclasts in the eighth century who were denigrating the use of icons and artistic images, deserve our thanks. He, like a myriad of individuals in the so-called Dark Ages, stood up for art, beauty, and aesthetic worship. He gives us an example, and there are many more besides. We can thank God for the faithfulness of the Orthodox Christians who, until the fall of Constantinople, preserved classical Greek and Roman thought as well as Christian teaching within the walls of the Byzantine Empire. We should praise God for the Medici family who snatched, like brands from the burning, the great library of Constantinople before the city's fall to the infidel.

We can look back with thanksgiving to the Jewish scholars who, while in forced servitude to the Muslims who had conquered Granada, Spain, preserved Roman learning and law that later became the basis of modern scholarship when the texts were transferred to Europe's first medieval university at Bologna. Jewish scholars and translators such as Ibn Da'ud made this generational continuity of truth possible. Because of Jews like Da'ud, the enlightened Roman concept of the rule of law and the classic scholarly disciplines survived.

We should offer up thanks for the people who, like King Charlemagne along with his principal scholar Alcuin, defended and then proclaimed knowledge and Roman-Jewish-Christian thought against the darkness of illiteracy. We should be grateful for the monks of Ireland and Scotland who, sitting in damp, cramped cells, copied the great texts of Scripture and classical literature, passing on to us literacy, salvation, and culture.

James Burke, in his book *The Day the Universe Changed* (Boston: Little, Brown and Co., 1985, 24), gives a lively description of the slender thread by which Western civilization hung in the eighth century.

> The rare sight of a passing monk was an event of note. These strange, cowled figures must have seemed to come from another world. They could read and write. They knew things beyond the ken of even the greatest barons. They lived in fortified stone monasteries, islands of knowledge in a sea of ignorance, protecting themselves where they could against the barbarian havoc, preserving what they knew against the day when there would be a world able to make use of it. (P. 24)

Now we, too, can join those who have gone before us in defending truth. The glorious history of the West, its knowledge, its art, its freedoms, are inextricably bound up with individual Christian and Jewish heroism in the face of darkness — a heroism we must imitate. Real heroes who reach out to us across the centuries are there to inspire us. The old fires may burn low, but they are not yet extinguished. The books, music, and art remain. The flames of Western light can be fanned to life once again. The idea of Western historical progress can be revived, newly directed, and even improved.

Opportunities

Christians in the arts should be invigorated by the fact that we *do* live in a pluralistic culture and that we *can* take advantage of this fact by using the breadth of opportunity afforded us to communicate our ideas freely in a still somewhat open society. We, too, can compete in the marketplace of ideas and history. To paraphrase Richard John Newhaus, the public square need not be naked.

Individuals can change history. When we look at the artworks of Tuscan, Italy before the Renaissance — before painters like Giotto and Masaccio and before the concerted efforts of the Medici family to uplift culture—we can see the difference they, as individuals, made in changing art. When we look at European architecture before the Gothic innovations we see a different imitative world of design into which burst a new light. Paul Johnson has argued in his book *Modern Times* (New York: Harper and Row, 1983) and elsewhere that individual human choices, not inevitable and mysterious historical trends, dictate what societies become. The Renaissance demonstrates this thesis well. La Fortuna, as they would have called it in Renaissance Florence, is not the only force directing history. Providence *and* men and women's ideas and actions shape history. The difference between pre-Renaissance Italian artwork and that of the High Renaissance is a vast and startling example of the power of ideas unleashed in a creative way by individuals as is the difference between pre- and post- Gothic architecture. The progress made toward artistic accomplishment and the beauty created in that period of history can inspire us in our time. The visual illiteracy concerning the accurate use of perspective and anatomy in paintings of Giotto's time was deep, yet he and others started a technical and spiritual reawakening in art, the profound implications of which they themselves did not fully understand.

Creating a cultural rebirth in the West from the cold ashes left us by the dogmatically secularized and failed twentieth century is no more impossible a task to realize than the revival of art and learning and the preservation of classical thought achieved by the men and women of the Middle Ages and the Renaissance.

Just as those such as Lech Walesa in Poland and other formerly Communist Eastern European countries consciously applied their deep Christian faith to questions of political freedom and change, we, too, have an opportunity to revive the West. Ideas *do* have the power to change and mold history. Art can communicate in universal transcendent terms, understandable to *all* people.

Ours is an immensely worthwhile cause. Knowledge, the arts, and progress of the human spirit and condition are worth the fight.

Augustine's vision of a single human family progressing toward enlightenment and instructed by God through history should be our vision today. It is an ancient and valorous vision.

In Aeschylus' *Prometheus Bound,* Prometheus mounts a spirited defense at his trial. He stands accused of bringing knowledge to mankind that enabled it to challenge the gods and progress. Prometheus' brief for himself rings as true today as it did to the ancient Greeks:

> But hearken to the miseries that afflicted mankind — how they were witless and I made them to have sense and be endowed with reason. . . . First of all, though they had eyes to see, they saw to no avail; they had ears but understood not. But, like to shapes in dreams, throughout their length of days, without purpose they wrought all things in confusion.

In our day, in our "length of days," we, too, stumble forward without purpose and in confusion. A self-inflicted blindness casts a shadow over what was once a bright sunlit plain. It is now up to us to "hearken to the miseries that afflict mankind," and to bring the light of Greco-Roman-Jewish-Christian culture, the West, back to those who are living in growing darkness in the West itself and elsewhere.

It is bitterly ironic that in the heart of the West today the keepers of the cultural flame, the "knowledge elite," are often the very people *leading* the advancement of anti-Western sentiment — this *at the very moment* in history when vast portions of the world's population are looking enviously to the West for new inspiration. There may be no more believing secularists, communists, and socialists in Eastern Europe — would that the same could be said of the American universities, the media, and art community!

Who has not felt how sadly sweet
The dream of home, the dream of
  home,
Steals o'er the heart, too soon to
  fleet,
When for o'er sea or land we roam?

    Sir Thomas More, *The Dream of Home*

11

OUR CHILDREN AND OURSELVES

At first glance, children, family, marriage, and home may not seem to have any direct bearing on our view of art and culture. Nothing could be further from the truth. If art is to communicate eternal, transcendent themes, then artists must experience life itself as a worthwhile, transcendent, humane enterprise. The empty, shallow, selfish life has little to communicate. To understand eternal themes and to make timeless artworks, the artist must be human first and artist second. The route to true artistic enlightenment is not to only look inward but to look outward and to live. Therefore our spouses, children, and ourselves are very fit, indeed, *the* fit subjects to examine in the context of a fruitful artistic life. If all we care for is our *career* in art, then we will be impoverished human beings and bad artists.

Childhood

Growing up in a Christian community in Switzerland (what would have been called a commune in the 1960s), L'Abri Fellowship, I absorbed the idea that it was normal to have an interest in and love of the arts. My late father, Francis Schaeffer, introduced me

167

to the arts, including film. He encouraged me to organize film
festivals for the L'Abri community. (This sometimes presented
problems for students visiting from evangelical-fundamentalist
colleges who had signed pledges promising not to, among a host
of other forbidden things, go to movies!) L'Abri Fellowship
would hire a local theater and rent movies to watch, then discuss
them. *Satyricon, The Pawnbroker*, and Bergman's various pictures
were some of the many films I remember watching. The reason
we watched them was not only to learn from them but also because we enjoyed them. L'Abri also organized art festivals and art
weeks — times of poetry readings, music, performances, art exhibits, as well as film screenings.

When I was fourteen years old, my father took me out of
school for three weeks and traveled with me to Florence, Italy. He
felt he had not spent enough time with me, his son, due to the
demands of his work. I recall walking through the Uffizzi Gallery,
standing in awe before the works of Botticelli, walking into the
Academia and looking at Michelangelo's *David* for the first time,
and having Renaissance art history from the early works of Giotto
and Masaccio up to the late High Renaissance of Raphael knowledgeably explained to me by my dear father as we tramped
through the galleries and churches.

Because of my mother's and father's positive attitude toward
the arts and humanities, I took it for granted that enjoyment of art,
beauty, and history was naturally part of the Christian life. I thought
that to be interested in Roman history or in a film about the Roman
Empire's decline (like Fellini's *Satyricon*) was natural and good. I
did not then appreciate the fact that I was living in an oasis.

At sixteen, with my father's blessing and encouragement, I
took my first paying job related to media. I worked on a light
show for the Led Zeppelin *acid rock* band at the Montreux jazz-
rock festival. My father invited the rest of the light show crew and
I up to L'Abri to put on a light show in the chapel one evening.
(To recorded music; we couldn't afford the band!)

While working at the festival, I remember noticing Jimmy Page, the Zeppelin's lead guitarist, reading Dad's book *Escape from Reason* backstage before a show. I found that he liked it when I asked him about it. He had been given the book by Eric Clapton, of The Cream, who in turn had received it from a British rock critic who had become converted to Christianity at L'Abri. (Dad had an early interest in and appreciation of acid rock, and often listened to it and discussed it and other contemporary music with his students and myself at L'Abri.)

As a child growing up in L'Abri, I never knew that there were R-rated movies. I only knew there were well-made films and poorly made films. I never knew nudity portrayed in art and film was "evil." I never knew that four-letter words invalidated someone's book or film, and made it "unacceptable," (though I was taught not to use profanity in polite conversation). I thank God for my ignorance during those formative years. When my father expressed himself at all on the subject of narrow fundamentalist and evangelical attitudes toward art and culture, it was to bewail the lack of vision and harsh treatment of artists.

I was taught by my father and mother to judge artwork on its artistic merits and that the rightness or wrongness of things, such as nudity, violence, or profane language in the arts, depended on their context, the honesty of the work, its quality, and the subject matter.

As a result, it never occurred to me to confuse what was right, as far as personal moral behavior went, and what was appropriate to portray in the arts and media. Violence was part of life; therefore, I was given to understand, it should be portrayed in art forms when necessary to the story. Some people used "bad language" in life. They, too, had stories honestly worth exploring through the arts and film — stories that could not be told if the syntax and phrases of profanity were eliminated from the characters' vocabulary. But this did not result in my being violent in my behavior or thinking that profanity in conversation was licit.

It was my parents' encouragement, through their own interest in the arts and their practical financial help, that led me to seriously pursue my own career, first in painting, then later as a movie director and screenwriter. To be a director, painter, or writer seemed a very natural career to choose for someone raised in a family that loved art, books, and movies, as well as the people who made them. For years my parents generously purchased art supplies for my use in my painting, sculpting, and woodcuts. My father always found the time and money to help me in my early, experimental super 8 mm. films. He sat for hours in my studio workshop at my film-editing bench criticizing my early film efforts and special effects' experiments. I remember him helping me one afternoon mix up a batch of "blood" mix for a "suicide" I was filming using his secretary as my "actress" and "stunt woman." She survived, though it took her two weeks to get the red paint stains out of her hair!

There were others in the L'Abri community who also encouraged my interest in the arts — opera singer Jane Stuart Smith and writer Betty Carleson, for instance. I well remember Jane sitting me down on her couch in Chalet le Cheselet and introducing me to the artwork of Brueghel the elder. At seven years old, I was rather bored, until she delightedly pointed out a detail in one of his paintings — of a man dropping his pants and relieving himself. Now here was an artist a seven-year-old could appreciate! This was fine!

On another occasion, Jane explained in detail the story of the opera *Norma* and then sat me down to listen to a recording. Knowing the story, following the libretto, and familiarizing myself with the music, I passed some unseen threshold from disinterest in opera to avid interest.

From an early age, my shelves were bursting with books about every subject imaginable. My mother spent hours reading aloud to her children. My dad and I often went to movies together. It was a good, full, and culturally rich life that I led, perched on a hill-side in that small, obscure, Christian community.

My father and my mother raised their children to be unafraid of ideas, unafraid of being challenged, quite an achievement for my mother who came from a very pietistic background. She was raised in a China Inland Mission home by parents who washed her mouth out with soap for using a *minced oath.* Minced oaths were even the subject of an earnest tract my missionary grandfather wrote. (A *minced oath* is any word used as an expletive that even *sounds* as if it *might* be bad. *Darn,* for instance, *might* be mistaken for *damn.* Get the soap!)

My mother made a series of conscious decisions to reevaluate what was and was *not* important for her children to learn. God bless her and my father for all the fundamentalist baggage they chose to leave behind so that their children would not have to carry it into that hard oblivion that awaits so many of the faithful.

Only later in life did I begin to meet the types of Christians who took it for granted that you were supposed to protect your children from "The World." Often this protection appeared to be an attempt to hide from reality and, above all, to not be challenged to answer your children's questions.

However, aside from the clear absolutes of Scripture, there *were* other taboos in my family. My parents protected me as best they could, not from art or hard questions, but from mediocrity. That was why we had so few contemporary evangelical or fundamentalist books in the house. That was why we had no television set — thank God! That was why my parents never played contemporary Christian music of the gospel variety, let alone trash pop. I grew up thinking that the label of "sacred music" referred to Bach, Buxtehude, Mahalia Jackson, and Handel. For me, contemporary music was Miles Davis' jazz or the poignant singing of Billie Holiday. My father's favorite "contemporary music" was Bob Dylan songs like "Route 66" and later the Beatles "Sergeant

Pepper's," which he listened to endlessly and discussed avidly and sang along with in his terrible off-key voice upon occasion.

In recent years, it has amazed me to hear my father referred to — in some quarters, by some people who should know better — as a "fundamentalist" (with the anticultural content which that label now deservedly denotes). One can believe in the fundamentals of the Christian faith without carrying the cultural know-nothing baggage of fundamentalism. I remember my dad as the man who took me to Fellini's movie *La Dolce Vita* and discussed it with me over a cup of coffee while lending me twenty centime pieces to feed the jukebox so we could listen to The Mothers of Invention's latest hit, *Brown Shoes Don't Make It.* I remember sitting on the steps of the Duomo in Florence at two in the morning and discussing the design competition which resulted in Ghiberti creating the panels for the east door of the Baptistery, the *Doors of Paradise* as Michelangelo later dubbed them. Was forty years too long to spend on one artwork? Judging by Ghiberti's results, we decided it wasn't!

My father never protected his children from ideas, from art, from intellectual challenge and stimulation or contrary thinking, even anti-Christian, anti-Biblical art, thought, and culture. Believing that Christianity was truth, he welcomed honest questions. If this was "fundamentalism," then let there be more of it!

I was raised in a family that read books, went to movies, talked, and did *not* watch television. It is an abiding irony that many of the evangelicals and fundamentalists who welcomed, often misreading, parts of my late father's critique of certain aspects of secular culture, never understood, let alone shared, his basic love of the artworks, books, and movies he was critiquing. My father spent his life feeling uncomfortable with the evangelical establishment, even as they made his books into best-sellers. "Life," as he was apt to say, "is strange."

Today

Now, years later, married and with my own children (as I write, ages nineteen, sixteen, and nine), I have come full circle to stand in the place of a parent. My wife and I have done everything we can to pass on the treasure of both open-minded, sensible inquiry and orthodox Biblical Christianity to our three children. In raising children there are no guaranteed results. Yet there are ways of improving their chances of succeeding in life as full human beings. There are also ways of almost guaranteeing bad results. At least we as parents can try to avoid that.

Having children has forced my wife and I to think a lot about education. In America today, there seems to be an unintentional collusion between church and the state. This has produced ugliness and mediocrity in American culture and daily life. The state has failed to educate through its public schools and, the church has not met the challenge.

Secular v. Christian

The state's schools cannot educate because many of the people who run and teach in them no longer believe in their own culture, the West, or in moral absolutes informed by Jewish-Christian teaching. The church and its schools are governed by people who may believe in absolutes in a theoretical way, but have been so compromised by tasteless, artless, mundane, and plastic middle America that they have nothing fresh, interesting, or profound to teach their students beyond pietistic platitudes and second-rate "basics." In many cases, in the "religious" schools and the "secular" schools, there is no commitment to Western cultural and historical knowledge (beyond the most minimal American civics) and barely token interest in European Western history, culture, and art. In the main, our schools in America now inhabit a cultural wasteland of antiknowledge.

Thus, at the very moment when our bankrupt state, "secular" education system is producing tasteless, uneducated, barely literate young people, who graduate to become empty, lumpish adults, or worse, the church and its schools can do no better than to add a few pious teachings and Bible verses to the general chaos of ignorance and entertainment masquerading as education. We are now, therefore, paying the dreadful price for a twentieth-century brand of evangelical-fundamentalist Christianity that has regarded culture, history, art, and learning as "unspiritual," thus unimportant.

Today, most evangelical and fundamentalist Christian education is either of the Victorian Sunday school variety or simply secular noneducation with a few Bible verses thrown in, along with some tub-thumping, nationalistic "patriotism" for good measure. The blind are leading the blind. Ignorant, pietistic teachers are passing on a-cultural learning to the children of ignorant, religious parents. "Secular" or "Christian," our population all watch the same television programs; this is their only remaining "cultural" bond it would seem.

Perhaps there is less respect for learning today than in the gloomiest period of the so-called Dark Ages, during which there was at least a high degree of *reverence* for learning even by those who possessed very little themselves.

Opening the school day with prayer, having less swearing in the locker rooms, and "devotions" after lunch is not Christian education. Middle-class niceness is not to be confused with the example of civilization set us by the Renaissance men and women of Florence or their enlightened medieval forbears, let alone the life, teaching, death, and resurrection of our Lord Jesus Christ. The Reformation men and women of northern Europe, or other heroes of the faith like Sir Thomas More, William Shakespeare, Winston Churchill, and Rembrandt, were not produced by systems of education remotely resembling our own.

Just Coping

Today, many Christian families are so bogged down in attempting to cope with divorce, adultery, and all the other immoral plagues of our time, that Christian teaching directed at the family seems to be more of a Christianized psychological counseling service than real education that advances truth and human aspirations. *How to Cope with This or That* could be the generic catch-all title of most evangelical-fundamentalist Christian books. The problem is that the very leaders of the church that people look to for guidance are themselves caught in and totally enculturated by the tasteless supermarket wasteland that is middle America.

The pagan, non-Christian culture is crying out for aesthetic and cultural leadership, and all we Christians now offer is plastic pablum, formula "gospel." Christian education is aiding and abetting the cultural decline of the West. The church unwittingly joins hands with the graffiti-spraying gangs of the inner cities, just as the Visigoths joined hands with the Vandals in the pillage of the Roman Empire. We do not even know what we are throwing away.

Television programming, materialism, the a-historical, anti-Western, anti-education of most evangelical fundamentalist, Roman Catholic, and non-Christian schools alike — these form the vortex into which the sensibilities of our culture are inexorably sucked. Culture, education, art, and intellectual risk are abandoned in favor of easy materialism and lazy lives spent in light amusements. Disney's Epcot Center is a representatively horrible idea of "culture as we now understand it." Steven Spielberg's trivialization of the supernatural is now our idea of "spirituality." Scholarship and appreciating the arts is dismissed as irrelevant by "right thinking" political propagandists masquerading as intellectuals. Middle Americana, its valueless values, and its niceties, are often all that remain to us of our glorious past.

Christian educators congratulate themselves because some statistics show that they teach more children to read than their even less effective secular counterparts. To read what? To write what? To speak what? To see what? To listen to what? To discuss what? To change what? To challenge what? To become what? To love what?

Given the indifferent results of the Christian schools in providing a real cultural alternative to anti-Western secular education (a fact that is glaringly apparent to anyone like me who has traveled around the country speaking at the many evangelical colleges that dot the landscape), the Jewish or Christian parent must face the reality that it is imperative to find that rare thing, a good school, and enroll one's children. We parents must also face the fact that, even if our children are in a so-called good school, their primary source of moral and cultural education will be in the home.

Whether a school is Christian, secular, or a home school is not the point. Good education is what we must pursue for our children. And since most Christian and secular schools, from kindergarten through college, are today so lacking in a Jewish-Christian-Western worldview, we parents must compensate by becoming educators ourselves.

This means we have to spend a great deal of time with our children reading, discussing, and exploring. *It also means that we cannot be lazy in our own continuing education and reading.* We need to have a well-formed view of Western culture, history, and the arts ourselves if we are to help our children. If we are samples of most Christian homes and contemporary schools, to become educated ourselves will take a real effort of the will. By reading, studying, watching, and discussing, we will have to engage in our own courses of study. We are all deprived and ignorant to one degree or another. We have been cheated of our inheritance. We are *all* in the dark. And our efforts to find the light will be hard and clumsy. But we must persevere.

At various stages in our family life, my children have been home-schooled, in an evangelical Christian primary school, and in a secular, liberal high school. What my wife and I have pursued for our children is good teaching and a love of learning and culture, not ideological or theological purity on the part of our children's teachers.

All knowledge comes from one source — God. Truth, good teaching, and culture are where you find them. Truth about a subject taught by non-Christians is better than falsehood taught us by Christians, or vice versa. It is a question of truth — as in medicine, it is a question of good surgery, not "Christian" surgery. Better a competent, atheist cardiologist who will help you survive your heart attack, than a well-meaning, bumbling, and incompetent Christian doctor who will pray over your corpse once he's killed you!

That even good schools are so often imperfect is all the more reason to make the home a place of comfort and creativity. It seems to me that the importance of all education, especially formal schooling, should be kept in proportion to what makes up the rest of life. When school activities conflict with important family time, we take our children out of school, even if it means short-term academic setbacks. There are more important things than school, and schools, even good ones, will never compensate for mediocre or broken homes.

Activities

In our family, we have found it necessary to make sure that organized activities do not diminish precious family time. A long evening meal at the end of every day during which the day's ideas and events are discussed, reading aloud, a day off together — these are untouchable, sacred familial institutions to us.

To have time together, a family has to have the discipline to say no to many activities. Children who are allowed to treat dinner as a "pit stop" on the way back to other activities will never be around long enough for you to get to know, teach, or enjoy. Parents who constantly treat their children as burdens on their time, while they rush off to do Important Adult Things, will have children who do, in fact, become burdens.

In our family, we try to minimize irrelevant social interruptions. My wife and I have seen our children and our marriage as the priority in our lives. Whoever came up with the idea of "quality time" with children as a replacement for spending a lot of time with them was a fool.

I have often slipped out of meetings with my producer or agent, saying that I had "an important appointment to get to." The appointment was to take my wife and children to a museum or a movie, then lounge around a Chinese restaurant afterward discussing it. You have to beg, borrow, and steal family time from a world bent on distracting you from the most important things in life.

Religion

One of the challenges of being a Christian parent is to keep too much religion, as opposed to truth, out of the lives of your children — too many church activities, too much indoctrination, rather than discussion.

You can ask a child to memorize one Bible verse too many. You can share one little platitude as an answer to a real question once too often. There *is* a straw that breaks the camel's back. If you are teaching obedience to Christ and enjoying the ancient traditions of Christian liturgy and the eucharist, the meaning of the sacraments and worship, teaching the value of Western culture, its art, its thought, studying its history, discussing today's movies and politics, looking at the world of nature and nature's God (and *not* watching television), your children *will* be naturally surrounded by the fruit of Christianity and its thought. They will still have to make their own choices about what they believe to be true, but they will have something positive by which to judge the claims of the world. And who knows, they may even be able to think rationally in this fundamentally irrational age.

A child's interest in the gospel can be harmed by well-meaning parents. Bible verses taught out of context, devotional time as a pietistic duty, endless "churchianity" rather than actual worship — these are sterile and counterproductive activities when forced on children.

Many Christian parents are amazed that their children do not follow their footsteps in the faith. Often they have only themselves to blame. There is such a thing as too much of a good thing. So much of the church today is shallow and rootless, cut off from the faith of our fathers, sound doctrine, liturgy, teaching and practice, that it is no wonder that many children will abandon it as they grow up. Overabundant, fraudulent piety without content is no replacement for truth and the sacraments, and young people know or feel this instinctively.

Tasteless, glitzy, evangelical, "charismatic," and fundamentalist activities are no substitute for genuine sacramental worship, obedience to Christ, and tradition, any more than the kind of gospel quartets, that appear on thousands of church platforms every Sunday, are any substitute for music.

Today, the heart of the gospel has been cut out of much so-called Christian worship. And the children who rebel against this fraud are often right in doing so. They are not rejecting the truth of Christianity, but the silliness, harshness, and finally the lies of pietistic Christianity. Deprived of the glories of Western culture and the ancient changeless traditions of the church, these children have never seen the gospel in action, beyond calls to personal religiosity and worship as entertainment.

One way some people in the church kill our interest, children's and parents' alike, in the truth is by not being satisfied with the traditional church of the ages and trying to make it into something else.

Some pastors, either bored, misled, or trying to work out their own inner problems, lead their congregations on strange journeys. Inner healing, wholeness, renewal, signs and wonders, liberal theology, or other fads sweep the church. The church dilutes the gospel and the Holy Spirit's power when it embraces other things that replace Christ. Pop psychology and Christianity merge uncomfortably in many so-called inner healing ministries. The church loses sight of Christ as He becomes obscured by a myriad of social programs and activities or doctrinal emphasis foreign to the simple gospel and the ancient traditions and liturgies of the orthodox, ageless church. The church ceases to be the church when it becomes, for instance, a psychological counseling service advocating simplistic techniques on how to be "whole," "happy," or "fulfilled."

In much of the church today, Christ is presented as simply a superfriend to help us with our psychological problems. The hard edges of truth and the demands the real Christ makes are abandoned in favor of what amounts to religious group therapy. The body and the blood are abandoned in favor of the psychiatrist's couch. It is the "me," the ego, that such religion serves, not the living God.

People involved in such ecclesiastical diversions begin to look inward. They become selfish, professionally and permanently wounded and needy; "hurting" becomes a badge of self-centered honor. People dredge up their pasts to find out who or what was responsible for their problems. Church becomes a source of drama and entertainment to fill the empty spaces that life itself should fill when lived in daily obedience to Christ and in the enjoyment of other people, culture, and natural beauty.

Because of the failure of the secular religions, including psychology, to genuinely meet people's needs as sinners, the irony is that the nonbelieving world now turns increasingly to religion, through things like the New Age Movement, to help heal people's problems caused by sin. Yet pitifully, the church itself turns to psychological counseling, under many guises, to heal what *is* in fact sin that only Christ can forgive and cure.

Pietism and psycho-babble are perfect companions. The one maintains the outward niceties and virtues of middle America, while the other allows us to wallow in selfish, narcissistic contemplation. Sin and judgment are forgotten as endless sermons on "love" soothe our frayed nerves. Salvation is reduced to an alternative to Valium. Being "whole" or happy is seen as more important than being virtuous.

By my observation of the many distressed parents I have known, if you want to guarantee that your children finally abandon the faith, then bring them up in an overwrought church that is off on some inward-looking, self-conscious, anti-historical tangent. Any tangent, beyond the church's basic orthodox function, will do: inner healing, psycho-babble, charismatic gifts (of the circus variety), feminism, social work, antinuclear pacifism, harsh reformed doctrine, pietism, tough-minded fundamentalism, smarmy, self-satisfied, evangelical "churchianity," even an overindulgent sacramentalism in which the sacraments begin to take on the magical aura of a talisman—this last being the final refuge of ex-fundamentalist Episcopalian rascals who love the liturgy more for its aesthetic qualities than for its true meaning. The list of diversions is as endless as are the dollars to be raised from the flock, and the victims as numerous as the misguided, unstable people who are looking for "meaning" rather than for truth in their church.

When Christ, the Holy Spirit, and the ancient rites of the church are "improved upon," beware! When any fad is followed that creates a little circle of special, in-the-know, "anointed" Christians, separated from the historical apostolic church, speaking their own enlightened dialect—be it charismatic, psychological, or aesthetic and liturgical—the whole purpose of fellowship is thwarted. If we begin to associate only with people in the church who are like us, or "good for us spiritually," we are on the road to a cult, however enlightened its beginnings.

Perhaps T. S. Eliot summed it up when he sardonically observed, "Certain saints found the following of Christ very hard, but modern methods have facilitated everything."

Television

Television is a blood-sucking parasite, at least, when the set is switched on! Even if the programming was all of universally high caliber, the point stands. It is foolish to spend too much time in any passive pursuit which bombards the mind with a numbing series of unrelated imagery that cuts off rational communication with other people.

There are some serious scholars who have even argued that there is a direct link between the amount of television we watch and the abysmal educational standards that we in our country have come to accept. According to them, the visual stimuli of television and the disjointed avalanche of images, that often have little or no logical sequence, actually have affected, even changed, the very way people think. People raised in an environment of television's kaleidoscopic whirlwind of imagery will not be able to think in as linear and rational a manner as people trained to think, read, and question have been in the past. Neil Postman, in his book *Amusing Ourselves to Death*, brilliantly argues that television has changed our society for the worst. (See Appendix B.) Others have also made a similar case—for instance, Marshall McLuhan, Jerry Mander, Jerome Bruner, Jack Goody.

An acute problem that television exacerbates is the loss of the sense of immediate community—of family, church, town, even state and country—as it gives the viewer the instant reality of "news" that is usually accompanied by flimsy, if any, analysis. After being ceaselessly pounded by images, people then feel that they are informed but remain ignorant of any real content, background, or history surrounding the events they have "seen." They thus can feel "in touch" with the world without actually being in touch with anything other than visual impressions or have any understanding of what they are seeing. In the same way that the image culture replaces the book culture, emotional feelings are now replacing logic as a means of judging reality inside and outside of the church today. This is a poor substitute for real study, contemplation, and reflection.

But the very lie that *is* television is hard to see since the sheer volume of programs offered seems to indicate that there is more substance there than there is. Yet, like Shakespeare's idiot full of sound of fury signifying nothing, television leaves us with a hollow feeling.

One can watch endless "live" reports from some hot-breaking news story, yet gain less from the hours of television images than from a thirty-minute reading of a comprehensive explanation and history of the same event in some good journal of current affairs, such as *Commentary* or *First Things*. Yet the lure and lazy ease of television's accessibility is more than many people seem able to resist, for themselves or their children.

Just because our culture seems to be moving away from rational discourse to the imagery of emotionalism, and just because the church itself seems to be joining in this wholesale abandonment of logic and rationality as it embraces emotionalism, does not mean that we or our children are condemned to follow the trend. The off switch on the television set and the simple action of reading widely and consistently to ourselves and our children are the beginnings of a quiet revolution for truth we can undertake in our homes.

Perhaps a few enlightened, educated believing Christians and Jews who read while others watch will be the last of a dwindling band of people who can think in linear, rational terms. Perhaps, too, these same people can become the leaders of a new Western renaissance. The apathetic majority will always be led by the dedicated minority. It is therefore our job to be that minority.

Reading Aloud

Reading aloud to our children, by the hour, has been one of the most positive things that we have done together as a family. *Huckleberry Finn, Oliver Twist, The Bible, Animal Farm*, P. G. Wodehouse, *Emille and the Detectives, A Hitchhiker's Guide to the Galaxy, The Lord of the Rings, The Odyssey, The Chronicles of Narnia, A Brave New World, The Lord of the Flies, Wind in the Willows, Alice in Wonderland, The Adventures of Sherlock Holmes, King Solomon's Mines, Babar the Elephant, The Medici, The Last Lion, Modern Times, Art of the West*, articles from *Commentary* and *First Things*, Beatrix Potter's books, history and art history only begin to cover the short list of books we have read together aloud. Biographies and many other books read aloud, literally hundreds of them, have provided an anchor for our family times and a means by which to introduce our children to the West and its culture. Children are surprisingly attentive when raised in a family that reads aloud. Children understand far more than most people think they do. We have read hundreds of books aloud in our family; many of them were passed on to me from my mother, who read hundreds of books to my sisters and I when we were children.

My mother is not alone in extolling the virtues of reading. Neil Postman writes:

> From Erasmus in the sixteenth century to Elizabeth Eisenstein in the twentieth, almost every scholar who has grappled with the question of what reading does to one's habits of mind has concluded that the process encourages rationality; that the sequential, propositional character of the written word fosters what Walter Ong calls the "analytic management of knowledge." To engage the written word means to follow a line of thought,

which requires considerable powers of classifying, inference-making and reasoning. It means to uncover lies, confusions, and overgeneralizations, to detect abuses of logic and common sense. It also means to weigh ideas, to compare and contrast assertions, to connect one generalization to another. (*Amusing Ourselves to Death*, 51)

Children who love books, stories, ideas, drama, and debate come alive as human beings. Children who want to reread *Alice in Wonderland* are in the end profoundly more human than children who want nothing more than to watch one more mind-freezing hour of badly animated cartoons. Children who are read aloud to in the end will read to themselves for pleasure.

For me as a parent, some of the most satisfying moments with my children have been the times when I have seen the fruit of my wife's and my own reading labors. For instance, I was reading aloud recently to my nine-year-old son from a book about art history. In one chapter on Greek art was an illustration of a Greek vase depicting a scene drawn from mythology. My little boy's excitement was no less than my own as he pointed to the picture and said, "I *know* what that is!" He identified the story depicted on the vase because we had been reading Greek mythology together some time before, and he had learned the story. He had also seen similar vases at the fine collection of the Getty Museum in Los Angeles. He was beginning to "connect the dots" for himself. Many times my own interest in self-education, reading, and cultural exploration has been kept alive by having the privilege of guiding my children as they discover the wealth that their Western culture has to offer them. My love for them has been a much needed inducement to combat my own laziness.

History

An understanding of history through reading, especially the reading of biographies, is absolutely essential to understanding who we are and what Greek-Roman, Jewish-Christian teaching and art has created in our Western culture.

Children who grow up and leave their home unacquainted with Abraham, Winston Churchill, Douglas MacArthur, Charlemagne, Queen Elizabeth I, Lorenzo de' Medici, Homer, Leonardo da Vinci, and many other figures of art, political, or religious history are poorer than they need be. People without a knowledge and appreciation of their history are impoverished, rootless people open to every lie told them about their nation, civilization, and the world. As American parents raising our families in the United States, it is important to remember that the *West* is our heritage and that its history and culture encompass far more than America's short existence. What happened in Florence in the Renaissance is, for instance, just as vital to us today and to our children as what happened recently in American history. St. Augustine, Dante, and Charlotte Brontë are just as much our *founding fathers* (mothers) as are Jefferson and Washington.

Music

Performing music, learning an instrument, reading the biographies of the composers, listening to and attending concerts, and learning to read music all draw out the best in children and their parents.

The Jewish-Christian West has produced unrivaled glories in the field of music. Christians who waste their time listening to most so-called contemporary Christian music, contemporary sacred music—and songs of praise, the staple of so much evangelical Christian radio—are like the starved victims of a concentration camp subsisting *voluntarily* on moldy potatoes when a feast is set before them after liberation! Certainly there are serious Christians engaged in making good contemporary music, but those who limit themselves to contemporary popular "Christian music" seem to be unaware that the horizons are so much broader.

The classical music of the West belongs to *us,* up to and including jazz, the classical music of the twentieth century. Thus, children raised in a musical environment of Christianized ditties are being cheated of their aesthetic and spiritual inheritance.

Bach, Mozart, Vivaldi, Debussy, Verdi, Billie Holiday, B. B. King — the list of composers and performers who created our musical inheritance is almost endless. The music of the West *is* Christian culture. Sadly, there are Christian families who fail to raise their children with an understanding of this fact — this triumph of artistic truth with its power to lift the human spirit above the urban sprawl.

Not all the good music is from the past. A great deal of modern jazz with its roots in the joyful celebration of New Orleans jazz and black spirituals, some country and bluegrass music, a number of contemporary film scores, and some rock and roll (Hendrix, Clapton, etc.) come to mind as artists well worth listening to, studying, and enjoying.

The Home

Children can and should pass from childhood to young adulthood. While many normal young adults do tend to act rather imbecilic at some point in their development (as I certainly did), nevertheless, the concept of out-of-control "teenagerhood," as we know it today, is an invention of our failed, middle class, television saturated society. It is a concept used as an excuse, as if it were a force of nature beyond our control, to explain parents' and educators' failures to discipline children and introduce them to the world of ideas. "Teenager-hood" is a handy excuse to use when explaining the resulting chaos caused by these "children" as they are let loose on society by parents who have failed to be good stewards of this most precious gift, their children.

If we want interesting, obedient children, we as parents have to be interesting ourselves and obedient to Christ. We have to read, watch, and listen. If we want children who are interested in culture, then our children must see our interest. If we want the truth about Jesus Christ to be interesting to our child, then, our own lives, which we claim are based on the truth, must compete with the interest, diversity, beauty, artistic creativity, and intelligence often found in the non-Christian community. If we want children who are fully human, then we must set our sights and expectations higher for them than the world does. We can do more for them than giving up the moral high ground and teaching them to use condoms! If these objectives seem hard to achieve, they are. We may have to rearrange our own lives, change jobs, lower our standard of living, make less money, change churches, or move our residence to accommodate the breadth of life and learning that will help our families and ourselves be fully human. However, there is no more pleasant cross to bear than that of giving up the materialism of the "Yuppie" fascism that has come to dominate our time, and instead, putting our children ahead of our ambitions.

My wife and I have, for our children's sake, made practical choices that have often been in some ways sacrificial. In our case, for instance in one not-so-sacrificial example, I have chosen to live in a small New England town, not in Los Angeles or Hollywood. The fact that I do not live in the heart of the movie industry means that my career, such as it is, has suffered. I make much less money. I am not often in the "right place at the right time." In our particular case, the school situation, the large garden for the children to play in, the friends and church that God has given us have all added up to good reasons to make a lot less money. My wife and I have enjoyed a rich existence together *because* she has not worked outside the home but instead has chosen to raise a family. She and I have found genuine fulfillment in the home—a home in which her well-read, articulate, luminous presence is like a bright, clear light.

Beauty

Beauty in the home is important. Tastes vary, and anyone who ventures to discuss taste, let alone bad taste, is running the risk of sounding pompous. Yet it should be self-evident that a home filled with books, art, music, solid old furniture or well-designed modern furniture, or gardening tools, or just plain nothing at all but clean white walls, is preferable to, for lack of a better word, the all-too-familiar *kitsch* of middle Americana, which is too often the evangelical-fundamentalist trademark. A stranger to our culture might be pardoned if he assumed that bad taste was the distinguishing mark of the evangelical and fundamentalist Christian, as circumcision is the mark of the Jew!

Visual aesthetics do make a difference in our daily lives. We can either deaden and damage our aesthetic senses or stimulate them by what we see and hear. We are not alone as we make aesthetic choices; we are not starting over. We have our Western inheritance and its traditions to study and to inspire us. We can examine what others, perhaps better informed aesthetically than we, found pleasing to the eye and ear, and emulate them.

There are, of course, many rewarding avenues of exploration (beyond our scope to examine here) open to us in helping our children discover the rich generosity of a full life. The appreciation of art museums, sports, nature study, and languages come to mind as things that should be an integral part of our lives. All of these will increase our interest in our fellow men and women and point toward our creative God who is, after all, Lord of all we are, see, and do.

Love

It should go without saying that above all in the home there should be love. Love verbally expressed. "I love you," spoken to our children many times a day. Hugs aplenty for all — for babies *and* sixteen-year-old boys heading out to the varsity soccer game. Kisses from mothers *and* from fathers. Plenty of apologies when we are wrong. Plenty of "I don't knows," when we don't. Love and humility with our children and each other. Generous doses of physical affection and mental affection verbally expressed should be the redemptive norm in our homes. This should include a lively and pleasant sexuality between husband and wife — that precious routine of intimacy.

We should possess enough love to combat our natural laziness and to give us an incentive to do better for our children than we might otherwise, left to our own predilections. We should have enough love for our children to motivate us to provide a taste of the fullness of life for them, beyond the boundaries of a safe middle-class church. Enough love to put our careers second and children first. Enough love to provide discipline. Enough love to turn *off* the television. Enough love to provide the *reasons* for being alive and not merely provide the means to stay alive. Lastly, enough love to decide what is and *is not* important to teach our children. And, if need be, enough love to leave a fundamentalist, or liberal, or just plain weird local church body that is crippling our sense of the divine and giving our children false, cultic, and compromised ideas about Christianity.

*The advances in human rights of
which we Americans can be justly
proud (however partial they might
yet be) can be traced to the fact
that they were successfully advocated as a development out of the
traditions which long predate the
founding of the American republic.*

David Novak, *First Things,* March 1990

*The Holocaust was, in largest part,
the consequence of ideas about
human nature, human rights, the imperatives of history and scientific
progress, the character of law, the
bonds and obligations of political
community.*

Richard John Neuhaus, *First Things,*
March 1990

12

TRUTH VERSUS PIETISM

There are two opposite traditions present in the history of the church and in the lives of individual Christians today that coexist and often seem to overlap. One tradition has produced, in various forms, the positive fruits of Western culture — the art and commerce that the whole world, including today much of the once communist world, is trying to imitate in order to produce Western-style freedom and prosperity in their own nations. The other tradition has produced a lasting legacy of human, social, and artistic problems.

The first tradition declares Jewish-Christian teaching to be truth, the explanation of existance itself. This tradition holds that God is the Lord of all reality and that He created all that is visible and invisible. Because of this, we live in an orderly universe that can be rationally investigated and understood through science and the arts.

The second tradition declares Judaism or Christianity to be a mere *religion* and, today, often a form of psychotherapy. It only believes Christianity is true in the sense that it is helpful personally or gives religious answers to certain psycho-spiritual questions. This tradition declares that life is divided into compartments, some "spiritual," others not; it does not affirm reality as one indivisible whole.

These two traditions run through all church history in all denominations, including present-day evangelical-fundamentalist and
charismatic Protestant denominations. These two competing traditions are also apparent in the historical and current Roman Catholic and Orthodox churches. These two worldviews vie for our attention, for the direction of the church, and the direction of
individual Christians' lives. Many Christians are unaware that
their faith is informed by one of these points of view.

For our purposes here, I shall call the first tradition *Truth* and
the second tradition *Pietism.* The faith of most Christians is not
clearly informed by either Truth or Pietism but is in some way a
mixture of the two. However, the results and quality of the
Christian's individual life depend on which worldview he or she
espouses.

The battle between Truth and various forms of Pietism has
taken many historical twists and turns. This is not a history book,
nor am I a historian. However, it is appropriate that we should
look at one specific historic confrontation between the forces of
Truth and those of false spirituality. Thus, it can serve as an example of the wider, more prevalent conflict between Truth and
Pietism we are examining now.

What better guide than G. K. Chesterton and what better example of true Christian faith than that embodied in the noble life
and work of Saint Thomas Aquinas. Chesterton examines the
ideas of Aquinas as he combated the false spirituality of Manichaeism. In his time this belief had divided reality into the "spiritual," thus important, and the "temporal," the unimportant, in
much the same way as today's pietists emphasize irrationality and
"spirituality" at the expense of reality and Truth.

> If we wanted to put in a picturesque and simplified form what
> he [Aquinas] wanted for the world, and what was his work in
> history, . . . we might well say that it really was to strike a blow
> and settle the Manichees. . . . What is called the Manichean phi-
> losophy has had many forms. . . . But it is always in one way or

another a notion that nature is evil; or that evil is at least rooted in nature. . . .

Now it was the inmost lie of the Manichees that they identified purity with sterility. It is singularly contrasted with the language of St. Thomas, which always connects purity with fruitfulness; whether it be natural or supernatural.

In truth, this vividly illuminates the provincial stupidity of those who object to what they call "creeds and dogmas." It was precisely the creed and dogma that saved the sanity of the world. These people generally propose an alternative religion of intuition and feeling. If, in the really Dark Ages, there had been a religion of feeling, it would have been a religion of black and suicidal feeling. It was the rigid creed that resisted the rush of suicidal feeling. . . . [W]hat kept [Aquinas'] thought in touch with healthier and more humanistic thought was simply and solely the Dogma. He could not deny that a good God had created the normal and natural world; he could not say that the devil had made the world; because he was not a Manichee. A thousand enthusiasts for celibacy, in the day of the great rush to the desert or the cloister, might have called marriage a sin, if they had only considered their individual ideals, in the modern manner, and their own immediate feelings about marriage. Fortunately, they had to accept the Authority of the Church, which had definitely said that marriage was not a sin. . . .

In this sense St. Thomas stands up simply as the great orthodox theologian, who reminded men of the creed of Creation, when many of them were still in the mood of mere destruction. . . . [M]edieval men did not care about being medieval and did not accept the authority of a mood, because it was melancholy, but did care very much about orthodoxy, which is not a mood. It was because St. Thomas could *prove* that his glorification of the Creator and His creative joy was more orthodox than any atmospheric pessimism, that he dominated the Church and the world, which accepted that truth as a test. (*Saint Thomas Aquinas* [New York: Doubleday, 1956; first published by Sheed and Ward, 1933], 102-111)

If this all has a very familiar ring, it is because this age-old battle never changes, only the players do. Those who regard Christianity as a mere spiritual experience and those who regard it as Truth are still locked in combat today as they were is Saint Thomas Aquinas' time.

(I should point out that as I use the word *pietism* I am not only referring to the historical and theological movements associated with people such as Madame Guyan and her weird brand of pietism, known by her contemporaries as "Quietism;" nor am I referring to those Pietists such as Jacob Spencer, August Hermann Francke, and Count Zinzendorf, all of whom were seventeenth- and eighteenth-century Christian leaders of pietistic movements. While not specifically discussing them here, nevertheless their ideas were part of a negative tradition in the church to the degree that they developed a theology of pure experience unchecked by reference to Scripture—a theology that separated life from truth just as its opposite, dead orthodoxy, ran the reverse danger of separating truth from life. Others, for instance, Menno Simon and a group of Anabaptists, were also known as "pietists." However, my use of the word *pietism* is to identify a way of thinking—or more accurately, of feeling—that runs through all church history, not simply to identify a handful of individual theologians.)

Truth

The tradition of Truth affirms life as a whole; it sees reality as a whole. There is no sacred and no secular—all of creation is God's. God's commands are not merely moral commands affecting our moral standing before Him; they are rather the instructions provided by God telling us how we, as His creatures, work best. God's law is not only a means of identifying what is right and wrong as it is commonly understood, but also as a question of what works and what does not. From the point of view of Truth, this makes sense. If God has created reality, then He will know how it functions.

In creating human beings, God did an odd thing. He made a biological machine, similar to the rest of the biological world, which He then infused with a conscious mind and soul. (Something like the computer robot creature in the movie *Short Circuit*: "Number five *is* alive.") We are biological machines that can choose: Choose to read God's instruction manual and live by it, or choose to disregard it and pay the price of self-destruction.

Law and creation have the same source: God. They are part of reality that God has made. God's law as expressed in the Scriptures, His instruction, is not a series of moral or pious sayings; it is a set of practical rules by which our biological, mechanical bodies and our nonbiological spirits can function and prosper.

The Results of Truth

If Truth *is* true, then it *should* work to whatever extent it is understood and obeyed. This has practical applications. For instance, the prosperity and freedom in the West, which the world envies and seeks to copy, is not merely an economic system that came into being by accident. Whether they know it or not, what the underdeveloped countries wish to copy are the fruits of Truth rooted in the ideas of Jewish and Christian teaching.

As Michael Novak, (author and George Frederick Jewett Scholar in Religion and Public Policy at the American Enterprise Institute), wrote in *Commentary* (September 1989) in an article entitled "Boredom, Virtue and Democratic Capitalism":

> Democratic capitalist societies are rooted in certain spiritual values without which they could scarcely have been imagined, let alone have come into existence.

> From the beginning the claim was made of democratic capitalist societies that they were built to the pattern of "the system of

natural liberty." The implication was that such a system would belong to all humans, wherever they might be. It would be adaptable to local customs, histories, traditions, and cultures, provided only that these opened the institutional ways to universal human capacities for reflection and choice — in politics, economics, and the realm of conscience and culture. The system was not designed for Jews or Christians only, for Anglo-Saxons or Frenchmen; it was designed for all human beings.

This claim is not forfeited by the historical fact that the insights and practices which originally led to the developments of the necessary institutions arose first in lands deeply shaped by the teachings of Judaism and Christianity. That democratic capitalism was embryonically realized first in such lands was, of course, "no accident." Judaism and Christianity are, in an important way, religions of history and consequently, religions of liberty. Although no one sees God, and no one can form an idea of God commensurate with His reality, humans are led by the Bible to imagine that He sees, chooses, acts. And humans, according to the Bible as well, are made in His image. In their capacity to reflect and to choose — and to create, in the sense appropriate to their limits — they are made like unto Him. Time itself is imagined as revealing the narrative of His compact with them — a compact into which they have freely entered. History is the story of how humans live out their end of this bargain.

In this philosophical-theological vision, every single human being has dignity, is in a way sacred, because of his capacity to reflect and to choose; a covenant freely entered into is the highest model to which human communities aspire. Civilization is imagined to be an ideal city in which humans address one another, not through force or coercion, but through the conversation of reason.

It was out of such beliefs that the words of Thomas Jefferson in the Declaration of Independence ultimately flowed: "We hold these truths to be self-evident: That all men are created equal; that they are endowed by their Creator with certain inalienable rights; that among these are life, liberty, and the pursuit of hap-

piness; that to secure these rights, governments are instituted among men, deriving their just powers from the consent of the governed; that whenever any form of government becomes destructive of these ends, it is the right of the people to alter or abolish it, and to institute new government, laying its foundation on such principles, and organizing its powers in such form, as to them shall seem most likely to effect their safety and happiness."

To say, however, that a "system of natural liberty" seems to flow directly from the convictions of Jews and Christians about human nature and destiny, is not to say that free societies are limited solely to those who hold such beliefs, nor that the details of such societies actually were or could have been worked out only by believing Jews and Christians.

As Novak wrote, ideas, in this case theological ideas, bear results in the practical world. While a Jewish-Christian tradition leads to certain economic and political results, these benefits can also be shared in part by non-Christian, non-Jewish societies because reality *is* one, and men and women *are* made in God's image, whether they acknowledge Him or not. Just as the rain falls on the just and the unjust, so even those who are *not* followers of Truth still live in a cause-and-effect world, in which, through trial and error if not through a commitment to theologically accurate ideas, they can benefit from and work with the natural order of things. Nature and history carry a cause-and-effect message from God. Revelation is a short cut to that message.

But the opposite can also be true. Cultures that have known the Truth can choose to abandon their principles. As the West abandons Jewish-Christian descriptions of reality and Truth and follows other ideas, it, too, could regress and join the so called Third World. Those who lift their voices in the chant "Ho, ho, Western culture has got to go!" are attacking not only Western culture but Truth, and the progress, prosperity, and freedom that follow from that Truth. They are committing spiritual, artistic, and economic suicide. The smoking ruins of inner-city gang warfare, illiteracy, and immorality are their legacy. Truth does work, and its opposite — lies and deception — leads to destruction and chaos. The human race is not divided along ethnic or racial lines; it is divided between those who follow true ideas and those who do not.

Western culture is not *the* Truth, but to the degree it has succeeded in producing a system that feeds, clothes, and defends its citizens and upholds their civil liberties, the West has benefited from a *belief* in the principles of Jewish-Christian Truth. (A fact amply demonstrated by a growing body of scholarly literature, including: P. T. Bauer, *Equality, the Third World, and Economic Delusion* [Cambridge, MA: Harvard University Press, 1981]; Julian Simon, *The Ultimate Resource* [Princeton, NJ: Princeton University Press, 1981]; Warren T. Brooks, *The Economy in Mind* [New York: Universe Books, 1982]; Michael Novak, *The Spirit of Democratic Capitalism* [New York: Simon and Schuster, 1982]; Paul Johnson, *Modern Times* [New York: Harper and Row, 1983]; and Robert Nisbet, *History of the Idea of Progress* [New York: Basic Books, 1980].)

Christian-Jewish principles of freedom, individual accountability, the rule of law, humanity, and compassion have produced magnificent results applied to political institutions and economic practice, a fact underscored again by the many church-led revolutions against communist tyranny of recent memory. The people of what was once Communist East Germany, Romania, Poland, Hungary, and Czechoslovakia have struggled to replace the yoke of the superstate and communist dictatorships with Western and Jewish-Christian institutions. Thus, while some in Western academia, the media, the "knowledge elite," (and members of the American Democratic party), continue to be enamored of socialist ideas, the people of the world, when given any chance at all, beat a path to the door of the West and its *religious* institutions for guidance.

The West they seek to emulate is the West founded on the concept of Biblical Truth.

Pietism

Those whose Christian opinions are informed by Pietism regard life as a moralistic quest for spiritual experience. For Pietists, the results are unimportant if only the motivation is correct. It is the *heart* and experience that concerns them, not the mind or the soul. Pietism is a process of constantly looking inward and searching for correct motivation and right-thinking, spiritual feelings. Pietism seeks to obey not only the Laws of God, but also a host of petty rules lifted up as "absolutes" by those to whom freedom is a threat. Content, truth, and logic take second place to experience, fervor, sincerity, and rule-keeping. In this regard, Pietism is in perfect tune with the times. This piety often turns into a sour experience, one of being "pious only when I'm bilious," as Thomas Hood puts it in his "Ode to Rae Wilson" (l. 43). Inner analysis and endless guilty agony are its results since one can never be sure one "feels" spiritual enough.

Because of the premium often put on feelings and emotion by pietists, those in this frame of mind may seek out many experiences which are fundamentally irrational, thus anti-Christian. These experiences will help them, they hope, in their rather desperate quest for a religious "high," the emotion and *feelings* they imagine to be holiness. Thus, worship often becomes hysterical. Mood, feelings, and "sensitivity" replace real discourse about ideas and content. Since the pietist looks to emotion to validate his or her faith, almost anything that heightens that emotion is perceived as good. This has opened pietists to abuse and false teaching in large numbers. This has also led to many pietists becoming disillusioned as things get out of hand, or when the promised results from their "walk with the Lord" fail to materialize. Many finally abandon their faith altogether, throwing out the baby with the bath water. This is why one meets so many ex-fundamentalists and hedonistic pagans who were raised in "charismatic" or evangelical homes.

Chesterton writes of the destructive trend toward pie-in-the-sky Pietism in the historic church as he related Aquinas' battle against this undermining philosophy. In his day, Aquinas locked horns with a certain wrong-headed gentleman by the name of Siger of Brabant.

> Siger of Brabant said this: the Church must be right theologically, but she can be wrong scientifically. There are two truths; the truth of the supernatural world, and the truth of the natural world, which contradicts the supernatural world. . . . In other words, Siger of Brabant split the human head in two . . . and declared that a man has two minds, with one of which he must entirely believe and with the other may utterly disbelieve. . . .
>
> St. Thomas [by contrast] was willing to allow the one truth to be approached by two paths, precisely *because* he was sure there was only one truth. Because the Faith was the one truth, nothing discovered in nature could ultimately contradict the Faith. Because the Faith was the one truth, nothing really deduced from the Faith could ultimately contradict the facts. It was in truth a curiously daring confidence in the reality of his religion; and though some may linger to dispute it, it has been justified. . . .
>
> Thomas Aquinas had struck his blow. . . . He had insured that the main outline of the Christianity that has come down to us should be supernatural but not antinatural; and should never be darkened with a false spirituality to the oblivion of the Creator and the Christ who was made Man. But as his tradition trailed away into less liberal or less creative habits of thought, and as his medieval society fell away and decayed through other causes, the thing against which he had made war crept back into Christendom. (*Saint Thomas Aquinas,* [New York: Doubleday, 1933, 84-91)

In our time the same battle rages; St. Thomas would be at home in our church. He would recognize in the liberals those who, like Siger of Brabant, want to have Christianity be religiously "true" though not true in all things. And he would do battle with some more conservative thinkers like Allan Bloom who think Christianity useful but not true. Aquinas would also hear—in our charismatic movement and our evangelical trend toward psychological well-being at the expense of Truth—echoes of the Manichaeism he labored so long to combat.

Pietism gives people a fractured reality, one in which the physical world, the body, the arts, economics, the sciences, the humanities, and sexuality are believed to be at war with the soul. A world in which fact is seen to be at war with religious experience. One can see a guilt-ridden motivation at work in the actions of many who have abandoned their "secular" talents in favor of "serving God"—an attitude embodied in the "I used to be a night club singer but now I'm a missionary" variety of Christian. Many a missionary and missionary's child has suffered because of the tragic mistake of pursuing the missionary calling out of some false sense of guilt—guilt fostered by a church that pushes people into "the Lord's Work" as if it were something special, separate, and better from "ordinary" life. Thus, pietists develop a hierarchy of values in which "spiritual" activities and full-time religious service are seen to be on a higher plain than ordinary life and activities. This is contrary to the teachings of Scripture.

Those Christians who have subscribed to the pietistic view of life can be recognized by the fact that they are driven by an inner, guilty need to Christianize all they do, to somehow make it "holy" in order to justify it. For them, for something to be worthwhile, it must be *made* to mean something spiritual or at least to *feel* spiritual. In our day, this impulse is seen in everything from bumper stickers, which Christianize cars; and Christian TV, which Christianizes the airwaves; to *The Christian Mother Goose*, a book that simultaneously Christianizes literature while bastardizing it.

War

In a fifteenth-century manuscript recounting a thirteenth-century incident, there is an entertaining account of the "miraculous" events leading up to the battle between two rival Tuscan cities, Florence and Siena, that took place on September 3, 1260. In the battle of Montaperti, the Sienese swept the Florentines from the field of battle like chaff, as "God and Mary marched before them." For those who think that Pietistic irrationalism is only an unfortunate phenomenon of the modern church, consider the events described below. With the powerful Florentines marching on the gates of the city, the holy people of Siena did thus:

> Our spiritual father, my lord the bishop, caused the bell to ring to summon his clergy. And he made to come together all the clergy of Siena, priests, and canons, and friars, and all the religious, to the duomo [the cathedral], and being there he made a short sermon to them, admonishing them and comforting them, and bidding them pray to God and His Most Holy Mother, the Virgin Mary, and to all the saints . . . for the people of the city; . . . that as he had spared the people of Ninevah because of its fasting and repentance, so it would please Him to free Siena from the fury and pride of these knaves of Florentines [fellow Christians who lived barely 30 miles away]. And so he ordained that every one should make bare his feet, and should go devoutly in procession through the duomo, singing with a loud voice and invoking ceaselessly the pity of God. . . .
>
> And no sooner had he said these words than this Buonaguida stripped himself to his shirt. And, being barefooted and bareheaded, he took his leathern girdle and fastened it round his neck with a slip-knot. And in this guise, at the head of the procession of the citizens, he set out towards the duomo. And behind him went all the people; and whomsoever they met by the way went with them, each man being shoeless and without cloak or hat. . . . And as they went they ceased not to cry "Mary Virgin, succor us in our great need, and deliver us out of the claws of these lions, and from these haughty men who seek to devour us." And all the people prayed, "Oh, Madonna, most holy Queen of Heaven, we miserable sinners entreat your mercy. . . ."

And taking one another by the hand, my lord the bishop and Buonaguida went up to the altar of our Mother, the Virgin Mary, and there they kneeled down with great lamentation and bitter tears. And this venerable citizen, Buonaguida, lay all prostrate on the ground, and so did all the people, with much weeping and many sighs. And so they remained for a quarter of an hour. Then Buonaguida raised himself to his feet in front of our Mother, the Virgin Mary, and uttered many wise and prudent words. And amongst others he spake these following: "Oh, Virgin, glorious Queen of Heaven, Mother of sinners! I, a wretched sinner, give, grant, and yield to thee, this city and contado of Siena, and I pray thee, sweetest Mother, that it may please thee to accept it, notwithstanding our great frailty and our many sins. Regard not our offenses, but guard, defend, and deliver us, I beseech thee, from the hands of these perfidious dogs of Florentines. . . (Ferdinand Schevici, *Sienna* [New York: Charles Scribners, 1909], 81-84)

On the next day the Christian Sienese drove the Christian Florentines out of Monteperti in a bloody slaughter and returned rejoicing to their fair city blessing God and Mary as they went!

Pietism has existed throughout history and has always produced excess. As we can see from the tale related above, not all Christian lunacy belongs to the twentieth century. The people of Siena, preparing to face their Christian neighbors, the Florentines, in battle, would have been at home, at least in spirit, with the ranting histrionics at many a charismatic evangelistic crusade, the kind of goings on that Shakespeare called "cruel irreligious, piety!" (*Titus Andronicus* I.i., 130).

The pious mysticism of the Middle Ages also led to the establishment of many new monasteries in Tuscan, Italy in the eleventh, twelfth, and thirteenth centuries, as Christians tried to become "holy" people, uncorrupted by daily and mundane life, which was seen to be less holy than a cloistered one. I hasten to add that many of these institutions did admirable work. But the idea that a cloistered life is more holy than an ordinary one sometimes produced the bitterness of false guilt with which we are so familiar. Indeed, wandering friars like Saint Thomas Aquinas, Saint Francis, and Saint Dominique were often harassed and looked down upon by the more "holy" and cloistered monks.

Today, in the evangelical fundamentalist and charismatic movements, these impulses manifest themselves in attempting to make everything fit into an evangelistic or so called Spirit-filled mode, or some other pious formula. Carried to an absurdity, the urge to Christianize things is the reason behind the Sienese invocations of Mary and God to help them in a war against their Christian neighbors, and, in our own day, such nonsense as the publication of *The Christian Mother Goose* and other "Christian" works of fiction. Thus, we see Mother Goose and a territorial war baptized in the spirit of piety. Both actions are cruel and irreligious.

In our own time, Pietism has been dominant in evangelical and fundamentalist circles. It has also deeply affected the American Catholic Church in a slightly different way. The Catholic Church is riddled with leftists driven by Marxist guilt. This, too, is Pietism, a separation of reality from truth in the name of religion. Thus, to these Catholics, the experience of Marxism and identifying with the poor, becomes a pietistic ritual of "helping the poor." This attitude also divides life into a hierarchy of more or less spiritual actions. Thus, a growing segment of the Christian community on the political left and right is weird and cultic, narrow, politicized, and downright strange.

Because of this, there is a tension between individuals who believe in Truth and those who believe in Pietism. Those who believe in Truth often wonder if they are truly Christian since they seem so out of step with and so different from the far more numerous Pietists, of both the political left and right, who appear to live in a sort of spiritual Disneyland of experience.

This tension, this sense of unease with the cultic face of Christianity that so many people of integrity feel, comes from the fact that the dogma of Pietism, not Truth, now dominates a great deal of the church — both Protestant and Catholic. Because of this there are many reasonable Christians who *do* love and follow the Lord but dislike being with other Christians who appear to them to be playing without a full mental deck of cards! The prospect of spending time in a church that is apparently a lunatic asylum for the pious is an unattractive prospect for many reasonable Christians.

Garbage of the Soul

The little Bible verses stuck on refrigerators, the bad Sunday school illustrations, the feeble and bland Sunday school texts of the "be nice to everybody" variety that Christian publishers specialize in, the many church programs, the lack of interest in the arts or their propagandistic misuse, the many little rules that have been added to God's few and sensible instructions, the "niceness" of so many Christians when toughness of mind is called for, the lack of courage, the laws of God that have been abandoned, the strange tangents churches go off on, the obnoxious bad taste, the contents of the average evangelical Christian bookstore, the predominance of hair-sprayed charlatans who lead much of the church, the cultic overtones of the evangelical-fundamentalist school movement, the lesbian-feminist inroads into the liberal denominations, the feminized wimps who pass for men in the evangelical world, the insular closed minds, the easily shocked sensibilities of the middle class and their taboos, the harsh rules of the fundamentalist churches, the increased New Age emphasis on inner healing and so called counseling, the "Liberation" theology — these things, and the list could go on, are related in one way or another, to the unnatural, pietistic division of life into religious versus secular, sacred versus rational. The chaos in the church is the result of removing normal, rational Biblical standards to judge the world by and replacing them with "spiritual" standards. The pietists have created a desert where a garden should be growing. They are tragically wrong.

The Real World

Reality is one and it is all God's. There is *nothing* intrinsically more spiritual about saving a soul than filling a tooth. And there is nothing more spiritual about feeding the hungry than taking a walk with your children or working hard to earn some money.

Creation, art, marriage, work, sex within marriage, church, the family, and all human activities have intrinsic value as does all of nature. These things have value in themselves because they are part of God's creation, which itself is no more or less spiritual than physics. It is physics, biology, nuclear science, cinema, feeding the poor, the Eucharist, and housekeeping. God's reality includes everything, though we are told that He does not approve of everything we choose to do. And let me add, Christianity is *not* pantheism; God is not *in* everything. Creation stands separate from God. Christianity is *not* syncretism; there are not many ways *to* God, though there are many avenues through which to explore truth.

God has an abiding interest in mankind, reaffirmed by His supernatural intervention in choosing the Jews to become the light of the world, and in the life, death, and resurrection of Jesus. Easter morning gives new meaning to the value of reality and all human life — meaning that faith-in-faith Pietism can only muddy.

The pietistic need to Christianize reality indicates a worldview that does not fundamentally understand or believe that reality is already God's and that Christianity is truly Truth.

We do not need to Christianize breakfast by memorizing a daily Bible verse. Breakfast is already God's. We do not need to Christianize our refrigerator by putting a small piece of plastic on it with a magnetic backing, stamped with the words, "Jesus Loves You." And if we want to fight the Florentines for control of

Monteperti, we do not need to dress that up as a church function carried on by force of arms! We do not need to feel compelled to put our children in Christian schools in order to Christianize academic subjects. A good school with good teaching about truth is what is required. The truth that encompasses math, physics, and history is part of the same reality as the truth about what happened historically one afternoon when Jesus fed five thousand bewildered people.

Results

To bring the subject specifically back to art, good art, like good science, describes the truth of a small or large part of reality without regard to maintaining the respectability of the artist. The fit subject for Christian art, therefore, is *reality*. This is the concept that, applied to art, science, the humanities, and political thought, created the West, the West that the world envies.

Democracy, free markets, freedom of expression, modern medicine, modern science, literature, art, and scholarship follow in the wake of belief in Truth and the practice of that belief. An understanding of the fact that we live in an orderly universe created by an orderly, personal God and that all of His creation is open to us creates different results from Hinduism, Animism, Marxism, or other religions that do not describe reality truthfully. If we throw away the instructions, we pay the price. The rusting Mercedes Benz by the side of some post-colonial road symbolizes more than merely a return to tribalism. Philosophy and popular mechanics are related. Closer to home, the failure of government programs that seek to legislate away sin in our super-welfare state also bears testimony to the failure of Socialist and other ideas that run counter to the nature of people — their need for charity, forgiveness, motivation and self-discipline.

The economic and human ruin spawned by the expansion of Big Government, often under the guise of a secularized compassion, has shown that even in the West there is no immunity from bad ideas translated into misguided programs. Aid to dependent mothers, many affirmative action programs, a host of social welfare programs, and now child-care legislation, all have produced bitter, unintended consequences. Worse, such programs attempt to impose a vision of "right thinking" from the top down, often at the instigation of special interest groups that have a vested interest in some particular government program. For instance, child-care professionals seek to, by law, eliminate the competition of informal child-care providers, such as relatives or "the lady down the street," so that they can establish a state-imposed monopoly on child care in the name of providing "safe" facilities. In the West, as it has lost its Christian-Jewish religious-philosophical bearings, such utopian, often jaded Statist ideas are hard to resist. Nature abhors a vacuum, and as Western men and women forget or reject the robust truths of Christianity and Judaism, the moral vacuum will be filled by government programs and creeping dependency. An extension of government into every area of life, including the arts, has become the menace of the free West. Big government has become the testament of secular religion.

The Vacuum

Others besides Christian apologists have noticed the decline in discourse in the Christian community, a decline caused by Christians imitating the general culture as it abandons rationality in favor of "experience." Yet, it was not always so. Once, to be a Christian was not to automatically be irrational. Pietistic Christianity was *not* always the norm. As Neil Postman writes concerning the shift from rationality to Pietism in the church:

Unlike the principal figures in today's "great awakening" — Oral Roberts, Jerry Falwell, Jimmy Swaggart, et al. — yesterday's leaders of revivalist movements in America were men of learning, faith in reason, and generous expository gifts. . . .

The doctrinal disputes among religionists not only were argued in carefully drawn exposition in the eighteenth century, but in the nineteenth century were settled by the extraordinary expedient of founding colleges. It is sometimes forgotten that the churches in America laid the foundation of our system of higher education. Harvard, of course, was established early — in 1636 — for the purpose of providing learned ministers to the Congregational Church. . . . The Presbyterians founded, among other schools, the University of Tennessee in 1784, Washington and Jefferson in 1802 and Lafayette in 1826. The Baptists founded, among others, Colgate (1817), George Washington (1821), Furman (1826), Denison (1832) and Wake Forest (1834). The Episcopalians founded Hobart (1822), Trinity (1823) and Kenyon (1824). The Methodists founded eight colleges between 1830 and 1851, including Wesleyan, Emory, and Depauw. . . .

In the eighteenth and nineteenth centuries, religious thought and institutions in America were dominated by an austere, learned, and intellectual form of discourse that is largely absent from religious life today. (Neil Postman, *Amusing Ourselves to Death* [New York: Viking Penguine, 1985, 54–56)

That Western countries, with a history of commitment to Truth, even if abandoned for some time now, are not completely riddled with graft, corruption of every kind, tyranny, double standards, State theft, agrarian disaster, complete stagnation in the arts and culture, viciously inhuman institutions, and filthy water is not a fluke. It is not to be explained by some simple North-South equation or mere resource availability. As P. T. Bauer has argued so eloquently in his book, *Equality, the Third World and Economic Delusion* [Cambridge: Harvard University Press, 1981], that Mozambique, Angola, and Cuba are qualitatively different from France, Switzerland, and Holland is not an accident of race,

natural resources, colonialism, or luck. The vast differences between nations has everything to do with the application of theological, secular, and religious *ideas* by the people of those
countries. It has everything to do with the commitment to the
Truth and its practice. It has to do with arranging societies along
lines that fit the way mankind and the physical world really functions, instead of creating societies based on inaccurate moral or
scientific theories into which people fit with difficulty.

The success of the West and those nations that have imitated
it, or like Japan were forced to adopt Western ideas at gunpoint, is
the result of and in direct proportion to the understanding of the
fact that reality works a certain way. Ideas produce results. The
acceptance of Christianity at some point in a nation's history, or
at least rational, Jewish-Christian thought patterns about cause-
and-effect reality, is the key difference between the *developed
world* and the *third world*. Even the vague memory of Jewish-
Christian thought has proved a better basis for society than non-
Christian philosophy. The West is not only different from the rest
of the world, it is measurably better — a fact that may be disputed
by leftist ideologues in Western universities and the media, but is
driven home by the millions who seek refuge in the West from
the "other traditions" and cultures.

The West has been at its most horrible when it has abandoned
its own Jewish-Christian traditions and embraced other ways of
seeing things, as Germany did when led by the rabidly anti-Catho-
lic, anti-Jewish madman, Hitler. Or as the Iberian Catholic Church
did in being influenced by the harsh Moslem views of the Arabs,
who conquered, then dominated much of Spain. In Fernand
Braudel's classic history *The Mediterranean (And the World in
the Age of Philip II)*, he writes about how Spain inherited more
than buildings and irrigation techniques from the Moslems.

One of the problems of the Mediterranean, and one of the
causes of its traditionalism and rigidity, was that . . . newly ac-

quired land remained under control of the wealthy. . . . Spain had inherited [from the Moslems] the labor force of *fellahin* [serfs and slaves]. . . . Spanish masters cared for . . . them in the same spirit as they would their livestock and exactly as they were to protect their slaves in the New World. ([New York: Harper and Row, 1966], 75)

Japan an Object Lesson

Even the imitation of the imitation of the Jewish-Christian West produces better results than a philosophy that bears no resemblance to the Truth as embodied in Jewish and Christian ideas. For instance, Japan's present prosperity can be directly traced to the new political-philosophical shape that General Douglas MacArthur *forced* on Japan from 1946 to 1952.

The Japanese, in 1946, may not have believed in Jesus of Nazareth, but they did come to believe in Douglas MacArthur. MacArthur, who was a believing Episcopalian Christian, very self-consciously applied Christian ideals to the radical restructuring of post-war Japanese society. Toshikazu Kaze, the Japanese diplomat who was charged to report directly to the Emperor, speaks of his first impression of MacArthur: "Here is a victor announcing the verdict to the prostrate enemy. He can exact his pound of flesh if he so chooses. . . . And yet he pleads for freedom, tolerance, and justice. For me who expected the worst humiliation, this was a complete surprise."

MacArthur spoke of the Japan he faced: "If we do not devise some greater and more equitable system, Armageddon will be at our door. The problem basically is theological and involves a spiritual recrudescence and improvement of human character that will synchronize with our almost matchless advances in science, art, literature, and all material and cultural developments of the past two thousand years. It must be of the spirit if we are to save the flesh." At another time the general said he would like to be remembered as, "One whose sacred duty it became, once the guns were silenced, to carry to the land of our vanquished foe the solace and hope and faith of Christian morals."

And that was exactly what MacArthur did. Later, in the controversy surrounding the end of the Korean War, some Americans forgot what the grateful Japanese remembered: that one man had saved them by the power of ideas — ideas of freedom, women's rights, economic empowerment, free markets, human rights, and the sanctity of the individual. All of these are Jewish-Christian-Western attributes, totally foreign to the Japanese in philosophy and practice until MacArthur imported them.

Arthur M. Schlesinger quoted a Japanese as saying, after the Emperor, Hirohito, had renounced his divinity, "We took MacArthur as the second Jesus Christ."

Roger Baldwin of the American Civil Liberties Union commented as he left an interview with MacArthur in Japan, "Why he knows more about civil liberties than I do!"

The *New York Times* observed, "MacArthur's administration is a model of government. . . . He has swept away an autocratic regime by a warrior god and installed in its place a democratic government."

MacArthur wrote the new Japanese constitution. William Manchester tells us, "He wrote his first memorandum on the subject, starting: 'Four points for a Constitution.' Later the General wrote, "It is undoubtedly the most liberal constitution in history." Under MacArthur's messianic influence, Japan's national income passed prewar levels within five years. MacArthur understood the power of Western ideas as perhaps no other twentieth-century leader besides Winston Churchill. MacArthur said, "The more missionaries we can bring out here . . . the more occupation troops we can send home." Ten million Bibles were imported on his order, and he said that he had contributed to "the greatest spiritual revaluation the world has ever known." By this he did not mean the acceptance of Christian doctrine itself per se, though two million Japanese did convert, what he was referring to was the acceptance of Western democracy, which he understood to be a spiritual manifestation of the Christian ideas of Truth. Later, MacArthur said that the struggle for Asia lay between imperialistic communism and Christian democracy, an idea sadly vindicated by the boat people of Vietnam and the silent dead of Cambodia that followed in the wake of the wholesale western retreat from Asia after the Vietnam debacle.

MacArthur's influence in Japan provides a unique example of just how well ideas rooted in Jewish and Christian belief work on a practical level, even when people are not individually believers. (The quotations above on MacArthur are cited from *American Caesar,* by William Manchester [New York: Little, Brown and Co., 1978], 452-551.)

The story of MacArthur in Japan is one of the shining examples of Christian statecraft, an example of culture-building without parallel since Augustine and the early missionary thrusts of the first to fourth centuries into the remains of the Roman Empire.

Conflict

Since the seventeenth century, the time of the so-called Enlightenment, Christians have had the conflict thrust upon them by a group of secularized thinkers and artists who reject all forms and manifestations of Biblical truth. These thinkers' spiritual grandchildren continue to shape our culture, including our artistic culture, to this day.

Much of our post-Enlightenment art seems to have been directed against our own Western society. The same is true of the anti-Western nature of many twentieth-century scholars' work. Thus, for example, the stranglehold of secularism on our universities continues to this day (see Appendix A). This secularism often takes the form of a leftist, "New Age," or "Green" environmentalist ideology that rejects the West itself as the despised "sexist," "chauvinistic," "colonialistic," "polluting" stepchild of Judaism and Christianity.

By rejecting Jewish-Christian truth, many Western secularists have now come to reject their own civilization founded on that truth. It is no wonder, then, that feminists seek to rewrite not only literature and art history but even the Bible. It is no wonder that militant women and homosexuals seek ordination in the church. It is no wonder that feminists wish to make us refer to God as "She." They understand where our culture came from even if many pietistic Christians do not. "Ho, ho, Western culture has got to go!" is no idle refrain. It comes from those who understand the full meaning of the historical reversal implied in this slogan — the abolishment of the Jewish-Christian tradition. The fact that there are even some people who espouse views that they call "evangelical feminism" or "catholic homosexuality" tells us that the power of the modern world and its fashions seem to be greater than the power of the church to resist temptation at times.

Those who have rejected Christian and Jewish belief have rejected the democratic foundation of Western society itself — a society distinguished from other cultures by its ideas of progress and social advancement based on ideas that are divinely inspired and therefore true and non-negotable. Not only true in a religious sense, but true in the sense that they work.

History and Progress

Robert Nisbet (Albert Schweitzer Professor of Humanities Emeritus at Columbia University and scholar at the American Enterprise Institute for Public Policy Research) has written the seminal study on the relationship of the idea of progress and its historical foundation entitled *History of the Idea of Progress* (New York: Basic Books, 1980, 352–356).

His summary in the epilogue of his book is instructive. His remarkable analysis is essential reading.

What is the future of the idea of progress in the West? Any answer to that question requires answer to a prior question: what is the future of Judeo-Christianity in the West? For if there is one generalization that can be made confidently about the history of the idea of progress, it is that throughout its history the idea has been closely linked with, has depended on, religion or upon intellectual constructs derived from religion. . . .

For just as the century especially in its second half is almost barren of faith in progress, so is it almost barren of widespread and life-permeating religious faith. No prior age in the West's history comes even close to our own age in this respect. The Renaissance humanists detested much of the ecclesiastical structure of Christianity in their day, but they were profoundly concerned with Christian creed. True atheists were few and far between in the Enlightenment, though this takes nothing away from the philosophers' assault on Christianity as a power in society.

In our day, however, religion is a spent force. If God is not dead, he is ebbing away, and has been since the early part of the century. We have, in Jonathan Swift's coruscating words, "just enough religion to make us hate but not enough to make us love one another" — or, enough to make us see the flaws and cankers of the society around us but not enough to generate hope for the future. Just as religion has seriously waned, so have most of the systems of thought which for a time served intellectuals as surrogates. . . .

The question is, who has succeeded the philosophers? There is no ready answer. We appear to be destitute of any reigning intellectual class. Intellectuals and artists have gone the way of business and political titans, of clergy and philosophers, of scholars and scientists. When has literature been held in as low estate as it is today in the West? Never has the gulf between creative writer and the public been as wide as it is now. . . .

The reason for this condition, the debasement of literature and estrangement of writer and public, is our lack of a true culture. And fundamental to this lack is the disappearance of the sacred, always at the heart of any genuine culture—from ancient Athens to Victorian England. For some time we thought we could live off the yield of the sacred, even though it was gone or passing away. . . .

It was belief in the sacred and the mythological that in the beginning of Western history made possible belief in and assimilation of ideas of time, history, development, and either progress or regress. Only on the basis of confidence in the existence of a divine power was confidence possible with respect to design or pattern in the world and in the history of the world. . . .

But it is absent now, whether ever to be recovered, we cannot know.

The inherent irrationalism of Pietism is the worst possible response to those great grandchildren of the Enlightenment who reject the teachings of Judaism and Christianity. If all Christians can do is to help people feel better, so can secular psychologists. If all Christians can do is add pious interpretations to life and a spiritual dimension, so can Hindu gurus and New Age prophets. If all Christians can do is imitate the worst of the world and become "Christian feminists" or "Christian homosexuals," then they might as well drop the "Christian" label altogether and join in the headlong stampede to oblivion. If all Christians can do is come up with pious platitudes, so can the makers of fortune cookies. Pietistic Christianity is the "spent force," not Christianity itself. Pietism and Christianized secularism, is not remotely related to the robust philosophy and political economy that an earlier Christianity inspired.

At least secular Western rationalism, a Jewish-Christian derivative, appeals to the reality of some part of the truth, inasmuch as it is concerned with science, the arts, and knowledge. It is, therefore, often more attractive than a pietistic Christianity, and even works better inasmuch as it is, ironically, taking advantage of the fruits of the Truth more effectively, whether it affirms the Truth or not. The same might be true of nations. If Japan, for instance, lives by the rules of Jewish-Christian ethics of work, thrift, and honesty better than the "Christian" West, then we can expect Japan to be more prosperous.

In that sense, some secular rationalists are closer to Truth than the many pietistic, cultic, irrational Christians who seem to dominate such large portions of the church today.

Truth Betrayed

The Christian who abandons the hard edges of reality and Truth in favor of a more comfortable, respectable, sheltered Pietism has abandoned the great eternal witness of the real world and the universe for just another religion, another form of psychological counseling to make him or her feel better. This is not a commitment to reality or obedience to Christ, this is a drug called *irrational spirituality.*

To the extent that much experiential Christianity, pietism, and the like appear to be out of sync with reality, they mirror a drug-like spiritual high that is fundamentally anti-reality. This is orgasmic spirituality for experience's sake, not love of the Truth.

To the extent that the church is pietistic, it will reject, or at least be uncomfortable with, art and science, not to mention real people! Art and science ask hard questions; real people are not all respectable. Art and science address complex problems; genuine people behave in unrespectable ways that often raise perplexing questions. Pietists, like all tribalists, long for cultic simplicity and easy solutions: lists of dos and don'ts; radio programs or shamans that tell them how to do everything from having a happy marriage, to happy children, to a happy church group, to a happy retirement. The original, true, odd, creative person in such a context is a nuisance regarded with suspicion.

Pietism invents far more rules for itself than God ever mandated. Because freedom is sometimes frightening, the pietists make their circle of life smaller, not bigger, with every successive generation. Thus life becomes narrow, ugly, strange, and cultic. Such narrowness does not reflect well upon Christianity, though perhaps many caught in its web believe in Christ as their Savior. And in that sense they are saved from Hell in the next life, while they busily create their own sentimental plastic hell in this one. Their salvation has been truncated and stunted in terms of any fruitful, humane, cultural results it could have borne. Thus, cut off from the real world, even real people, the pietistic church has little or no influence in the lives of the people who are creative. The Christian presence in the arts, politics, and the academic disciplines is sadly lacking, perhaps even diminishing.

However ineffectual the middle-class church is, it is nevertheless always attentive to the outward trappings of respectability. It wants its members to be clean, wholesome, to use only "good" language, to be predictable and comfortable. Yet, even as we middle-class Christians have become experts at maintaining our respectability, we have forgotten true virtue. An extreme example of this can be found in the instance of one evangelical pastor I know of who urged his daughter—even forced her—to have an abortion to save him from the *disgrace* of having an unwed mother for a daughter. The mind boggles at the contradiction implied by a man who would murder his grandchild to safeguard his standing in a church. Sadly, this example is not fictitious or unique, nor is the middle-class addiction to respectability in the church only limited to such dramatic extremes. (Remember the "Biblical scorecard" for movies?) If you don't fit in, look, taste, smell, act like a middle-class Christian, you will not find much of a welcome in a great deal of the church today as an artist or a human being. The one thing that the middle-class evangelical-fundamentalist church will not forgive is embarrassment.

Given Douglas MacArthur's historic opportunity in Japan, the pietists of today would merely have held religious rallies, taught people Bible verses by rote, and preached platitudes or tried to "redistribute" the little wealth that remained to achieve "justice." There would have been no historic-cultural-political-economic vision, no rebirth, no renaissance in Japan under such sterile tutelage. The average graduate from an evangelical-fundamentalist Bible school or Christian college will, sadly, never be confused with a MacArthur (that eccentric, sometimes vulgar, titan of nineteenth-century virtue striding into the twentieth century, brimming with Western self-confidence, well-read, informed, opinionated, caustic, and emboldened by a sense of the power of the Truth) nor will the well intentioned Roman Catholic leftest who ignores the lessons of history in favor of experiencing an identity with the poor.

The Truth is like a rock — you either are willing to break yourself on it or it will crush you, because we do live in an orderly, cause-and-effect universe. The Truth is not only a spiritual lesson but has to do with history, economics, and nations as well. Pietism lacks the courage to cast itself on the rock and yet is afraid of being crushed. It, therefore, hides within itself and the church. Thus Jewish-Christian truth begins to take on the trappings of a superstitious talisman.

Truth in the Church

In this book I have used the word *church* in its widest application: to describe Christians in general, the whole body of believers, Catholic, Protestant, or Orthodox. Here, however, I shall turn to the church as a formal, organized, and local institution.

I believe that if the organized local church is led by a pastor who preaches obedience to Christ's teaching by word and example, offers pastoral care, worship, and the Eucharist, practices the clear preaching of the gospel, affirms the real rules and instructions of God, and carries on the apostolic tradition, this church is in good order. The faithful, local church and its true mission needs no justification, no dressing up. Just as artists should not seek to be evangelistically propagandistic, the congregation and minister of the local church do not need to be culturally "relevant" in their worship. They do not need to incorporate contemporary art into their worship: second-rate mime troops, third-rate guitar playing, or modern dance at Mass! The formal church and its orthodox traditions are good in themselves; they are part of God's creation and fulfill the need for Biblical instruction, the serving of the sacraments, teaching, and inspiration. But the local church, too, is only a *part* of the whole of reality, all of which comes from God. Just because the local church is instrumental in bringing people to Christ and in nurturing their faith, does not mean that the rest of reality is less godly or less important.

The people and leaders of the local church are at their weakest and most futile when they are not satisfied with the basic function of the church and seek to justify themselves by becoming "relevant." The needs of the professionally wounded notwithstanding, the church's mission is not to stage "meaningful worship experiences." The true church is not a social welfare agency or a psychological touchy-feely, hold-your-hand counseling center. It is something entirely different.

The church, like the arts, needs no rationalization to exist. It does not need to fulfill some societal function beyond its own unique calling. It has been instituted by Jesus to give spiritual food and grace to His children, to call lost people to obedience by preaching the gospel, seeking new converts, serving the sacraments, jealously guarding the apostolic succession, teaching the Scriptures, passing on orthodox belief and tradition to the faithful, and standing for what is moral, right, and true at whatever cost to itself.

The church has been charged with explaining God's rules and the way of salvation. It has not been instituted by God to be a soup kitchen or a drama club or a dance company or a social event, a good movie, a self-help venue for A.A., or a place to practice the guitar in—let alone as a forum for the expression of "diverse opinions" or as a place for "learning from other traditions." The last thing that the church should be is an institution that keeps up with the times or that strives to be fashionable. The church is the foundation of Western democracy because it is itself the undemocratic guardian of certain eternal truths that should never be subjected to some right-thinking committee or put up for a vote. The church is the guardian of our souls and certain nonnegotiable truths. The church need not "dialogue" with the world or its fashions. Instead, it should teach by word and deed.

The true church is not "relevant;" it is eternal. It alone can offer the blood and the body of our Savior. It should keep its altar uncluttered and its mission clear. Naturally, the formal church may at times engage in extracurricular activities directed by a compassionate response to the needy, for instance, in pro-life activities on behalf of unborn babies or in work with the sick and needy. But, finally, even these good works are not *why* the church exists. The church exists to serve God, not man, and does this by bringing man into more perfect harmony with God, his creator.

If many churches today strike one as strange, cultic, inbred, and pietistic, it is because they are. This is not to judge individuals. *All* of us have fallen far short of the glory of God. And those who seek perfection in their local church are foolish. Yet, it is right to mourn the loss of beauty in so much of the organized local church and to mourn the passing away of the understanding that God is truly God and Christ truly Lord of all of life. It is also right to call ourselves to the fight to restore orthodox traditions and Biblical integrity in the church.

Conclusion

When God looked at creation and said that it was good, He was describing reality. Man's fall is part of God's reality, yet through Christ we can again say with God, "it is good" — a cosmic "amen" to Truth forever. When the church sets out to serve God rather than the whims of men and women, it serves people best.

I am the way, the truth, and the life.

John 14:6

13

FREEDOM — SANITY

F or Christians, the adoption of a worldview based on the concept of Truth results in freedom from false guilt and other
dreadful burdens.

The first freedom is the freedom to be *normal.* The follower
of the Truth need not be a guilt-ridden weirdo, part of some small,
separated band of desperate Christian flagellants seeking personal
holiness and spirituality by abandoning life in the modern world
or by adopting it too thoroughly.

To the believer in Truth, the *normal* everyday events of life
are received as gifts from God, not in some odd spiritual sense,
but directly, literally. The normal relationships of life are sustained. Husbands, wives, children, friends (Christians and non-
Christians alike), co-workers, and our other friends who have
died, now in the cloud of witnesses, authors, statesmen, composers, beggars, painters, and poets all stand together before our God.
We share in one historic reality.

The follower of Truth does not need a relationship with a sect
or cultic body of believers to be sanctified. He does not need to
attach himself to some fleece-the-flock ministry led by some
evangelical or "charasmatic" Christian "leader" or "spiritual counselor" who is on a quest for personal power and acts as if he or
she had special, extra-Biblical revelations for the flock. To the

227

follower of the Truth, the glory of life is *in* life, in thankfulness to the Creator, in a simple childlike relationship to Christ, his Lord and Savior.

His work, his obedience to Christ's teaching, his art, his family, his love of nature and science, his love of the historic and orthodox church, worship and the Eucharist, these are simple, straightforward, *outward-looking* realities that give joy to the believer in Truth. Few of us, certainly *not I*, have achieved this ideal state. But it is what we struggle for with the inner hope the Holy Spirit gives us.

The follower of the Truth is not mired in inward-looking self-analysis. The believer in Truth can be at peace in his vegetable garden tending his tomato plants, savoring a glass of wine, or writing a screenplay, and need not worry as to whether there is not some more "spiritual" way that he should be spending his time. I am free to lie in the arms of my beloved wife and revel in all the senses of sexual intimacy and arousal without any guilty sense that there are activities that are more Christian than making love to her.

The follower of Truth is free to seek quality and integrity in the music he or she enjoys. He does not need to confuse the mandatory "god-words" of Pietism with Truth. He can listen to Mozart instead of the Christianism of so-called contemporary Christian music — usually nothing more than warmed over, second-rate "pop" music. He can appreciate the music of both Bach and the old Mothers of Invention, each for what it is. He can be free to use his mind and senses to sort through what he hears, as regards its truth and beauty. He can appreciate the artisitic merit even in an art work whose reflections on reality differ with his own.

The follower of the Truth is free to apply *one standard* to all things, to all reality: that is, to simply ask, "Is it true?" "Is it false?" "Is it good?" "Is it bad?" "Does it work?" "Is it excellent?" "Is it mediocre?"

The follower of Truth has no strange, weird, or wonderful, special, magical, or spiritual standard by which to judge life, the arts, beauty, and people. Such a follower does not need some special spiritual counselor to give him words of knowledge. The practical, straightforward, unvarnished teaching of Christ is more than sufficient.

The follower of Truth need not be a strange, mystic oddity. He is a flesh-and-blood person—a real person who may curse when he hits his thumb while adding an extension to his kitchen, but does not blaspheme by saying "Praise the Lord," unless he means it.

He does not need to dress up an argument with out-of-context Bible verses. He deals in the plain currencies of truth and common sense. He lets his yes be yes and his no, no. If Western democratic capitalism, for instance, produces prosperity and freedom, the follower of the Truth does not need to scavenge the Bible for support of his thesis in favor of free markets. Economics, too, is a creation of God through man. Prosperity and well-fed children are good ends to seek in themselves. A society that allows entrepreneurial freedom, allows choice of professions, allows people to use their minds and talents to create wealth for themselves and their families does not need to be theologically justified beyond ordinary, logical, humane arguments.

We can discuss the pros and cons of all questions as *already* part of the total reality that comes from God. God is the God of logic and common sense, of science, and of rational discourse as well as of feelings.

The believer in Truth is free to state his case on the basis of its merits. There may be "new" and "old math," but there is no "Christian math." Math itself is already God's. Reality, logic, progress, what works—these things are not the enemy of faith. Reality needs no pious overlay to redeem it.

Sanity

The follower of Truth is free to be sane. He can simply say, "I got a job as a farmhand because I needed the money." He does not have to take God's name in vain and say, "The Lord led me to become a farmhand."

He can give good, common sense advice to his friends; he need not indulge in well-meant lies and presumptuously tell them that "the Lord laid thus and so on my heart to tell you."

The follower of Truth can begin a letter with "Dear friend . . . How are you?" He needn't pretend he is writing an epistle to the church at Corinth and open a letter with "Greeting, Brother! In the name of our Lord Jesus Christ, can you send me your recipe for Tortellini al Pesto?"

He understands that reality — the ordinary, the simple, the straightforward — *is* God's. He does not have to be a spiritual lunatic caught in some permanent spasm of sneezing out pious phlegm.

Christ is not a mystic. Most of His parables involve scenes from everyday life — secular stories — not religious examples. Christ saw Truth manifested in the ordinary. We can too.

When those who reject Jesus look at those who say they follow Him, it is not necessary for them to see people who appear to be deranged. What they should see are truly *normal* people: husbands of one wife, of good repute; wives who love their husbands; couples who love their children; people who dare to tell the unpopular truth about the true evils (like abortion on demand) confronting our society; people who treasure nature and creation; people who love art and beauty; open people; people who will fight for what is right and against evil at cost to themselves; people who are easily accessible; and people who do not speak in some private, blasphemous, "Spirit-filled" code of "God-told-me-so" and "thus says the Lord" babblings.

Truth is not madness. However, Pietism finally leads to a type of insanity, a split personality in which reality, carved into incompatible parts, is believed to be at war with itself—a madness of guilt-ridden people trying to out-do each other in their pietistic exhibitionism, people who *directly disobey* Christ's instruction to *not* parade one's spiritual life in public like a circus act (see Matthew 6:16–18). Pietistic evangelicalism, fundamentalism, and Catholicism, Left and Right, charismatic and Reformed, have often turned Christianity into a sideshow. It it no wonder that this looks crazy to the world at large. It is.

Jesus

Jesus the Jew *is* a historical figure. He is indeed God become man. Jesus' teaching and the laws of God are basic, common sense instructions to ordinary people that, if believed and obeyed, produce life now and eternally.

We believe in Jesus because He is a real figure in history who came from God to save us from the self-destruction and the folly of having thrown out our instruction booklet, our owners' manuals. We can test His teachings against the evidence of the real world. We can look at what people's lives look like who *truly* obey God and, conversely, at the lives of those who have deliberately departed from God. Jesus came to us to give us a second chance. Through His life, death, and resurrection, He enables us to enter into the favor of our artist, maker-creator God — a God who is justly angry at seeing His work of art hacked to pieces.

Jesus does not occupy some strange spiritual dimension. He is alive in a real place we call Heaven. There, He is building and designing yet another creation, perhaps even inventing a new spectrum, new colors, new biological species, new atomic structures. He is also building a city, a *real* place with measurable dimensions.

Like all artists and creative persons, Jesus, God the Father, and God the Holy Spirit are partial to those who like their creation. They regard with favor humans who don't break their world, lives, bodies, and souls to pieces by deliberately not following the instructions. Since no fallen men and women have yet succeeded in keeping their world and themselves whole, God has punished Himself through Jesus instead of us. Thus we acknowledge God as a loving God. This punishment on our behalf is the mystery of the gospel and the means by which we can be restored to the good graces of a just Creator. The moral universe trembled but stood.

God does love us, as evidenced by the fact that He didn't just trade us in for newer models that work better. Instead, the Jewish authors of the Bible inspired by God, the prophets, and finally His Jewish Son, God made flesh, were sent to show us the way back, to repair us, to reissue the lost instructions, and, in the case of Jesus, to suffer death for us.

Because flesh, blood, and reality are part of God's creation, His Son worked through flesh, blood, and suffering to reach out to us. God gave us a second chance through a Jewish girl called Mary — a real girl who was really pregnant and endured all the physical ramifications of pregnancy.

Reality, flesh, blood, tears, amniotic fluid, suffering: this is the stuff of Mary's motherhood and of Christ's life. The stuff of Jesus' travail. If Mary had had an abortion, then Jesus would have died. There would have been no Savior of the world. There was only one fetus that was the Christ. He was a real baby like you and I once were. He was, and is, irreplaceable. Truth is very untheoretical. Truth is truth. Truth brings freedom to human beings, not spiritual chains.

God is not an ice cream parlor. There are not thirty-one flavors. *There is only one way to God,* and that is through his Jewish Son, Jesus of Nazareth. Other "ways of salvation" and other religions are false, or in the special case of God's chosen people, the

Jews, incomplete. However unfashionable it is in our inclusive, egalitarian age to believe in *exclusive* Truth, Jesus is just that — unique, exclusive, not *a* way but *the* way to God. There are not numerous covenants, but only one, and it comes to us through the Jews. Jesus the Jew loves us; He will feed us with genuine pearls — pearls that can turn sham people, hollow men, into full human beings.

*Feminist literary critics, starting
out in the conviction that women
writers had long suffered at the
hands of male critics, have ended
up fostering an image of women at
least as insulting as any they set out
to protest.*

Peter Shaw, *The War Against the Intellect*

14

THE CHALLENGE TO THOSE OF US IN THE ARTS

I have argued in this book that propaganda makes bad art. Yet today we see that the nearly complete politicization of art and culture is well under way. Pre-twentieth-century art and literature are being reinterpreted through new ideologically motivated political methods by feminists, Marxists, and others. New works are being produced as mere political tracts, old works obliterated by ideological creativity. As noted before, political views will sometimes manifest themselves in an artist's work. Yet there is a vast difference between the political or religious-moral views of an artist emerging naturally at times, along with a host of ordinary human and transcendent themes, and the drum-beating "artistic" moralizing to which we have become accustomed today. Many people in the arts now use their talents to propagate blatant messages and moralistic bombast.

The Problem

In the *Selected Letters* of Vladimir Nabokov (New York: Haracourt Brace Jovanovich, 1989), he addresses the problem of moralizing through art. "I never meant to deny the moral impact of art which is certainly inherent in every genuine work of art. What I do deny and am prepared to fight to the last drop of ink is the deliberate moralizing which to me kills every vestige of art in a work, however skillfully written."

Implicit in Nabokov's words is the sense of his own struggle to establish a balance between the temptation to propagandize and the honesty inherently necessary to real art. Today in many quarters this struggle has been abandoned in favor of accepting crude proselytizing as a form of art.

The idea of art being an expression of eternal, common, ageless, human themes is being lost. Therefore, art is being lost, pounded to death by the political-religious moralizers. Even those who one might suppose are equipped to judge the shortcomings of current artworks (produced along party ideological lines) often do not speak up for fear of appearing to be unfashionably out-of-step with the "right-thinking" majority in academic circles. Christians who know better have also shown cowardice in the face of a strident fundamentalist and/or pietistic or leftist Catholic juggernaut within the church. Academics in universities have shown similar cowardice in response to the fashions of feminism and deconstructionism. As a result, we now have supremely mediocre art and literature being taken seriously, even taught to students. *The Color Purple* is said to be required reading more often than Shakespeare in many college literature courses today! Art and literature are embraced or rejected nowadays because of "right thinking," instead of aesthetic or creative qualities. For instance, Alice Walker's novel *The Temple of My Familiar* can hardly be considered literature at all on its merits. It can only be understood to be literature if it is read as the feminist, black, lesbian "religious" tract that it is. It is such a bad book that its publication and acclaim seem to be motivated by some kind of literary affirmative action that has replaced old-fashioned ideas of quality and aesthetic merit. In the world of evangelical writing, one can hardly conceive of some new best-selling "Christian novels" finding as wide an audience as they have, except for the fact that they have propaganda value appreciated by many evangelical Christians.

Carol Iannone states the parameters of the problem very well in an article, "A Turning of the Critical Tide?"

> A major strategy in the current assault on the integrity of art from within the literary world has been the denial of the possibility of transcendence. Any claim that a writer can speak beyond his particular historical experience as lived by all men is considered spurious. What has been seen as the universal truth in literature, we are told, is nothing more than the disguised or unexamined assumptions of the ruling class, sex, or race.
>
> In no way have those making such accusations actually proved them. Do blacks, for example, find unrecognizable the mournful despair of the Trojan people at the death of Hector? Are women incapable of appreciating the restless dissatisfaction that drives Ishmael to join a whaling expedition? Is it beyond the capacity of a person born into the working class to fathom the overreaching ambitions of Macbeth? Of course not — in fact, such suggestions are *truly* "racist," "sexist," and "classist."
>
> Yet the notion that all literature [and art] is ideological has enabled its purveyors to clear the way for their own authentically political [and theological] approaches, entirely relieved of the burden of aesthetic justification. A whole academic/intellectual industry is now thriving on the infusion of politics into literature [and art], much as some people claim whole industries thrive on the manufacture of chemicals that pollute the environment and contaminate the food supply. (*Commentary*, July 1988)

The "pollution" Iannone writes of has affected every area of the arts (see Appendix A). Yet this is not the first time in history that the arts have been polluted by those who abused them as a means of political-theological warfare carried on by other means.

The Challenge

After the High Renaissance, seventeenth- and eighteenth-century art in most of Europe drifted toward pompous political and religious propaganda. In the age of supreme papal power, the sometimes reactionary Counter-Reformation (or Catholic Reformation), and later the Age of Reason, art was used as a tool for combating "wrong thinking" (in the case of the Counter Reformation, Protestantism) and promoting "right thinking" (in the case of eighteenth-century France, revolutionary themes). Gone was the sublime transcendence of the Renaissance or the earlier innocence of the High Middle Ages. In its place, painters, sculptors, and architects served to promote a threatened papacy, monarchists of all stripes, and finally, antimonarchist revolution. The florid, overwrought sentimentality of Bernini replaced Michelangelo's purity and truth. The ridiculous, pretentious monstrosities of Rubens stand in contrast to the tranquil luminosity of Botticelli. The beautifully rendered political tracts, masquerading as painting, of Jacques-Louis David contrast sharply with the humanitarian and universal symbols chosen by Michelangelo as his subject matter.

Yet in Holland, in the midst of pretentious propagandistic seventeenth-century Europe, a very different breed of artist worked. All was not lost. Holland's mercantile class continued to support painting, as it had since the early Renaissance. The elevated rhetoric of aristocratic propaganda via art had no allure for these educated, hard-working free people. Nor was there any need for them as Protestants to become caught up in the baroque experiential-irrational religious excess of the Counter-Reformation. In the tranquil work of painters like Jan Vermeer, Jan Steen, and Rembrandt, we see the true spiritual descendants of the Italian Renaissance and the High Middle Ages as well as the orderly, natural theology of Thomas Aquinas.

Eighteenth-century French painters such as Jacques-Louis David used art to serve political and revolutionary causes. In the nineteenth century, artists such as Eugène Delacroix and Ingres also politicized what they were painting. Yet other artists began to rebel against the straitjacket of nineteenth-century academic style and rigid political content. The impressionists, led by painters such as Manet, Monet, Degas, Renoir, Mary Cassatt, James Abot, and Turner, rediscovered freedom of expression, aesthetic imperatives, and transcendent *human* and natural meanings in their work. Painting was saved from the frozen sterility of politics.

In our own day, we face a similar situation to that of the seventeenth-, eighteenth- and nineteenth-century artists—we are surrounded by reactionaries. This time they come disguised as feminist literary critics, fundamentalist Christians, leftists, Green party "ecologists," black rights ideologues, liberation theologians and what have you. But their intent to misuse the arts and humanities is the same as that of the authoritarian manipulators of other times. The philosophical-artistic answer to them must be the same as that presented by the Dutch painters of the seventeenth century and the impressionists of the nineteenth and early twentieth centuries. They, through their work, produced a poignant rebuke to the idea that art was only for princes, revolutionaries, academics, or conquerors. The everyday scenes of Dutch and French life were infused by the light of transcendent, humane aspirations by these artists *in spite of* the received wisdom of the European elite of the day.

Now we in our own time must stand firm. We must battle against the politicization of art. We must produce, or at least work toward producing, works of transcendence in an age that no longer believes that this is possible—an age that has become *fundamentally* anti-Western, anti-heroic, and anti-human.

Robert Nisbet writes: "Only, it seems evident from the historical record, in the context of a true culture in which at the core is a deep and wide sense of the *sacred* are we likely to regain the vital conditions of progress itself [and] of faith in progress, past, present, and future" (*History of the Idea of Progress* [New York: Basic Books, 1980], 357).

As the woefully mediocre careers of the new secular ideologues, such as Alice Walker or Oliver Stone, remind us of the
limits of ideology, Christians and Jews who *do* believe in the sacred must carry on, as did the Dutch seventeenth-century painters.
As did the impressionists of the late nineteenth and early twentieth centuries, we must rebel against the ideological-artistic con-
ventions of our times. We must defend art and the humanities
even if we become outcasts for our pains and are ridiculed or
ignored by the people who are for the time being the official
keepers of the cultural flame.

However, we are not without allies. Just as Donatello and Michelangelo drew inspiration from the Roman ancients, we too may
look back in order to learn again how to go forward. We have our
heroes to emulate. We can, for example, study the creative spirit
that animated the Florentine Renaissance, Dutch seventeenth-century painting, and English seventeenth-century drama. We can reject today's destruction of the humanities by the professional critics with their political agendas. Such inspiration, as we find in our
rich past, will provide the direction for the long trek home.

President of Czechoslovakia and playwright Vaclav Havel, in
his remarkable 1990 New Year's address to the Czechoslovac
people, said the following:

> The worst thing is that we are living in a decayed moral envi-
> ronment. We have become morally ill, because we have become
> accustomed to saying one thing and thinking another. We have
> learned not to believe in anything, not to care about one another
> and only to look after ourselves. Notions such as love, friend-
> ship, compassion, humility and forgiveness have lost their depth
> and dimension, and for many of us they represent merely some
> kind of psychological idiosyncrasy, or appear as some kind of
> stray relic from times past. (*Newsweek,* June 15, 1990, 42)

He was speaking of the state of Czechoslovakia, long dominated by materialistic communist ideology. But his remarks could

equally apply to our own anti-Western contemporaries who no longer look for transcendent themes in art or believe in virtue, heroism, or even in the rationality of language itself. They risk dragging us all into a poisonous sea of uncertainty.

Beautiful Things

In ancient Greece, the Athenians decorated the Parthenon with the sculpted story of the Lapiths' battle with the centaurs. The Lapiths were a peace-loving tribe whose triumph over the war-like centaurs symbolized for the ancients the victory of civilization over barbarity. Later, during the Renaissance, this story was revived by those guiding the reawakening of learning and art. They believed, like the Greeks before them, that they could also conquer the forces of barbarity, ignorance, and chaos.

Today we, like the Lapiths of old, stand facing "centaurs" of politicized art, fundamentalist ignorance, and anti-Western academic bigotry. The church, liberal and conservative, so often the defender of culture in times past, has betrayed us, as has the majority of academics. Yet art does reach out and speak, even from the grave. Stripped of the new criticism, literature still can speak to us. Art *is* a universal language and does give us access to transcendent meaning, if we will forget what we *feel* and relearn what we *know*.

Plato, in the *Republic,* states of the arts:

> The man who has been properly nurtured in this area will be keenly aware of things which have been neglected, things not beautifully made by art. . . . He will rightly resent them, he will praise beautiful things, rejoice in them, receive them into his soul, be nurtured by them, and become both good and beautiful in character.

To which I add my own humble "amen."

But the Lord answered and said to her, "Martha, Martha, you are worried and bothered about so many things; but only a few things are necessary, really only one."

Luke 10:41–42 NAS

15

JESUS IN HOLLYWOOD

E veryone in the arts has their own struggles. Each person has their own story. Mine relates to Hollywood, others' to different places, people, and problems. Yet there are enough similarities between all artistic and spiritual struggles that my own odyssey may have served to be of interest, perhaps even of encouragement, to others as I have unfolded it in this book. Therefore, it is perhaps not inappropriate to conclude on a rather personal note.

Hollywood is a desert to me. No scene in *Dune* is more arid. A place of endless meetings with people whose only interest in you is to get something out of you before they discard you. Shakespeare would have understood the agents, producers, and con-men who populate my world.

> Everyone that flatters thee
> Is no friend in misery.
> Words are easy, like the wind;
> Faithful friends are hard to find:
> Every man will be thy friend
> Whilst thou hast wherewith to spend. . . .
> But if Fortune once do frown
> Then farewell his great renown,

They that fawn'd on him before
Use his company no more.

(The Passionate Pilgrim, v. 21)

In Hollywood, children are abandoned for careers and spouses discarded for other men or women. In *the business*, friends who are not "making it" are forgotten.

I work with people some of whom seem to believe that they have two lives: one to ruthlessly achieve their career ambitions; the other a mythical life in which living on the prestige and benefits of their career success, they will be human. In these second lives they will raise families, savor life, play with their children, lose weight, love one man or woman forever, and ride off into the sunset. For most of them, their lives are not long enough to be both *successful and human.*

Life in the movie business is an example of what happens when people really do try to "live by bread alone." Since the people I work with in Hollywood are created in God's image, even though they rarely acknowledge it, they do have souls. They crave some larger transcendent dimension to life for themselves. But because they will not make commitments to follow God's rules, much less make financial or sexual sacrifices or reorganize their priorities, they naturally gravitate toward easy, pseudospiritual solutions: false, feel-good gods, their many prophets for profit, gurus, psychics, New Agers, psychologists, spiritual counselors, scientologists, and superspiritual Christians of the superchurches. The so-called New Age theologies that Rabbi Harold Kushner, author of *Who Needs God* (New York: Summit Books, 1989), contemptuously dismisses as "religion for impatient, narcissistic souls that infantilizes our relationship with God."

Los Angeles is not a beautiful part of the world. But the physical ugliness of Beverly Hills, Hollywood, Burbank, and the Valley is easy to tolerate compared to the soullessness of many of the human life forms flitting through the Hades that is the movie industry, peopled by men and women with dead eyes.

At times I feel myself brutalized and prostituted. I despair of the chance to make the movies *I* want to make. I feel resigned to a fringe existence, making low-budget "B" movies, action movies, horror movies, mindless movies.

I work hard to make the scripts I am given into the best pictures I can. Sometimes it seems I am the only person involved who seems to care about the production. "It's only a little genre movie," or "The foreign market won't be worth more if you spend an extra day in the mix, who cares?" These are typical sentiments I battle.

I am fortunate, one of the lucky few; I have work as a screenwritere and director. That's a beginning. But I have no illusions that my work is *art*. It is merely commerce with some artistic overtones.

Once, long ago it now seems, I thought the only challenge was to get into the feature film business. Then I discovered that the greater challenge, once in it, is to be in a position to make a *good* movie, let alone a *successful* one. There are massive obstacles in the way. Since I am not well-known, I have limited access to scripts and actors.

I have not yet made a "great" feature film, and I do not know that I ever will, but I am slowly, painfully learning how to survive financially, spiritually, and professionally in the movie business. I am learning how to make movies that work within the limits of their budgets. At the same time, I am writing my own scripts for future projects, dreams beyond the present, dreams that may or may not become a reality, dreams of making the movies I would like to see.

"Success at Last!"

I remember back in my more idealistic (read, ignorant!) days living in Hollywood and having a series of meetings with people I thought could help me achieve my career ambitions. At that time I considered it a triumph to get an appointment with someone *important*—a person sitting at a desk in some dark tower surrounded by the casual trappings of power. How hopeful I was when some such person said they were *interested* in a project I was pitching. How exhilarated I was when they said they *liked* my work!

Once I thought I had had my *big break, the* big break! Steven Bach himself, the man then in charge of production at United Artists, agreed to meet me. I flew into L.A. expectant, *assured,* that "the Lord was now opening doors"; that I was *on my way.* I sat in an airport hotel room for ten days. Each morning Mr. Bach's secretary informed me that my meeting had been postponed to the next day. The meter was running. That room was becoming a small fissure into which I was pouring money.

Finally the great day arrived. "Mr. Bach will see you now." Steven Bach was very warm and friendly, gay—in both senses of the word—fashionable, young; ah, to be in his shoes (except for the gay part)! He offered me champagne, good champagne, too, out of a nifty little refrigerator he had in his office. This was the life! He handed me a book, the story of a Dutch art forger. Would I be interested in developing a screenplay out of this? You *bet* I would! A deal with U.A.! I'm here, this is IT!

Unknown to me, there was a worm in this apple. At the time U.A. had me writing my script for free, on spec, "we'll do the deal soon," they had another movie in production: *Heaven's Gate,* Michael Cimino's history-making financial fiasco, a boondoggle that would take the whole studio down. My small hopes were, unknown to me at that time, riding on this runaway, uncontrollable disaster. I finished the first draft of the script. I "Fed Exed" it to U.A. Why wait? They need it *now.* I can afford the cost of *"overnighting"* it! Soon I'll have millions! We'll be shooting by autumn! By the spring, the movie will open on a thousand screens! And my percentage of the adjusted gross will be . . .

The next day I waited for the phone to ring. It didn't. So I called. I had Steve's private number, the one that rang on *his* desk, the Desk of Power!

The phone rang and rang. Finally, an unfamiliar voice answered.

Me: "Steve?"

Voice: "Who dat?"

Me: "Steve?"

Voice: "Who dat?"

Me (annoyed now): "Mr. Bach, please!"

Voice: "He ain't here, he been fired dis mornin', I'se de security guard. I gotta make sure he doan come back 'n' steal scripts 'n' stuff, no one allowed in here dis mornin'."

My hopes went up in flames. I had had three long meetings with Steve. I had flown to L.A. twice and once to New York on my own nickel. I had spent at least $600 on script conference phone calls to various people at U.A.! I had spent three months living off my meager savings, writing a first script draft, and celebrating my coming and inevitable triumph.

Once during that time of blissful ignorance while I was "working for U.A.," I met with a friend of a friend and ate an overpriced and bad breakfast with him on Sunset Boulevard. This man was a struggling writer-producer. (He now has his own successful network TV show.) He told me that I would not get into the business until I had "suffered enough." I *had* suffered! What about all the hours of documentaries I made? What about all those meetings I was going to? What about . . . ? I was furious with him.

But he was right; I had *not* suffered enough. It took five years of seemingly endless disappointments, from 1980 until 1985, before I got my first feature off the ground. When released in 1986, my first picture did not do well at all, except in foreign sales. I had not suffered enough. It was eighteen months before I made my next movie. A project that took me to Africa for ten months. I'm still suffering; I'm not sure it's enough yet!

Steven Bach went on to write a best-seller, *Final Cut* (New York: Morrow, 1985), about the *Heaven's Gate* disaster. I'm still in the business; he's selling insurance or something. In the movie business you don't have relationships with companies. Your hopes rise and fall with the executives playing musical chairs between the studios, independent production companies, and oblivion. Your life is no more stable than theirs, and their lives are as stable as nitroglycerin in a cocktail shaker. You have to suffer.

I think that a lot of time spent in making movies is like a car crash — exciting, but nerve-wracking and dangerous. Dangerous to who I am as a person, to who I want to be to my wife, children, friends, and God. And yet, this is what the movie business *is.*

Since the episode with U.A., I have learned to take constant disappointment in stride though the slap of rejection still stings. Lost opportunities continue to hurt. Recently I have written a very good script. *The Foreigners* is the best story and screenplay I have authored. It is the sort of project I long to make and that would truly represent my philosophy *and* artistic ambitions. It is a story that takes place in Italy during the Second World War. It involves a priest as the hero and a story in which the principal characters wrestle with concepts of Christian justice, civil disobedience, mercy, and redemption. I would "kill" to make this picture. A few months ago Zoetrope Studios, the production company owned by director Francis Ford Copolla, called me. The head of production, Fred Fuchs (producer of the film *Tucker*), had read the script and loved it. He said that Zoetrope wanted to produce the movie with me directing. He said the script was "brilliant" and the sort of inspirational and uplifting material he wanted to make.

But . . . *But?*

On January 26, 1990 Zoetrope production filed for bankruptcy! Only days earlier my lawyer had begun to work on the contract with Zoetrope for my script. Now Zoetrope had had a court judgment against it in regard to debts incurred years earlier on the production of *One From the Heart.* My deal was stalled. The good side to this story is that potentially the Zoetrope deal is still open if they can make enough money out of their current production of *Godfather III.* Also, I have not "shopped" the script of *The Foreigners* elsewhere, so there are many other avenues to explore. But! . . . This is the story of my life — indeed, of the life of anyone in the arts. The players and situations change, but the disappointments are constant. Thus we grind forward grateful for what does occasionally work. Expecting the worst the rest of the time but . . . hoping, secretly hoping.

New directors work their way up in the system, making little, often silly pictures, or they don't work at all. People like me have to start somewhere. Beggars can't be choosers. Whether other believers in Jesus understand this or not, this is what I should be doing while working towards better things to come. If you are a fellow believer and you stumble across one of my silly little movies and are offended by it, forgive me. Have mercy. Have patience. I am trying hard to do better and so are thousands of other Christians in the arts. Bear with us. I trust God's creative judgment for what talent and skill He has given me. I trust Him for the projects, even the nasty little ones, He has helped me to secure work on.

Thankfully, there *are* areas I can control better than my bizarre career. Things such as fighting stingy producers for plane tickets for my wife and children so that we can be together on distant locations, so that I can try to be a good husband and father and not just a movie director earning a living. I *can* bring the brutality and harsh reality of my daily life, when in Hollywood or when doing "deals" or directing, and place them at the feet of Jesus and ask for His body and blood to protect me. I can ask for my fellow believers in truth to pray for me. God *does* provide; He *has* provided. The plane tickets have been part of the deals. My wife and children and I are still one family. Zoetrope and company may reorganize under Chapter 11 financially, but God is still in heaven.

Whatever I may *feel* at times, I know I am never alone. There are the fellow travelers, far and few between, who understand the inherent problems and battles of being in the film business. They know what it takes to pay your dues, to suffer in the business, *and* are believers who will discuss a script and pray with me. The people who encourage and lift up, who appear unexpectedly with a light in the dark place and say "this way." There are also the good friends who are not believing Christians or Jews but very decent, intelligent, and thoughtful human beings that stand ready to encourage. God provides such people, knowing that the way is indeed difficult.

The One Thing

In the end, it is not our careers but the ordinary, God-given human institutions of the local church, marriage, children, and friends that sustain us. In the end, things boil down to rather simple issues — issues of plain obedience to Christ, simple questions of fidelity to one's spouse and children, of remembering that life goes on in spite of our disappointments. And issues of honesty — of not passing the psychological buck for our failures to our parents, for instance, but being willing to admit our own sins and shortcomings, including the hardest admission of all: that our talent is limited and that we are who we are, miserable sinners. Keeping things in perspective is hard. Often I fail.

Hardest of all challenges is keeping any success we have in perspective. Remembering to consciously fight against the master-of-the-universe syndrome so well-described by Tom Wolfe in his book, *Bonfire of the Vanities.* It is hard to quell the adrenaline that even a modest success sends pumping through our veins, to remember that we are really very limited and that God's time and perspective is geologic in scope — a time reference in which all our huffing and puffing and effort is merely a fleeting whisper, a nod, a blink.

If the disappointments of failure and the sour aftertaste of ego-driven "success" have taught me anything, it is that nothing is ever what it seems to be and that neither I nor anyone else is dependable or good.

Jesus

Only Jesus is good when everything around us is evil, pale, and decayed, when the very work we do is rotten. It is Jesus who gives us understanding and a reason to live when it comes time to carry our cross, even our small artistic crosses.

When I long for dream producers, like some latter day Lorenzo de' Medici, who might say, "Make the best work of art you can, tell the truth about your subject matter, here's the money, go do it," Jesus understands this longing. He also understands the disappointments that drive us to despair.

I fall into gloomy depression at times. There is good reason for despair when you are a human being, a broken machine with a soul, an artist trapped for the time being in a nonaesthetic environment, a faithful spirit dwelling in faithless flesh. Depression is not bad. Jesus despaired; Jesus knows the groaning of a sleepless night. Jesus had His work "re-edited" and has had, throughout history, to endure the misinterpretations of His truth by His supposed friends.

According to tradition, when the young St. Thomas Aquinas visited St. Bonaventura, he asked from what books Bonaventura drew his deep knowledge of God. St. Bonaventura took Thomas Aquinas to the back of his cell and there drew back a curtain, revealing a crucifix on which Christ was depicted in all His suffering. It was from Christ's suffering, Bonaventura explained, that he learned of God, spirituality, and piety.

There is real sorrow, disappointment, and pain in personal setbacks and professional agony, but nevertheless there is hope. Jesus is that hope.

His was a greater suffering than ours. Jesus does not promise prosperity, but He allows us to join our suffering to His. His wounds will hide us even in despair. When my movie deal stalls or fails, when I have no way to tell my side of the story, Jesus hears my pleading.

Jesus knows what we must do to earn a living; He knows the desperate compromises we make in everyday life. He knows the imperfections of our lives. Jesus understands all of life, including the lives of artists. He understands the arts, even if today's Christian community does not.

Jesus is not a pietist. He came to save sinners like me, to save people who are moviemakers, musicians, painters, writers, tax collectors, and Roman soldiers. He came to save people who do real things in the real world for a living, people who are not always nice, people who suffer. Jesus came from death to life. Jesus can bring us into a new life of hope and help us to realize our dreams, even if they turn out different from what we hoped for.

APPENDIXES

APPENDIX A

The following is excerpted from *The War Against the Intellect* by Peter Shaw (Iowa City: University of Iowa Press, 1989) and is used by permission.

Introduction

Starting in the 1960s a change came over the rules of discourse whereby the marshaling of logic and evidence gradually lost its prestige. In its place right feeling and good intentions came to reign as the highest intellectual values and the most persuasive earnests of high seriousness. . . . The spirit of the 1960s, which favored the heart over the head, was making itself felt across the spectrum of argumentative writing and scholarship. This was the war against the intellect. . . .

Henceforth, as it developed, the willed suspension of the critical faculty in the service of a perceived cause or higher principle would come to be regarded as a mark of intellectual distinction. As this attitude seeped in the intellectual process, scholarship and intellectual discourse were invaded by what might be called theories of feeling and personal experience.

A virtually automatic suspension of the rules of proof, reason, and logic was now accorded to certain privileged kinds of discourse: the championing of artistic works by those newly designated as minorities or the oppressed; accusations of Western historical guilt toward the working class, minorities, or the Third World; assaults on established reputations or the elevation of obscure ones. . . . The war against the intellect had brought about a decline of discourse — slackening in the process of critical evaluation. . . .

Guilt and recrimination toward history, culture, government, and institutions became accepted scholarly attitudes. In the typical manner of orthodoxies, these attitudes ceased being put forth as arguments: they had become unstated assumptions, grown so familiar as hardly to merit comment. . . . In the universities especially, an atmosphere of intimidation came to prevail. Those who continued to uphold the standards of objectivity were regarded as insensitive and reactionary. Eventually there took place an institutionalization of resistance to authority of all kinds. Literary critics rejected traditional interpretations, scholars found the formal limitations of their disciplines stifling, and humanists objected to the established canon of great works. . . .

Thanks to the war on the intellect, special-interest groups — here a poet's cult following; elsewhere women, blacks, homosexuals, Chicanos — [have] had come to be regarded as immune from ordinary standards. . . .

[One can] trace the war against the intellect from late 1960s incursions of countercultural attitudes such as antitechnology and the patronizing of special-interest groups, to an escalated attack on America and Western values. . . .

It appears in retrospect that there emerged during the early 1960s a dissatisfaction and weariness with reason itself. . . . Then in the late 1960s, after nearly five years of the war in Vietnam, the war against the intellect intensified. The year 1968 saw challenges to settled attitudes of every kind. . . . Activism had to replace intellect, it came to be widely felt; at the very least, intellect had to be put at the service of activism — at whatever cost to intellect. . . .

These sentiments have since been recognized as epitomes of a particular response to the Vietnam experience. What has been little recognized — and least of all by the guardians of culture — has been their persistence in other forms through the 1970s and 1980s. Each of my essays argues that during these years the terms of discourse were altered to the detriment of objectivity and the spirit of disinterestedness.

The Decline of Criticism

The failed cultural revolution of the 1960s proved remarkably successful in its assault on the university, and especially on the humanities. . . . Practitioners of the new literary critical movement in question are divided over its precise definition, as well as over what it should be called. *Revisionist criticism* has been suggested, and also the French-derived term *deconstructivism*. . . .

They attempt to show that both literature and criticism are inevitably rife with ambiguities. Given the tendency of the reader or listener to confuse his own prejudices with the message being sent, they argue that all uses of words prove to be no less uncertain than the most abstruse poetry.

The tenuousness of language to which these critics refer has always been appreciated. What is being claimed for the first time, though, is that we must give up any illusion that we can gain a clear understanding of the written word. . . .

It follows from these new propositions that the moral attitude of a given work of fiction can in no case be made clear, least of all through the kind of explicit assertion favored by champions of traditional values in fiction. . . . The issue compromising academic criticism today is simply whether it is possible to mean

what one says and to convey that meaning to others. Anyone
wishing to answer in the affirmative must begin by confronting
the new language of indeterminism. . . .

This language, as it develops, has surprising similarities to that
currently spoken by instructors in college classrooms throughout
the United States. Here, too, certainty and piety of all kinds are
systematically undermined in favor of a universal relativism of
values and judgment. . . .

College professors thus share a skepticism about art and
knowledge, the intellect and culture, not only with revisionist critics but with anti-intellectuals outside academe as well. In the end,
from this point of view nothing makes any sense; everything is
relative, anyway; one person's opinion is as good as another's;
moral distinctions are useless. They all reduce to power and desire — to my own opinion, the way I feel, what seems right to
me. . . .

Critics who adopt . . . [this approach] come to believe that the
one thing a play [or painting or book] does not mean is what it
appears to mean. Nevertheless, despite the failure of all previous
interpreters to recognize this fact, the new academic readings
prove always to be successful, and to render superfluous all previous understandings of the play, character, or scene under examination. In one article after another in the most prestigious academic journals, the shared experiences of audiences and readers
for some three hundred years are regularly overthrown. . . .

However, just as the deceitfulness of language is exaggerated
into metaphysics by the revisionists, so the Renaissance speciali-
ties elevate themes into systems of infinite complexity. Ranging
among the themes with unaccountable ease, the critics affirm that
they have been able to identify and explain complexities completely different from anything their predecessors or even their
contemporaries have ever suspected. One, commenting on rival
interpretations of *Troilus and Cressida*, not long ago explained
that "the play, as I read it, is not 'about' love and war, or love and

honor, or policy and emotion. . . . Rather it deals with the single problem of corruption and its causes." Soon afterward this critic was dismissed by another, who confidently identified "Time" as the conclusive theme of the play. That critic was then superseded by yet another, who reinstated "the corruptive spirit.". . .

The disagreements among thematists thus quite definitively undermine any claim they might have to be taken seriously. From another point of view, though, their excesses deserve recital for the light they throw on the present state of literary studies, both in the academic journals and in the classroom. It is important that the readers of a respectable scholarly journal have been warned against the "misleading impression" that *Othello* "is about jealousy." And that one critic is barely willing to admit that the same play significantly concerns Othello and Desdemona: "Since I see the unresolvable appearance-reality dualism as the center of the *Othello* design, I regard Emilia-Iago as the play's central relationship." Such readings are regularly applied throughout English Renaissance drama. Levin's other categories or dramatic criticism — the ironic and the historical — yield equally fatuous absurdities.

For the ironist, virtually all heroes are flawed and all happy endings false. Hamlet, for example, is "a soul lost in damnable error . . . a serpent-like scourge . . . a profane fool." The marriage scene at the end of the comedy *A Midsummer Night's Dream* conveys "a ghastly reminder" of death — that is if we have read the sources and know that one of the marriages is reported in legend to have produced a child who later died. "Historical" critics reveal that the secret meaning of a given play lies in its having been composed for a special occasion — usually a supposed performance before King James. . . . In fact there is absolutely no evidence for these "occasionalist" claims, which recall the semimystical maunderings of the anti-Stratfordians — that lunatic fringe of readers who assert that Shakespeare of Stratford is not the author of the plays.

It is difficult to say which is harder to believe: that the claims of historical occasionalism can actually have been published, or that their significance, which would be spectacular if true, has gone largely unnoticed. . . .

If someone were to take the unprecedented step of reading the criticism of the past twenty years with a view to gaining a perspective on, say, *Romeo and Juliet*, what would be the result? That the pair would be exposed as anything but star-crossed lovers may be easily guessed in advance. But this is not all. One would learn that Romeo, who never achieves "true love" according to Saint Paul's definition, something he should have done, "took up the purchase of illegal drugs (which ultimately caused his own death)." Romeo, in fact, is "close to a mass murderer." In the character of Juliet, "perversion" and the "rawness" of "sexual hunger" prevail. (In this she resembles Othello's Desdemona, who according to another critic "shrinks from the reality of the whore within her.") An unnatural, indecent, sinful girl, Juliet must be condemned along with Romeo for the blasphemy of committing suicide. . . . The vulgarity of this conclusion, along with its fractured grammar, may give the impression that such opinions as it typifies are uncommon exceptions — the work of obscure hacks in the profession. But the abuses . . . have been committed by critics at every level of competence and reputation. Moreover, while they have been ignored in general, such readings have gained respectability and even fame within the specialty of Renaissance and Shakespearean criticism.

[The] tendency to debunk is built into each of the approaches. . . . But the devaluation of values that they share can as easily be seen as part of a wider phenomenon: the erosion of certainty about what is true and right. . . . Renaissance criticism has strayed so far from ordinary human impulses that most of it would hardly lead one to suspect that characters, actions, and feelings have anything whatsoever to do with the theater. Characters are made into vehicles of ideas; when they speak it is to "debate" and "discuss" the abstractions that are taken to be the real business of the plays. Marriages are "symbolic," and tragic endings convey no pain, even to the protagonists.

Students introduced to this universe learn to adopt the attitude toward it of their professors. They come to treat literary talk, that is, as a rarefied discourse that does not have to be tested against ordinary experience. Yet this does not necessarily insulate them from either the cynicism or the nihilism of their professors' critical dogma, for covert assumptions reach students more surely than explicit philosophies. Academic criticism starts with the assumption that there are no such things as admirable human beings, unequivocally admirable acts, or truly pure motives for acts. To prove that these do not exist, every conceivable method of questioning motives is employed. . . .

In view of this debased morality it would on the whole seem safest to keep one's college-age children away from the intellectual influence of most English professors. . . .

[T]he systematic dismissal of common sense by conventional critics and the programmatic uncertainty of revisionists have much in common. . . [I]n revisionist criticism the first consequence of calling discourse itself into question is the proposition that all criticism amounts to misreading, and thus one reading is as legitimate as another. . . .

[T]he charges leveled by opponents — of self-indulgent subjectivism, of thesis-ridden obscurity, of a purposely evasive use of terminology, and of an attempt to supplant the artist by shifting attention to the drama in one's own thought — are commonly received with a patronizing air.

[T]heirs is not merely an academic tendency, but rather a movement with political sources and aims. . . .

As in traditional radical politics, this new "politics of anti-realism," . . . assigns revolutionary tasks to art and criticism.

It is not at all inconceivable . . . that English studies, though at present the seemingly irreplaceable guardian of the Western cultural tradition, should decline to . . . marginal status. . . .

[T]he arts and literature have appeared to be flourishing in past epochs when in fact they were on the verge of extinction, and so it may be with literature and criticism today. For in the decay of cultural institutions, the moment of demise cannot be pinpointed until well after it has passed. . . .

[It] is difficult to pinpoint exactly when an institution has reached the end of its vigorous life. . . . In academe, they . . . have abandoned the citadel years before it came under attack. As a result, the professors' uncoerced embrace of absurdity and inconsequence amounts to the surrender of their role in the transmission of culture before a shot was fired.

The Politics of Deconstruction

The aim of Marxist literary criticism has always been to make whatever contribution it could to the overthrow of bourgeois society. . . . The crudities of such an approach were apparent at the outset. . . . Something more sophisticated was called for, and the continental theorist Georg Lukács supplied it. . . . Lukács recognized the need to write about art in terms that would satisfy the intellectual class with something more than the transposition of political slogans to literature. His ability to develop a respectably complex theory accounts for his current popularity among Marxist poststructuralists.

The still greater subtlety of deconstruction lies in its virtual abandonment of explicit politics. Radical ideas are no longer alluded to except through the invocation of certain apparently literary terms. For example, works of literature that have come to make up the canon of accepted masterpieces are referred to by deconstructionists as "privileged texts," the implication being not only that these works hold a special position in literature, but also that because of this they deserve the same suspicion and resentment that a revolutionary would be expected to direct at social privilege. . . .

Whoever hews to fixed meanings is said to participate in an act of "control" in literature analogous to the control that the imperialist-bourgeois state supposedly imposes on the exploited and the downtrodden. The State of Letters is conceived of as a surrogate for the political state, and as the battle against both escalates, so too does the language of deconstruction.

One user of this formula—the British Marxist Terry Eagleton—praises deconstruction for having helped to "keep the revolution warm," but dismisses it all the same. Revealingly, he traces the origins of deconstruction to the failed revolutionism of the 1960s, most particularly the student uprising of 1968 in Paris. "Unable to break the structures of state power," he writes, literary critics sympathetic to the student movement developed in poststructuralism a movement that "found it possible instead to subvert the structures of language.". . .

[D]econstruction now reigns as the one prestige subject capable of drawing graduate students of literature to extracurricular study groups in literary theory, where the subject inevitably devolves into poststructuralism. Generations of such students by now have written dissertations and built careers either wholly or partly under the influence of deconstruction. . . .

[D]econstructionist attitudes, especially skepticism about the existence of any firm knowledge and the replacement of rationality by subjectivity, have spread beyond literary theory to virtually every corner of literary study. A recent book on the subject of scholarly biography, for example, calls on the researcher to depend on "an intuitive sense of his subject, although this often means the manipulation of data." Such "freedom from fact," we are informed, "has recently become celebrated by contemporary biographers as a new methodology."

Not only biographers are celebrating freedom from fact these days, but also scholars throughout the humanities and social sciences, while some theorists of science edge in the same direction. Thus deconstruction proves to have provided the philosophical justification for a broad movement away from Western objectivity and rationality. In this perspective it has to be judged a success, having helped to bring about a number of results in the intellectual world; a retreat to relativism of values; distaste for the assertion of either intellectual authority or its correlate, social control; and an instinctive attraction to the delegitimizing tendency, whether in the intellectual, social, or political realm. . . .

[A]ny straightforward remark about . . . deconstruction in general . . . is certain to be greeted with the most powerful weapon in the academic arsenal: intellectual contempt. This contempt, moreover, is always likely to be compounded with the ever ready charge of political reaction.

Both of these techniques of intimidation were used against E. D. Hirsch, whose literary theory amounted to asserting that it is possible to arrive at a close approximation of an author's intended meaning. One critic called this assertion "the intellectual equivalent of aggressiveness and a wish to dominate" and branded it as "part of an ideology of society that is authoritarian and hierarchical." . . .

Just how much support Hirsch received from his non-deconstructionist colleagues can be surmised from the following remark by the deconstructionist Frank Lentricchia, in his book *After the New Criticism* (1980): "As a theorist who speaks unapologetically for rational values, E. D. Hirsch stands pretty much by himself in the landscape of contemporary theory." No more devastating reflection on the academic response to deconstruction could be made.

The supine intellectual posture of the academics will be familiar to anyone who recalls the variety of capitulations with which they had greeted the student movement out of which deconstruction grew. In the face of that assault, professors had swiftly abandoned their central pedagogical and scholarly convictions. They conceded that authority was by its nature coercive and that subjective impressions were as valuable as reasoned analysis. . . .

Once again the academics responsible for standards in their profession have been little more than bystanders as developments ran their own course. . . .

Feminist Literary Criticism

Although it presents a united front to the world, feminist criticism has long been divided internally and is at present undergoing a particularly far-reaching reassessment of itself. . . . Of these questions, the most troublesome is whether or not women's writing differs in some essential ways from men's. . . .

The debate represents a conflict between aesthetic theory, on the one hand, and the imperatives of the feminist movement from which feminist criticism sprang, on the other. The feminist movement has of course dedicated itself to the cause of women, whereas criticism is ordinarily supposed to represent a primary allegiance to literature. The allegiance, previously tested by political radicals in the 1930s and 1960s, is being questioned again by feminists. . . . Ironically enough, those who have put the cause of women before the cause of literature have harbored just enough residual loyalty to literary values to compromise their usefulness to the movement. . . . Can it be that feminist criticism has served feminism badly and has allowed literary values to be badly served in turn? If so, feminist criticism's relationship to feminism stands out as a major though not often acknowledged embarrassment. . . .

Feminists complain that their work goes largely ignored on account of what they call gender politics on the part of men, but they underestimate the degree to which they themselves discourage serious discussion when they claim to possess an order of understanding not available to male intelligence. . . .

Feminist critics, among others, appear to have borrowed the recherché vocabulary of poststructuralism chiefly as a handy form of certification in today's theory-ridden academy. They have assimilated the poststructuralist challenge to authority, for example, to their own attack on patriarchy. They have also extended poststructuralism's challenge to the literary canon into a call for the inclusion in the canon of more female-authored works. . . .

[G]ender theory has become, according to K. K. Ruthven, the "central hypothesis" of feminist criticism. . . .

The trouble [comes] with the attempt to make a case for an essential gender difference in the act of writing. For exactly where, they were forced to ask, can gender be identified as crucial in writing? Does it manifest itself in plot? In style? In setting? . . .

But feminist critics themselves pointed out that the sex of an author cannot be identified from literary style alone, even by professional critics, and that the same is true of plot.

Despite the practical and theoretical objections, some feminist critics have maintained their allegiance to gender difference in writing. . . .

Is [this] not issuing a license for the critic to supply the gender differences that the author herself failed to supply? If gender difference cannot be found, in other words, let us fabricate it. . . .

Such an outcome is the result not of any retreat from logical rigor but rather a commitment to politics. It was a political allegiance to the feminist movement of the early 1970s that produced woman-as-victim criticism in the first place. . . . In order to understand the evolution of feminist literary criticism, therefore, it is necessary to examine the role of politics. . . .

The chief considerations, in other words, must always be tactical because the movement is not primarily literary but political.

Feminist critics have been the first to state that feminist scholarship "candidly serves political or social ends." For example,

Toril Moi, in her explicitly titled *Sexual Textual Politics*, writes that "the principal objective of feminist criticism has always been political," and Elizabeth Meese specifies that its "motive" is "resistance in the interest of social transformation through interpretation." . . . But once political considerations dictated such a course, it was adhered to—thanks to an exertion of pressure, once again best described by feminists themselves.

The movement, in Sandra M. Gilbert's words, arose out of "anger and frustration at injustice" that "got italicized into shrieks." Carolyn Heilbrun has professed herself "amazed at how high a moral tone I take," and Elaine Showalter has concluded that in at least one of its modes feminist criticism is "righteous, angry and admonitory." As K. K. Ruthven observes, the "intimidatory rhetoric of radical feminism" is used to suppress certain kinds of dissent within the movement. Dale Spender, though she does not go so far as to adopt Ruthven's term "feminist terrorism," does seem to illustrate through her own experience what Toril Moi describes as "suppression of debate within the camp." Spender reports that she suffered unpopularity simply for "declaring that feminism has no greater monopoly on truth than does patriarchy."

A similar coercion has been directed outside the movement to achieve similar ends. "Our male colleagues," writes Sandra M. Gilbert, "are increasingly reluctant" to express hostility. . . .

Jean Bethke Elshtain, writing in the magazine *Salmagundi*, has offered a subtle analysis of how feminist literary thought can result in coercion. Feminism's "sexual manicheanism"—that is, its "universal presumptions of victim/victimizer; innocent/guilty; pure/tainted"—gives rise to a hectoring style of argument. As Elshtain explains, "In order to sustain the mask of purity, the feelings of victimization, [feminist] rhetoric must bear a heavier and heavier burden of rage." . . .

Coercion requires . . . closing ranks to . . . pass . . . muster as a feminist. In the introduction to *The New Feminist Criticism*,

Elaine Showalter endorses Rosalind Coward's requirement that, in order to be judged feminist, books written by women should display a "shared commitment to certain political aims and objectives." Coward added that "reading a novel can be a political activity" in which books are "interrogated" to determine their true commitment to feminism. . . .

The "only" way to "analyse the difference between feminist and sexist" criticism, therefore, is through "a political definition.". . .

Once loyalty and orthodoxy replace the ordinary norms of intellectual discourse, those who enforce the most Draconian standards tend to prevail. Not even the most orthodox themselves, even those who specialize in anathematizing other feminist critics, can feel safe. Thus, Toril Moi finds Annette Kolodny herself guilty of unwittingly serving the enemy. Kolodny is said to arouse suspicion by her "use of the somewhat masculinist-sounding adjectives 'vigorous' and 'rigorous,'" while her apparent belief in objective principles of literary analysis "betrays the traditionalism" of her thinking ("traditionalism" here serving as a synonym for "masculinist"). . . .

Yet not even the abandonment of aesthetic value in the service of a revolutionary political paradigm can satisfy the most demandingly radical of feminist critics. For them it is necessary also to abandon the humanistic tradition from which aesthetic value has sprung. "We have believed, I guess," writes Susan Gubar, "that women and men participate equally in a noble republic of the spirit and that both sexes are equal inheritors of 'a thousand years of Western culture.'" Now she knows better. "The treasures of Western culture" prove to be nothing more than "the patrimony of male writers.". . .

Showalter has . . . [identified] the common "enemies" of all "feminist, black, and poststructuralist critics, both male and female" — namely those who "urge a return to the 'basics' and the 'classics.'" . . .

Such are the results of what might be termed sexual politicization — that is, the bending of critical categories and arguments according to the needs of the feminist movement. . . . Historians of
feminist criticism are in agreement that its range of opinion extends no further than the distance from "liberal" to "radical" to
"socialist.". . . Elaine Showalter has stated that feminist criticism's
closest "theoretical affiliations" are with "Marxist sociology and
aesthetics." But, even putting Marxism aside, Left radical politics
have influenced American feminist criticism at least as much as
purely sexual politics. And paradoxically enough, radicalism's influence has also pushed feminist criticism at least as much as
purely sexual politics. And paradoxically enough, radicalism's influence has also pushed feminist criticism in the direction of de-
moting instead of elevating women. . . .

Radicals have taken the lead, for example, in depicting women
writers as victims on account of their exclusion from the literary
canon of recognized great works. Accepting this account, other
feminist critics have joined them in calling for the inclusion of
more women writers in anthologies and on college reading
lists. . . . Inasmuch as women's writing began to appear exten-
sively in print only about two hundred years ago, feminist critics,
in common with Helen Gardner, have been faced with the issue of
quality. In particular, should they call for the inclusion of the sentimental novels by women that dominated popular literature in the
nineteenth century and that made up the bulk of early women's
writing. . . .

In recognition of the problem, feminists initially treated the
nineteenth-century sentimental novel as a sociological phenomenon, being careful to make no claims for its literary worth. But
this necessitated calling for the introduction of second-rate writing
by women into the literary canon as an act of "affirmative action,"
creating an impression of women's inferiority once again. Seeking
to avoid this trap, the political radical falls into a worse one of
repudiating literary values altogether. For radical critics assert that

aesthetic standards are themselves a politically inspired imposition in the service of "interests." The privileged classes impose standards in order to install in the canon literary works calculated to help maintain the political and social status quo. Translated into feminist terms, the interests thus served are those of male literary critics acting to sustain patriarchy. . . .

In the meantime, Ellen Carol DuBois and the other authors of *Feminist Scholarship* explain that the proper approach to the sentimental novel "involves replacing the usual standards of 'excellence' with values that examine the extent to which a work reflects or serves the interests of women.". . .

What starts out as sexual politics in feminist literary criticism, then—replacing a concern to elevate women's condition before literary considerations—yields to radical politics, in which women's condition is glossed on a vaguely Marxist model of oppression and exploitation. At each radicalizing step, surprisingly enough, radical politics puts at least as much emphasis on gender as sexual politics did, advancing with equal if not greater insistence the ideas of a separate women's sensibility, a separate women's writing style, and a separate women's literary criticism. Moreover, where sexual politics had demanded ever more Draconian denials of specific literary values, radical politics demands the abandonment of literary value altogether. Where sexual politics resulted in a second-class status for women in literature, radical politics effectively fixes their status altogether beneath the level of literature. Radical politicization, in other words, escalates the demotion of women as writers and critics, and then treats apostasy with even greater severity than had merely sexual politics. . . .

Some black critics have gone beyond the feminist rejection of white male discourse to the rejection of feminist discourse itself on the grounds that critical categories based on analyses of white women characters are Euro-American in derivation. Black feminists believe that they have suffered as well from "the racism of white lesbian feminist theory," a complaint in which they are joined by black lesbian feminist critics. The feminist critics who have attacked, once again resembling male critics, have offered only the feeblest of responses to these charges. . . .

[T]o be safe from recrimination, a feminist critic at the present moment would need to have not only Third World credentials . . . (or credentials as a black or "Chicana" woman), but also be a lesbian, and preferably a Marxist or at least a *soi-disant* radical at the same time. Ordinary feminist literary critics can too easily be assailed as heterosexist, homophobic, racist, or guilty of "cultural imperialism.". . .

The sexually and politically ideal writer, it can be concluded, like the ideal critic, can never be found. . . . And the more radical the politics, the greater has been the need to assert a biological difference of one or another kind. . . .

Appropriately, it has fallen to the French, who have developed the most politically radical tendencies in feminist criticism, to make the most intransigent theoretical case for the proposition that women are weak-willed and weak-minded. Women's chemical and physical makeup, explains Luce Irigaray, a prominent French theorist, renders them "temperamental, incomprehensible, perturbed, capricious." Women writers, the French critic Julia Kristeva asserts, for these reasons function primarily as "hysterics," and their prose should be traced to "the predominance in them of drives related to anality and childbirth." Under the influence of poststructuralism, these critics have managed to arrive at the paradoxically reductive assumptions of what Toril Moi characterizes as "clear biologism"—the proposition that women's biological makeup dictates how they think, read, and write. Not hesitating to follow the biological imperative all the way, they have arrived at yet another characterization of women virtually identical with the hoariest of stereotypes.

Drawing on a second notion from Jacques Lacan—his characterization of the phallus as "the primary signifier"—French criticism does not hesitate, either, to ask the logical question (in words

of Sandra M. Gilbert and Susan Gubar): "If the pen is a meta-
phorical penis, from what organ can females generate texts? . . .

Luce Irigaray champions the vulva. In her theoretical system
the unique experience of pleasure derived from the labia. . . .

An American, Naomi Schor, holds that Irigaray tends to "'val-
orize the vagina' at the expense of the clitoris" — an evidently
more weighty objection. Schor seems to be suggesting that such
"valorization" falls into the patriarchal habit of delegitimizing the
clitoris — something radical feminists have taxed other feminists
with in the past. Schor calls on feminist critics to correct the
shortcomings of Irigaray's approach by developing a "clitoral hermeneutics.". . .

The French, furthermore, do not exactly claim that women's
writing is at present an expression of the female body: their bio-
logic formulation is advanced only as a prospective and utopian
construct. Other feminists have nevertheless perceived a danger in
positing the biological determinism of women's writing. Yet having done so, they stop short of dissociating themselves from the
French. Once again, it appears, the demands of solidarity, this
time thanks to the powerful lesbian, poststructuralist, and political
radical credentials of French feminism, have triumphed over literary judgment. . . .

Feminist critics . . . have repudiated the morality of the aesthetic. Seizing on the poststructuralist argument that we can never
achieve objectivity, or on the Marxist argument that all taste reflects social conditioning, they have justified their subordination
of literary values to the needs of the women's movement, or of
radical politics, or both. . . .

[This] prompts the question of whether traditional society ever
really went so far in denigrating women as feminist criticism itself
has gone. In the past, surely, stereotypes of the sexes were understood as tendencies, not absolutes. When men and women were
stigmatized, it was typically because of their occasional, not their

immutable, vulnerabilities. In feminist criticism, by contrast, women have come to be defined almost exclusively by their putative limitations.

Striking as the failure of feminist criticism is, with its seemingly fatal tendency to denigrate rather than elevate women, it is not the first literary movement to have suffered from its own theory. A comparably torturous path of self-contradiction can be traced in the development of Marxist criticism in this century. . . .

It is not surprising, therefore, that the extremes of critical self-contradiction in feminist criticism tend to correlate with extreme politicization, as in the case of the French feminists, most of whom are declared Marxists. . . .

By positing the theory of a separate, yet-to-be-recognized women's tradition of writing, feminist criticism has had and will continue to have the effect of excluding women from literature — and not only from literature. For, by asserting that language is for women "something like a foreign tongue," feminist criticism denies them their role in the development of human speech. . . .

The one broad avenue to participation in the life of the culture always thought to have been open to women — literature's noble republic of the spirit — is in one way or another effectively denied women by feminist criticism. Yet it was through literature that Mary Ann Evans, writing as George Eliot, could confront her world unfettered by any limitations that might be thought to attach to her as a woman. Through literature Emily Dickinson and Willa Cather were free to write poems and stories in which the "I" who speaks is male rather than female, thereby claiming their privilege to speak for any kind of human being their imaginations were capable of grasping. Feminist critics, in contrast, would in the name of liberation circumscribe women's participation in literature in exactly the fashion that they imagine women to have been circumscribed by society.

The Demotion of Man

In the twentieth century, the ordered universe broke apart into atoms, and man found himself alone. William Butler Yeats expressed the new sense of breakdown in the famous phrase, "the center cannot hold" (from his poem "The Second Coming"). . . .

The lost consensus . . . is one which stretched back, changes and permutations notwithstanding, for centuries. The Renaissance scholar E. M. W. Tillyard, in *The Elizabethan World Picture* (1943), describes the form it took in Shakespeare's time. As epitomized in Ulysses' speech on degree in *Troilus and Cressida*, a great chain of being was imagined, extending vertically in logical, hierarchical steps from the highest to the lowest spheres of the universe. On the earth, rulers held sway over their subjects, fathers over their families, and man dominated the lower animals. The essential order of things was expressed in harmonies of music and the rhythm and rhyme of poetry.

It was precisely the loss of this sense of order and authority that Eliot and Yeats mourned, a loss that found formal expression in the early twentieth century in musical disharmony and free verse. . . . The new picture is, in fact, modeled exactly on the old idea of an ordered hierarchical universe, except that the terms have been systematically reversed. Where once man was at the top of this order — only a little lower than the angels — now he is somewhere near the bottom; and where once his authority was taken to be divinely inspired and ordained, now it has come to be seen as a kind of usurpation. . . .

The unfavorable comparison of man with cockroach has become a familiar staple of biological discussion — although Stephen Jay Gould is ready to take a stunning step even further down the scale:

> Evolution is a copiously branching network, not a ladder, and I do not see how we, the titular spokesmen for a few thousand mammalian species, can claim superiority over three quarters of

a million species of insects who will surely outlive us, not to mention the bacteria, who have shown remarkable staying power for more than three billion years.

Here we have very nearly the ultimate demotion of man, the inferior not only of primitive peoples, other mammals, and the cockroach, but even of bacteria. . . .

Most writers on these subjects are so committed to the relativist view that they routinely put quotation marks around the key terms of the discussion, "civilization" and "primitivism." The marks indicate that the writer rejects any tendency to elevate the one or to fail in appreciation of the other. . . .

The vocal equivalent of such quotation marks can be heard in the tones of narration employed in television documentaries about animals and primitive peoples. The title of one of these, "Testament to the Bushmen," may stand for all, with their invariable presumption of a widespread and deplorable tendency toward feelings of civilized human superiority. His voice dripping with sanctimony, the narrator at once gently castigates the audience and renders homage to the rare, underappreciated values to be found among the peoples and species who have been photographed.

Interestingly enough, however, what we see on the screen is often a picture of destitution, disease, or blank despair. As a narrator intones the virtues of Masai tribal life, for example, the camera may be revealing naked children covered with sores and beset by cattle flies so persistent that the children have ceased to pay attention as they crawl over their open eyes. Or the Maori will be extolled for their devotion to art and respect for nature while the camera roams over ancient carvings depicting a people living in fortified villages and constantly at war.

In a film about Nigeria, a solemn respect is accorded to "traditional healers," long spurned by "orthodox [Western] medicine"; it is wrong, we are told, to think that "one is better than another," when what is needed between the two is "mutual respect." Without irony, the camera shows a traditional bone setter, who helps heal his patient by breaking a cock's leg; when the cock heals, the patient's leg will heal as well. With the mentally disturbed, we are informed, the native way in Nigeria is to keep them in village surroundings rather than exiling them to the indifferent confines of institutions. In the village, they are cared for by a traditional healer, who uses incantations and herbal concoctions. The camera now takes the viewer to the dirt area behind the healer's hut. Here sit approximately a dozen mental sufferers in a line (the camera shoots only in close-up, making it impossible to view conditions in the dirt enclosure or to see how many are held in it). Some of them are shackled, some drugged; all straddle a ditch; none moves. . . .

This is not to say that there are no discriminations to be made *within* Western civilization; the new world picture has as many gradations as any previous world picture. But once the principle of reversal is understood, it is easy to arrive at the contemporary view on any number of matters. Simply elevate students with low grades and poor test scores, for example, over high achievers (the former are talented, the latter unimaginative). Find virtue in the criminal, stodginess in the law-abiding citizen. For the highest accolades, move quickly to what used to be thought of as the bottom of society: children and the insane.

The Dark Age of the Humanities

Those clinging to the still-dominant, low view of man increasingly have resorted to the unverifiable to sustain their case, positing eons-old explosions in space, fanciful interpretations of prehistoric hieroglyphs, putatively destroyed documents, conjectures about the mind processes of inarticulate primates. When their slenderly supported metaphysical constructs are refuted, they respond with recriminations against the bearers of bad tidings.

The much-discussed crisis of the humanities actually has two parts, the more serious one of which is the less noticed. First there is what might be called the traditional crisis. It goes back some thirty years, and has had to do with the dominance first of modern science and then of social science, with a consequent falling off of student interest in nonscientific and nontechnical studies, with drops in literacy, and with diminishing knowledge of the past. . . .

The second crisis has to do with the . . . nominal guardians of the humanities. These . . . college presidents, foundation directors, members of institutes of the humanities, concerned educators, professors, deliverers of commencement speeches, and testifiers before congressional committees—have succeeded in raising money to save the humanities. . . . But their clichés of revitalization betray the presumption of an intellectual class confident that it has everything to teach and nothing to learn from the past. What these self-appointed saviors really intend to teach is that the usual assumptions about the nature and use of the humanities are mistaken. Rather than a renewal, they have undertaken an undermining of the humanities. . . .

Rejected by the new guardians of culture, in fact, have been his very notions of "the best," of disinterested inquiry, and of spiritual uplift. Anyone familiar with current academic fashions will recognize at work here the questioning . . . of all normative values. . . .

The inversion of values whereby the guardians of tradition have gone from attempting to cure a perennial crisis in the humanities to fostering a far more serious one of their own is an amazing event in intellectual history. . . .

Like a class preparing for its own demise, wherever well-funded programs professing to save the humanities are in place, the present guardians of the humanities can be found at work "decolonizing" and otherwise overthrowing their humanistic heritage. In the glossy brochure put out by the Humanities Council of New York University, for example . . . the . . . brochure does occasionally touch on subjects actually having to do with the humanities, and some of these subjects, remarkably enough, are (or appear to be) distinctly Western. For the most part, though, the well-endowed Humanities Council has spent its money on non-Western subjects and on social and political themes quite outside any previous age's definition of the humanities. . . . "The Future of Socialism in the Advanced Societies" (a very rosy one, one may guess), and "Nuclear Disarmament." The council's awards are given for the study of nuclear war. Its symposia and colloquia, too, concentrate not on the humanities but on "The Spanish Civil War," "Sex and Gender Studies," "War and Peace Studies," "Immigrant Mobility in New York," "Comparative Social History" (that is, working-class subjects considered from Marxist and quasi-Marxist points of view), . . . and yes, "AIDS." . . .

Together, the trivialization of the classical tradition and the act of giving the West second place in humanities programs are intended as indirect attacks on the heroic ideal, on bravery, on loyalty, and on patriotism. . . . At present . . . the very idea of high civilization distinguishing itself by its art and philosophy is denounced as elitist and chauvinistic. . . .

[W]e need to recognize that we are in an exceedingly bad period for the humanities: a period . . . that deserves to be called a Dark Age of Humanities.

In the dark ages of Europe after the Roman Empire, the danger to the humanities had to do with the destruction and neglect of the great texts. In our own dark age, the texts are suffering from the wrong kind of attention. They are being subjected to a system of interpretation that is extinguishing their spirit quite as effectively as if they were again literally under assault by Vandals and Goths. We are probably not in a position to wrest the tradition back from its . . . interpreters, at least for the time being. But there are some things we can do while awaiting another Renaissance.

Much . . . follows from the minimal acknowledgment that the past cannot in some respects be improved upon. . . . Once a truth has been expressed, or a work of art created whose quality cannot be improved upon, we sense that it should be allowed to stand. . . .

[T]he commitment to preserve these works amounts to a message to our children that in the future they may hope that whatever works they create will not be swept away so long as the culture values something more than the present. . . .

From the same assurance other benefits flow as well. First, he who would leave a mark on society is likely to conceive an interest in the preservation of society—no small achievement in our day. Second, he who recognizes what might be called the precedence of the past—its having already thought our thoughts—is likely to be rather skeptical about startling departures from social and cultural norms. In politics such a person will tend to be anti-utopian—another distinct gain. Third and last, he who has some sense of the achievements of the past begins to have a sense that there is something more appropriate than our evaluation of it, and more important than anyone's attempt to "deconstruct" it. This something is the way in which the past begins to measure *us*. *It follows that for those who recognize this measuring function, the past becomes a kind of superego or restraining influence.*

All three benefits—the wish to preserve society, becoming skeptical of departures from its norms, and feeling more judged than judging of the past—flow naturally from the idea of precedence. It is only with the introduction of interpretation as a method of instruction that the past can become subject to co-optation by the ephemeral purposes of the present. . . . This belief which itself constitutes a civilized value, also provides the best reply to the challenges of the now triumphing antihumanists: in the final analysis the tradition will judge us, and not we it. . . .

In a dark age one is at least permitted to see clearly what is being lost by hostility to the humanities. And thanks to this clarity, one is reconciled to playing the only role that is truly respectable in a dark age: that of a curator of values. A renaissance cannot be mandated, but it can at least be prepared for.

APPENDIX B

What follows is a series of excerpts from *Amusing Ourselves to Death* by Neil Postman (New York: Penguin Books, 1985) and is used by permission.

≈ ≈ ≈

To say it, . . . as plainly as I can, this [is] an inquiry into and a lamentation about the most significant American cultural fact of the second half of the twentieth century: the decline of the Age of Typography and the ascendancy of the Age of Television. This change-over has dramatically and irreversibly shifted the content and meaning of public discourse, since two media so vastly different cannot accommodate the same ideas. As the influence of print wanes, the content of politics, religion, education, and anything else that comprises public business must change and be recast in terms that are most suitable to television. . . .

There is no poverty so abject that it must forgo television. There is no education so exalted that it is not modified by television. And most important of all, there is no subject of public interest—politics, news, education, religion, science, sports—that does not find its way to television. Which means that all public understanding of these subjects is shaped by the biases of television. . . .

Twenty years ago, the question, "Does television shape culture or merely reflect it?" held considerable interest for many scholars and social critics. The question has largely disappeared as television has gradually *become* our culture. This means, among other things, that we rarely talk about television, only about what is *on* television—that is, about its content. Its ecology, which includes not only its physical characteristics and symbolic code but the conditions in which we normally attend to it, is taken for granted, accepted as natural.

There is no more disturbing consequence of the electronic and graphic revolution than this: that the world as given to us through television seems natural, not bizarre. For the loss of the sense of the strange is a sign of adjustment, and the extent to which we have adjusted is a measure of the extent to which we have been changed. Our culture's adjustment to the epistemology of television is by now all but complete; we have so thoroughly accepted its definitions of truth, knowledge, and reality that irrelevance seems to us to be filled with import, and incoherence seems eminently sane. And if some of our institutions seem not to fit the template of the times, why it is they, and not the template, that seem to us disordered and strange . . . that television's conversations promote incoherence and triviality; that the phrase "serious television" is a contradiction in terms; and that television speaks in only one persistent voice—the voice of entertainment. Beyond that, I will try to demonstrate that to enter the great television conversation, one American cultural institution after another is learning to speak its terms. Television, in other words, is transforming our culture into one vast arena for show business. It is entirely possible, of course, that in the end we shall find that delightful, and decide we like it just fine. That is exactly what Aldous Huxley feared was coming, fifty years ago. . . .

Television does not extend or amplify literate culture. It attacks it. If television is a continuation of anything, it is of a tradition begun by the telegraph and photograph in the mid-nineteenth century, not by the printing press in the fifteenth. . . .

American television is, indeed, a beautiful spectacle, a visual delight, pouring forth thousands of images on any given day. The average length of a shot on network television is only 3.5 seconds, so that the eye never rests, always has something new to see. Moreover, television offers viewers a variety of subject matter, requires minimal skills to comprehend it, and is largely aimed at emotional gratification. Even commercials, which some regard as an annoyance, are exquisitely crafted, always pleasing to the eye and accompanied by exciting music. There is no question but that the best photography in the world is presently seen on television commercials. American television, in other words, is devoted entirely to supplying its audience with entertainment. . . . The problem is not that television presents us with entertaining subject matter but that all subject matter is presented as entertaining, which is another issue altogether. . . .

No matter what is depicted or from what point of view, the overarching presumption is that it is there for our amusement and pleasure. That is why even on news shows which provide us daily with fragments of tragedy and barbarism, we are urged by the newscasters to "join them tomorrow." What for? One would think that several minutes of murder and mayhem would suffice as material for a month of sleepless nights. We accept the newscasters' invitation because we know that the "news" is not to be taken seriously, that it is all in fun, so to say. . . .

There is no conspiracy here, no lack of intelligence, only a straightforward recognition that "good television" has little to do with what is "good" about exposition or other forms of verbal communication but everything to do with what the pictorial images look like. . . .

When a television show is in process, it is very nearly impermissible to say, "Let me think about that" or "I don't know" or "What do you mean when you say . . . ?" or "From what sources does your information come?" This type of discourse not only slows down the tempo of the show but creates the impression of uncertainty or lack of finish. It tends to reveal people in the *act of thinking,* which is as disconcerting and boring on television as it is on a Las Vegas stage. Thinking does not play well on television, a fact that television directors discovered long ago. There is not much to *see* in it.

I do not say categorically that it is impossible to use television as a carrier of coherent language or thought in process. William Buckley's own program, "Firing Line," occasionally shows people in the act of thinking but who also happen to have television cameras pointed at them. There are other programs, such as "Meet the Press" or "The Open Mind," which clearly strive to maintain a sense of intellectual decorum and typographic tradition, but they are scheduled so that they do not compete with programs of great visual interest, since otherwise, they will not be watched. . . .

It is in the nature of the medium that it must suppress the content of ideas in order to accommodate the requirements of visual interest; that is to say, to accommodate the values of show business.

Film, records, and radio (now that it is an adjunct of the music industry) are, of course, equally devoted to entertaining the culture, and their effects in altering the style of American discourse are not insignificant. But television is different because it encompasses all forms of discourse. No one goes to a movie to find out about government policy or the latest scientific advances. No one buys a record to find out the baseball scores or the weather or the latest murder. No one turns on radio anymore for soap operas or a presidential address (if a television set is at hand). But everyone goes to television for all these things and more, which is why television resonates so powerfully throughout the culture. Television is our culture's principal mode of knowing about itself. Therefore—and this is the critical point—how television stages the world becomes the model for how the world is properly to be staged. It is not merely that on the television screen entertainment is the metaphor for all discourse. It is that off the screen the same metaphor prevails. As typography once dictated the style of conducting politics, religion, business, education, law and other important social matters, television now takes command. In courtrooms, classrooms, operating rooms, board rooms, churches and even airplanes, Americans no longer talk to each other, they entertain each other. They do not exchange ideas; they exchange images. They do not argue with propositions; they argue with good looks, celebrities and commercials. For the message of television as metaphor is not only that all the world is a stage but that the stage is located in Las Vegas, Nevada. . . .

As reported with great enthusiasm by both WCBS-TV and WNBC-TV in 1984, the Philadelphia public schools have embarked on an experiment in which children will have their curriculum sung to them. Wearing Walkman equipment, students were shown listening to rock music whose lyrics were about eight parts of speech. Mr. Jocko Henderson, who thought of this idea, is planning to delight students further by subjecting mathematics and history, as well as English, to the rigors of a rock music format. In fact, this is not Mr. Henderson's idea at all. It was pioneered by the Children's Television Workshop, whose television show "Sesame Street" is an expensive illustration of the idea that education is indistinguishable from entertainment. Nonetheless, Mr. Henderson has a point in his favor. Whereas "Sesame Street" merely attempts to make learning to read a form of light entertainment, the Philadelphia experiment aims to make the classroom itself into a rock concert.

In New Bedford, Massachusetts, a rape trial was televised, to the delight of audiences who could barely tell the difference between the trial and their favorite mid-day soap opera. In Florida, trials of varying degrees of seriousness, including murder, are regularly televised and are considered to be more entertaining than most fictional courtroom dramas. All of this is done in the interests of "public education.". . .

Prior to the 1984 presidential elections, the two candidates confronted each other on television in what were called "debates." These events were not in the least like the Lincoln-Douglas debates or anything else that goes by the name. Each candidate was given five minutes to address such questions as, What is (or would be) your policy in Central America? His opposite number was then given one minute for a rebuttal. In such circumstances, complexity, documentation and logic can play no role, and, indeed, on several occasions syntax itself was abandoned entirely. It is no matter. The men were less concerned with giving arguments than with "giving off" impressions, which is what television does best. Post-debate commentary largely avoided any evaluation of the candidates' ideas, since there were none to evaluate. Instead, the debates were conceived as boxing matches, the relevant question being, Who KO'd whom? The answer was determined by the "style" of the men—how they looked, fixed their gaze, smiled, and delivered one-liners. In the second debate, President Reagan got off a swell one-liner when asked a question about his age. The following day, several newspapers indicated that Ron had KO'd Fritz with his joke. Thus, the leader of the free world is chosen by the people in the Age of Television.

What all of this means is that our culture has moved toward a new way of conducting its business, especially its important business. The nature of its discourse is changing as the demarcation line between what is show business and what is not becomes harder to see with each passing day. Our priests and presidents, our surgeons and lawyers, our educators and newscasters need worry less about satisfying our demands of their discipline than the demands of good showmanship. Had Irving Berlin changed one word in the title of his celebrated song, he would have been as prophetic, albeit more terse, as Aldous Huxley. He need only have written, There's No Business But Show Business. . . .

Imagine what you would think of me, and this book, if I were to pause here, tell you that I will return to my discussion in a moment, and then proceed to write a few words in behalf of United Airlines or the Chase Manhattan Bank. You would rightly think that I had no respect for you and, certainly, no respect for the subject. And if I did this not once but several times in each chapter, you would think the whole enterprise unworthy of your attention. Why, then, do we not think a news show similarly unworthy? The reason, I believe, is that whereas we expect books and even other media (such as film) to maintain a consistency of tone and a continuity of content, we have no such expectation of television, and especially television news. We have become so accustomed to its discontinuities that we are no longer struck dumb, as any sane person would be, by a newscaster who, having just reported that a nuclear war is inevitable, goes on to say that he will be right back after this word from Burger King; who says, in other words, "Now . . . this." One can hardly overestimate the damage that such juxtapositions do to our sense of the world as a serious place. The damage is especially massive to youthful viewers who depend so much on television for their clues as to how to respond to the world. In watching television news, they, more than any other segment of the audience, are drawn into an epistemology based on the assumption that all reports of cruelty and death are greatly exaggerated and, in any case, not to be taken seriously or responded to sanely.

I should go so far as to say that embedded in the surrealistic frame of a television news show is a theory of anticommunication, featuring a type of discourse that abandons logic, reason, sequence and rules of contradiction. In aesthetics, I believe the name given to this theory is Dadaism; in philosophy, nihilism; in psychiatry, schizophrenia. In the parlance of the theater, it is known as vaudeville. . . .

The result of all this is that Americans are the best entertained and quite likely the least well-informed people in the Western world. I say this in the face of popular conceit that television, as a window to the world, has made Americans exceedingly well informed. Much depends here, of course, on what is meant to being informed. I will pass over the now tiresome polls that tell us that, at any given moment, 70 percent of our citizens do not know who is the Secretary of State or the Chief Justice of the Supreme Court. Let us consider, instead, the case of Iran during the drama that was called the "Iranian Hostage Crisis." I don't suppose there has been a story in years that received more continuous attention from television. We may assume, then, that Americans know most of what there is to know about this unhappy event. And now, I put these questions to you: Would it be an exaggeration to say that not one American in a hundred knows what language the Iranians speak? Or what the word "Ayatollah" means or implies? Or knows any details of the tenets of Iranian religious beliefs? Or the main outlines of their political history? Or knows who the Shah was, and where he came from?

Nonetheless, everyone had an opinion about this event, for in America everyone is entitled to an opinion, and it is certainly useful to have a few when a pollster shows up. But these are opinions of quite different order from eighteenth- or nineteenth-century opinions. It is probably more accurate to call them emotions rather than opinions, which would account for the fact that they change from week to week, as the pollsters tell us. What is happening here is that television is altering the meaning of "being informed" by creating a species of information that might properly be called *disinformation*. I am using this word almost in the precise sense in which it is used by spies in the CIA or KGB. Disinformation does not mean false information. It means misleading information — misplaced, irrelevant, fragmented or superficial information — information that creates the illusion of knowing something but which in fact leads one away from knowing. In saying this, I do not mean to imply that television news deliberately aims to deprive Americans of a coherent, contextual understanding of their world. I mean to say that when news is packaged as entertainment, that is the inevitable result. And in saying that the television news show entertains but does not inform, I am saying something far more serious than that we are being deprived of authentic information. I am saying we are losing our sense of what it means to be well informed. Ignorance is always correctable. But what shall we do if we take ignorance to be knowledge? . . .

All that has happened is that the public has adjusted to incoherence and been amused into indifference. Which is why Aldous Huxley would not in the least be surprised by the story. Indeed, he prophesied its coming. He believed that it is far more likely that the Western democracies will dance and dream themselves into oblivion than march into it, single file and manacled. Huxley grasped, as Orwell did not, that it is not necessary to conceal anything from a public insensible to contradiction and narcoticized by technological diversions. Although Huxley did not specify that television would be our main line to the drug, he would have no difficulty accepting Robert MacNeil's observation that "Television is the *soma* of Aldous Huxley's *Brave New World*." Big Brother turns out to be Howdy Doody. . . .

Terence Moran, I believe, lands on the target in saying that with media whose structure is biased toward furnishing images and fragments, we are deprived of access to an historical perspective. In the absence of continuity and context, he says, "bits of information cannot be integrated into an intelligent and consistent whole." We do not refuse to remember; neither do we find it exactly useless to remember. Rather, we are being rendered unfit to remember. For if remembering is to be something more than nostalgia, it requires a contextual basis — a theory, a vision, a metaphor — *something* within which facts can be organized and patterns discerned. The politics of image and instantaneous news provides no such context, is, in fact, hampered by attempts to provide any. A mirror records only what you are wearing today. It is silent about yesterday. With television, we vault ourselves into a continuous, incoherent present. "History," Henry Ford said, "is bunk." Henry Ford was a typographic optimist. "History," the Electric Plug replies, "doesn't exist."

ABOUT THE AUTHOR

F rancis Schaeffer (aka Franky Schaeffer) lives in Massachusetts with his wife and three children. He is a movie director and screenwriter.

In 1974, he produced and directed his first documentary film series, *How Should We Then Live?* The success of this led him to further documentary film work on such projects as the *Whatever Happened to the Human Race?* series (with Dr. C. Everett Koop and Franky's father, the late Francis Schaeffer), which he wrote and directed.

While making his many documentaries, some twenty-five in all, he authored several best-selling books including *Addicted to Mediocrity* and *A Time for Anger.*

In 1985, Mr. Schaeffer changed careers and began directing full-length feature films. His first feature was *Wired to Kill* (winner of four Golden Scroll Awards from The Academy of Science Fiction, Fantasy and Horror Films, including that of Best Director). To date he has directed four feature films for theatrical, video, or cable release. He is currently engaged in numerous movie production projects and continues his screenwriting, as well as speaking and teaching as time and opportunity permit.

The typeface for the text of this book is *Times Roman*. In 1930, typographer Stanley Morison joined the staff of *The Times* (London) to supervise design of a typeface for the reformatting of this renowned English daily. Morison had overseen type-library reforms at Cambridge University Press in 1925, but this new task would prove a formidable challenge despite a decade of experience in paleography, calligraphy, and typography. *Times New Roman* was credited as coming from Morison's original pencil renderings in the first years of the 1930s, but the typeface went through numerous changes under the scrutiny of a critical committee of dissatisfied *Times* staffers and editors. The resulting typeface, *Times Roman*, has been called the most used, most successful typeface of this century. The design is of enduring value to English and American printers and publishers, who choose the typeface for its readability and economy when run on today's high-speed presses.

Substantive Editing:
Michael Hyatt

Copy Editing:
Susan Kirby

Cover Design:
Steve Diggs & Friends
Nashville, Tennessee

Page Composition:
Xerox Ventura Publisher
Printware 720 IQ Laser Printer

Printing and Binding:
Maple-Vail Book Manufacturing Group
York, Pennsylvania

Dust Jacket Printing:
Strine Printing Company Inc.
York, Pennsylvania